Performance Manag
in the Public Sector

Tackling the key topics of reform and modernization, this important new book systematically examines performance in public management systems. The authors present this seminal subject in an informative and accessible manner, tackling some of the most important themes.

Performance Management in the Public Sector takes as its point of departure a broad definition of performance to redefine major and basic mechanisms in public administration, both theoretically and in practice. The book:

■ situates performance in some of the current public management debates;
■ discusses the many definitions of 'performance' and how it has become one of the contested agendas of public management;
■ examines measurement, incorporation and use of performance information; and
■ explores the challenges and future directions of performance management.

A must-read for any student or practitioner of public management, this core text will prove invaluable to anyone wanting to improve their understanding of performance management in the public sector.

Wouter Van Dooren is Assistant Professor of Public Administration at the Department of Political Science, University of Antwerp, Belgium, and Research Fellow at the Public Management Institute at the Katholieke Universiteit Leuven, Belgium. He researches performance measurement and management.

Geert Bouckaert is Director and Professor of Public Management at the Public Management Institute at the Katholieke Universiteit Leuven, Belgium. He is President of the European Group for Public Administration and he researches performance management, financial management and public sector reform.

John Halligan is Professor of Public Administration at the University of Canberra, Australia. His research interests are comparative public governance and management, performance management and public sector reform.

ROUTLEDGE MASTERS IN PUBLIC MANAGEMENT

Edited by Stephen P. Osborne, Owen Hughes and Walter Kickert

Routledge Masters in Public Management is an integrated set of texts. It is intended to form the backbone for the holistic study of the theory and practice of public management as part of:

- a taught Masters, MBA or MPA course at a university or college;
- a work-based, in-service, programme of education and training; or
- a programme of self-guided study.

Each volume stands alone in its treatment of its topic, whether it be strategic management, marketing or procurement, and is co-authored by leading specialists in their field. However, all volumes in the series share both a common pedagogy and a common approach to the structure of the text. Key features of all volumes in the series include:

- a critical approach to combining theory with practice which educates its reader, rather than solely teaching him/her a set of skills;
- clear learning objectives for each chapter;
- the use of figures, tables and boxes to highlight key ideas, concepts and skills;
- an annotated bibliography, guiding students in their further reading; and
- a dedicated case study in the topic of each volume, to serve as a focus for discussion and learning.

Managing Change and Innovation in Public Service Organizations
Stephen P. Osborne and Kerry Brown

Risk and Crisis Management in the Public Sector
Lynn T. Drennan and Allan McConnell

Contracting for Public Services
Carsten Greve

Performance Management in the Public Sector
Wouter Van Dooren, Geert Bouckaert and John Halligan

Performance Management in the Public Sector

Wouter Van Dooren,
Geert Bouckaert and
John Halligan

Routledge
Taylor & Francis Group

LONDON AND NEW YORK

First published 2010
by Routledge
2 Park Square, Milton Park, Abingdon, Oxon OX14 4RN

Simultaneously published in the USA and Canada
by Routledge
270 Madison Avenue, New York, NY 10016

Routledge is an imprint of the Taylor & Francis Group, an Informa business

© 2010 Wouter Van Dooren, Geert Bouckaert & John Halligan

Typeset in Bell Gothic and Perpetua
by Keystroke, Tettenhall, Wolverhampton
Printed and bound in Great Britain
by TJ International Ltd, Padstow, Cornwall

British Library Cataloguing in Publication Data
A catalogue record for this book is available from the British Library

Library of Congress Cataloging in Publication Data
Dooren, Wouter van.
    Performance management in the public sector / Wouter Van Dooren, Geert
    Bouckaert and John Halligan.
        p. cm.
    Includes bibliographical references and index.
    1. Government productivity—Evaluation.   2. Performance—Management.
    3. Public administration.   I. Bouckaert, Geert.   II. Halligan, John, 1941–
    III. Title.
    JF1525.P67D66 2010
    352.6'6—dc22   2009045304

ISBN 13: 978–0–415–37104–9 (hbk)
ISBN 13: 978–0–415–37105–6 (pbk)
ISBN 13: 978–0–203–03080–6 (ebk)

ISBN 10: 0–415–37104–X (hbk)
ISBN 10: 0–415–37105–8 (pbk)
ISBN 10: 0–203–03080–X (ebk)

Contents

Figures, tables and boxes

FIGURES

TABLES

BOXES

Chapter 1

Introduction

LEARNING OBJECTIVES

- To be able to position the performance debate in contemporary public administration: public sector reform, public management and public policy.
- To understand the controversy around performance management.

KEY POINTS

- The concept of performance has many meanings, which can be classified based on the value judgements they imply.
- Performance is not only a concept, but also a contested agenda of change which calls for a balanced treatment of the issue.
- A clear distinction between measurement, incorporation and use of performance information is vital.
- Performance management is embedded in debates of reform, management and policy.

The subject of this book is the core of public management, certainly in its New Public Management (NPM) form: is it possible to envisage management in the public sector without due regard to the pursuit of results and the measurement of performance? Nevertheless performance management lacks a coherent treatment that explicates its significance, analyses its several dimensions as a working system, compares its application internationally, and challenges its shortcomings. The purpose of this book is to develop this comprehensive understanding of performance management as a concept and phenomenon that has swept through OECD (Organisation for Economic Co-operation and Development) countries, to examine how it has been applied in practice and to review the relationship to public management and public policy.

The aim of this first, introductory chapter is to situate performance, performance measurement and performance management in some of the current debates in public management. We discuss the many meanings of the word 'performance' and how it has become one of the main but contested agendas in public administration. We also introduce the sequence of measurement, incorporation and use of performance information, which reflects the structure of the book. We finally argue that performance measurement has become pivotal not only in reform, but also in daily public management and policy-making. We end the chapter with an outline of the book and summaries of the chapters. The discussions are deliberately sketchy since we primarily want to outline the relevance and controversies surrounding the performance debate. We will seek more definitional precision in the next chapter.

1 PERFORMANCE AS A CONCEPT

In many public sectors, performance is the talk of town. As with many much-debated concepts, performance accumulates multiple and often ambiguous meanings. Dubnick (2005) asserts that:

> outside of any specific context, performance can be associated with a range of actions from the simple and mundane act of opening a car door, to the staging of an elaborate reenactment of the Broadway musical 'Chicago'. In all these forms, performance stands in distinction from mere 'behavior' in implying some degree of intent.
>
> (p.391)

In science, connotations vary according to disciplines. For example, psychology, social sciences and managerial sciences use different definitions depending more on individual, or societal, or organizational and system performance. Clearly, performance has many meanings and our task is to characterize this variation.

From Dubnick's observations of car doors and musicals, we can infer a universal definitional ingredient. Performance is about intentional behaviour, which can be individual or organizational. Based on this understanding of performance as deliberate action, a classification of performance perspectives can be built. The two dimensions in Table 1.1 reflect the importance that a perspective attaches to quality of performance; does a definition imply a statement on whether performance is good or bad? Quality is either (a) the quality of the actions being performed, or (b) the quality of what has been achieved because of those actions. This allows us to distinguish between four perspectives on performance.

The first perspective of performance focuses the attention on tasks being carried out by the performing agent (P1). Performance then includes all actions that are performed. A police patrol, a vaccination campaign, a medical treatment, teaching a course, judging in courts, all are examples of performances, irrespective of whether they were successful. Performance is intentional behaviour of government actors. As such, this conceptualization is relatively neutral in nature, but also very broad.

The other dimensions of the concept 'performance' contain a value judgement. Performance has a quality that can be either high or low. First, when performance is about the quality of the actions, and not as much about the quality of the achievements, performance is conceptualized as *competence* or *capacity* (P2). Under the assumption that a highly competent performer will be more likely to generate more and better quality output from an activity most of the time, performance becomes associated with the competence of the performing institution (Dubnick 2005: 392). There is a substantial literature on high performing public sector organizations and governments that roughly equals performance with superior capacity of the performing institution. The Government Performance Project, initiated by Syracuse University, studies for example the performance of US states by measuring their management capacity (Maxwell School of Citizenship and Public Affairs 2002).

Second, when performance is about the quality of the achievements and not as much about the quality of the actions, performance equals *results* (P3). The capacity of the organization is not the focus of this conceptualization. The opinion that only results matter is emblematic for this position (see Box 1.1 for a narrative reflecting this perspective). Below, it is argued that results may be both the outputs and the outcomes of the public sector. Many NPM texts see performance like this. As long as the results are proven, it does not really matter how they came about.

Finally, when performance is conceptualized with attention for both the quality of actions and the quality of achievements, it may be typified as sustainable results. Performance refers to the productive organization, i.e. an organization that has the capacity to perform and converts this capacity into results – outputs and outcome. Performance in this text refers to the last conceptualization. We will study how measurement of both capacity and results is embedded in public organizations.

Table 1.1 *Four perspectives on how performance is understood*

		Does the perspective imply quality of achievements?	
		No	Yes
Does the perspective imply quality of actions?	No	Performance as production (P1)	Performance as good results (P3)
	Yes	Performance as competence/ capacity (P2)	Performance as sustainable results (P4)

Source: based on Dubnick 2005

3

BOX 1.1 ONLY RESULTS MATTER

A priest and a taxi driver both died and went to heaven. Saint Peter was at the Pearly Gates waiting for them.

'Come with me,' said St. Peter to the taxi driver.

The taxi driver did as he was told and followed Saint Peter to a mansion. It had anything you could imagine from a bowling alley to an Olympic size pool.

'Wow, thank you,' said the taxi driver.

Next, Saint Peter led the priest to a rugged old shack with a bunk bed and a little old television set.

'Wait, I think you are a little mixed up,' said the priest. 'Shouldn't I be the one who gets the mansion? After all I was a priest, went to church every day, and preached God's word.'

'Yes, that's true. But during your sermons people slept. When the taxi driver drove, everyone prayed.'

Lesson: only results count.

taken from Hatry 1999

2 PERFORMANCE AS AN AGENDA

Performance is not only a concept, but also an agenda. The term 'performance' expresses a programme of change and improvement, which is promoted by a group of like-minded actors that are usually only loosely coupled. In chapter 3, these groups of actors sharing a performance agenda are called *performance movements*.

In Western societies, the promise of increasing performance has been one of the dominant agendas in the public sector. Ingraham (2005) observes that 'for much of the twentieth century – and certainly for the last 25 years – performance has been a siren's song for nations around the world' (p. 390). The post-war expansion of the welfare state has raised expectations about the role of government. In the 1980s, this expansion was no longer supported (Pollitt and Bouckaert 2004). Fiscal stress pressured the public budget and legitimacy crises pressured the politico-administrative system. In those days, US president Ronald Reagan marked government as the problem rather than the solution. As a response, governments pledged to do more with fewer resources – a government that works better and costs less (Gore 1993).

Government across the globe reformed in the name of performance. In the UK and the USA, this led to cutback management and a reduction of the size of government (Dunleavy 1986). Other countries followed other trajectories. Pollitt and Bouckaert (2004) identify four strategies: to minimize (privatize), to marketize (bringing private sector techniques and values into government), to modernize (changing public sector techniques and values) and to maintain (using the old techniques more intensely). The societal demand for a high-performing public sector resonates until today, and filters through to the organizational level.

3 A CONTESTED DEBATE

The roots of the performance agenda lie well beyond NPM. It should however not be forgotten that quite distinct, but maybe less eye-catching agendas exist in public administration such as establishing the rule of law, eradicating corruption, safeguarding equity, transparency and democratization. One of the most persistent lines of attack on the performance agenda is that it does not take these other values into account. Performance may even be at cross purposes with other values. As a result, positions on performance management have been quite polarized with opponents contending against the dissenters who argued that the fundamental premises were wrong and produced dysfunctional behaviour.

With time and experience, attitudes have matured and some convergence is apparent. Yet performance management is at a turning point with close scrutiny and questioning by both external observers as well as practitioners wrestling with the challenges in practice (Bouckaert and Halligan 2008; Flynn 2007; Moynihan 2008).

A new generation of studies is addressing the age of performance characterized by its pervasive influence on governments wrestling with complexities and issues. This growing middle ground of analysts see the limitations of performance management but believe there is something worthy of careful investigation through examining assumptions and exposing faulty thinking as a means of narrowing the gap between rhetoric and practice (Moynihan 2008; Radin 2006). The OECD (2009) has also been exploring a range of performance questions. At the same time more private debates have been occurring among officials in several jurisdictions about the efficacy of existing arrangements.

There is general acceptance that performance management will continue to be central to government. The reliance on highly developed official frameworks in various countries indicates that these systems continue to serve important purposes for public sector management. At the same time there is considerable evidence of issues about how well performance management is working in practice (KPMG 2008) and of the need for improvements. Several factors – institutional, cultural and administrative tradition – assist in accounting for different levels of commitment to performance management.

Although it may be too early to assess its definite impact, it seems that the financial crisis may further institutionalize performance management. The nature of the crisis has already changed from a financial to an economic crisis. It is unclear how it will transform in the future, but it seems plausible that a fiscal crisis will follow upon current deficit spending. With public finance under pressure, the need to assure and demonstrate value for money of public programmes will be reinforced.

5

4 MEASUREMENT, INCORPORATION AND USE OF PERFORMANCE INFORMATION

This book is structured around the notions of measurement, incorporation and use of performance (Bouckaert and Halligan 2008). It is a logical sequence of collecting data, integration of data into the management systems and, finally, putting information at work. Measurement could also be seen as the supply side whereas the envisaged use is the demand side. Supply and demand will not automatically adjust to each other, so incorporation assures the link between both (see Figure 1.1).

Measuring performance means systematically collecting data by observing and registering performance-related issues for some performance purpose. There could be a causal reason, e.g. there is a law or a regulation which requires an organization to collect specific data. There could be an organizational objective, e.g. a need to use data for improvement.

Incorporating is intentionally importing performance-related data in documents and procedures with the potential and purpose of using them. The purpose is to create the possibility of including performance-related information in the discourse and ultimately in the culture and the memory of the organization. An inventory of tools and techniques used to generate and anchor data and information into procedures, documents and organizations gives an overview of the incorporation capacity, which makes it possible to use performance information functionally. Measuring performance data is necessary but not sufficient for incorporating performance information. The capacity of anchoring instruments to institutionalize performance information will create the conditions to use this. Examples of these tools and techniques could be in financial, personnel or organizational legislation, and related handbooks for implementation. So there are levels and degrees of incorporation.

Using incorporated performance information refers to debates and institutionalized procedures for stakeholders for the purpose of designing policies, for deciding, for allocating resources, competencies, and responsibilities, for controlling and redirecting implementation, for (self) evaluating and assessing behaviour and results, and for substantiating reporting and accountability mechanisms. Incorporating performance data is necessary but not sufficient for using performance information. There is a need for fit-for-purpose infrastructure (i.e. incorporation), and of an accommodating and motivating performance culture as supra structure. In such a way, performance is fully institutionalized.

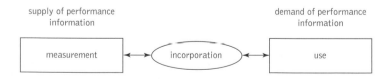

Figure 1.1 *Measurement, incorporation, use*

To the extent that information is available across organizations, benchmarking and bench learning could be used to upgrade systems to specific standards (single loop learning), to adjust standards (double loop learning) or even to adjust systems constantly as learning how to learn (meta learning). Using also suggests abusing and misusing and therefore there is a legitimate concern for increasing potential value added and for reducing possible dysfunctions (like new red tape or gaming), and to equilibrate costs and benefits. This results in looking at general and specific use (reporting, learning, accountability), but also at costs (dysfunctions) and benefits (value added) of using incorporated performance information.

5 PERFORMANCE MEASUREMENT AND PUBLIC SECTOR REFORM

Performance measurement has played a pivotal role in reform initiatives. Box 1.2 includes a sample of some key texts that served as catalysts for public management reform with a performance agenda. England in particular witnessed a boost in indicators by the end of the 1980s (Pollitt 1993). Reform initiatives such as the Financial Management Initiative, the Next Steps agenda, and the Citizen's Charter led to the creation of performance indicator systems for most public services, central and local. League tables have been created for, among others, schools, hospitals, health trusts, ambulance services and local authorities. No other country went so far in the use of performance indicators in governance regimes. The intrusion of indicators in the fibres of the public sector has led Hood to conclude that it is English exceptionalism (Hood 2007). Even Scotland and Wales opted for a softer approach.

In general, Continental Europe has not used performance indicators with the same intensity as the Anglo-Saxon world. Yet, there are considerable variations between countries. In Germany, the 'New Steering Model' (*das Neues Steuerungsmodell*) stressed the importance of performance indicators (Naschold and Bogumil 2000). However, the reform has only been applied in some big cities, city-states and *Länder*. Nowadays, the reform enthusiasm seems to be over and there is increasing acknowledgement of reform fatigue. In France, the Loi Organique Relative aux Lois de Finances (LOLF) introduced a form of performance budgeting (Calmette 2006). In Sweden, having a highly decentralized public sector, performance measures mainly played a role in the steering of agencies. In Norway, the Management by Objectives and Results system has been widely adopted, albeit after a transformation and translation by the agencies (Laegreid *et al.* 2008). The country with the strongest tradition in performance measurement in continental Europe is probably the Netherlands. The first initiatives were taken in the 1970s and by the 1980s, several local governments implemented NPM-like measurement-based reforms. The first large-scale implementations of performance-oriented reforms at a central level took place in the 1990s. The series of reforms culminated in 1999 with the 'VBTB' initiative – an outcome-based budget structure.

BOX 1.2 PERFORMANCE AND PUBLIC MANAGEMENT REFORM – SOME KEY TEXTS

This box presents some key texts that propagate reform and link it directly to performance. These are not academic texts, but policy documents by governments and their think tanks.

1   1993: US vice president Al Gore publishes the National Performance Review. The title is revealing; 'From Red Tape to Results: Creating a Government that Works Better & Costs Less'. The report was accompanied by the Government Performance and Results Act (1993), which imposed performance plans and reports as a basis for managerial accountability in the federal government. It was strongly indebted to Osborne and Gaebler's (1993) *Reinventing Government*.

2   1997: The OECD's Public Management Service (PUMA) publishes a study titled 'In search for results, performance management practices' (1997). It is a case catalogue of performance-oriented reform practices in ten, mainly Anglo-Saxon and Scandinavian OECD countries. The performance practices are a blend of financial management, HRM and accountability reforms. The activities of the PUMA were later critiqued for imposing a NPM framework, regardless of context (Premfors 1998).

3   1999: The British PM Tony Blair launches 'modernizing government', a reform agenda which confirmed the use of targets and indicators in the British public service. In 2001, the publication 'Choosing the Right FABRIC – A Framework For Performance Information' substantiated this agenda. It was issued jointly by the main players in the field of measurement: the Treasury, the Audit Commission, the National Audit Office, the Office for National Statistics and the Cabinet Office.

4   2003: The UK House of Commons' Public Administration Select Committee brings out a report titled 'On target? Government by measurement'. The committee documented an over-strong focus on the performance measures at the expense of performance itself. The report proposes a shift from a measurement culture towards a performance culture.

5   2008: The election of the Rudd government in Australia in 2007 produces an agenda to improve budget transparency (termed Operation Sunlight) (Tanner 2008). It critiques the outcomes and outputs framework for being unable to shift the focus of financial reporting from inputs (programmes, expenses and recipients) to outputs and outcomes (i.e. actual results). Basic information on inputs was lost in the changeover, and reporting of outcomes is seriously inadequate.

Bouckaert and Peters (2002) argue that performance measurement is the 'Achilles heel' of many public sector reforms. The availability of performance information is a necessary – but not sufficient – condition for the success of many reform initiatives. Yet, often the availability of performance information is assumed. The presence of performance information is one of the most decisive and susceptible aspects of the recent tide of public management reforms. This observation legitimizes a scientific focus on measurement of performance. Yet, performance measurement goes beyond public sector reform. It is found in recurring activities in public management and public policy.

6 PERFORMANCE MEASUREMENT AND PUBLIC MANAGEMENT

Performance information is not only pivotal in public sector reform. It also plays a role in daily management practice. The Government Performance Project (GPP), a six-year research initiative evaluating the management capacity of federal, state and local government entities in the USA, provides some insight in the role of performance information in organizations (Ingraham *et al.* 2003). The most visible part of the project was the graded reports of the 50 states. The underlying model of the assessment identified four management subsystems that contribute to management capacity – defined as the potential for performance: financial management, human resources management, capital management and information technology management. The GPP identifies two crosscutting levers; leadership and information. First, leadership is the driver since leaders are able to make informed decisions, to provide guidance and direction, to develop the institution's mission, vision and values, to communicate these to the members and to coordinate organizational components. Second, information and a focus on results are connectors. Information connects the management sub-systems with each other. It also connects the management system with the outside world through measurement of programme delivery and performance.

Besides performance information, other connectors in the management of organizations may be identified. The 60-year old Friedrich–Finer debate on accountability systems points to an important addition (Bouckaert and Halligan 2008). Finer championed a system based on objective accountability. He would support performance information for its integrative potential. Friedrich advocated a system based on professional 'fellowship' between practitioners. Pride-related arguments of these professionals allow for a subjective accountability mechanism derived from their values, which could also be seen as a connector between subsystems.

7 PERFORMANCE MEASUREMENT AND PUBLIC POLICY

Performance measurement also plays a role in public policy. Performance measurement and policy evaluation are adjacent fields. Wholey *et al.* (2004) see a role for performance data in the evaluability study that may precede an evaluation. Weiss (1998) points to performance data as a data source for evaluators (see also Wholey *et al.* (2004)). Some authors go further and advocate an integration of performance measurement and evaluation. McDavid and Hawthorn (2006) assert that performance measurement may be seen as an approach to evaluation. The basic programme evaluation tools are also useful for performance measurement. They are complementary evaluation strategies. Yet, some important differences remain (see Box 1.3).

Not only evaluators are using information from performance measurement systems. Performance measurement also plays a role in actual policy processes. At several points in time, the quest for rationalization of policy decisions led to substantial measurement efforts. In the 1960s, the social indicators movement aspired to provide policy-makers in the welfare states with objective facts on their performance. Social indicators were to be integrated into a system of social accounting that paralleled the national income accounting system. Social indicators should also serve as a tool for programme evaluation and social engineering (Rossi and Gilmartin 1980). In hindsight, the movement seems to have been too ambitious.

BOX 1.3 THE DIFFERENCE BETWEEN PERFORMANCE MEASUREMENT AND EVALUATION

McDavid and Hawthorn (2006: 293) point to seven differences.

1   Performance measurement systems are ongoing while evaluation is episodic.
2   Performance measurement addresses general issues while programme evaluation is issue specific.
3   Performance measures are routinized while evaluation measures are customized for each evaluation.
4   Performance measurement generally takes attribution for granted while for evaluation it is a central issue.
5   Resources for performance measurement are usually part of the organizational infrastructure while resources for evaluation are targeted.
6   Managers often play a key role in performance measurement while evaluators and managers are less connected.
7   The uses of performance information evolve over time while the intended purposes of programme evaluation are usually negotiated up front.

8 APPROACH AND OUTLINE OF THE BOOK

The book aspires to a deeper understanding of performance management, its strengths, weaknesses and context. Several choices have been made in writing this book:

1 Performance management is a contested field with advocates and opponents in both the academic and practitioner community. This book assumes that it is not necessary to take sides. A combination of a critical attitude with openness towards the inherent potential of measurement is possible.
2 Key for critical believers of performance management is an understanding of the conditionality of successful performance management; what works when and under which circumstances? This text will pay ample attention to contextual variation.
3 A common but accurate saying states that there is nothing more practical than a good theory. More than in typical how-to manuals, we use theories for a deeper understanding of performance management. The practical relevance of theoretical argumentation lies in the capacity to discover regularities in the relation between performance management and its context. The book does not envisage a grand theoretical scheme. Rather, middle-range theories are suggested when appropriate.
4 The book does not discuss the technicalities of measurement. Discussions on analysis techniques and ICT (information and communication technologies) support are not included in this text. Performance management is seen as a social process in a political and administrative context. A strong focus on the use, users and non-use of performance information follows from this viewpoint.

The outline of the book is as follows (see also Figure 1.2).

Chapter 2 develops and extends the concepts. Key concepts are performance, performance measurement and performance management. Questions include: What is performance and how does it relate to public values? What is micro, meso and macro performance? What is performance measurement? Is everything measurable? What is performance management and what is it not?

Chapter 3 describes the history of performance management in the twentieth century. Several performance movements are identified. A chronological account of those movements is followed by a discussion of elements of change and continuity in performance management.

Chapter 4 is about performance measurement. The subsequent stages of deciding what to measure, identifying indicators, analysing, reporting and safeguarding quality are discussed in detail. This chapter deals with the major design parameters for a performance measurement system.

Chapter 5 discusses how performance information can be incorporated into policy and management. Policy and management cycles are the target for the incorporation of performance information. If successful, incorporation should bridge the gap between the provision of information through measurement (chapter 4) and its use (chapter 6).

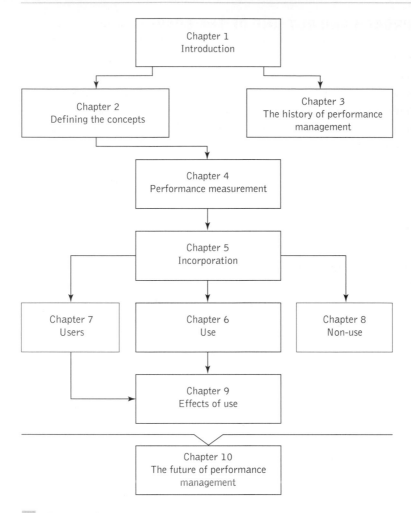

Figure 1.2 *Outline of the book*

Chapter 6 then deals with the use of performance information. Three modes of use are distinguished: learning, steering & control, and accountability. The chapter further argues that the design parameters of a measurement system (see chapter 4) need to vary according to the use that is envisaged.

Chapter 7 looks at performance information from the perspective of the users: public managers, politicians, citizens, oversight agencies and media. The actor perspective on use is intensely intertwined with the thematic approach in chapter 6.

Chapter 8 reflects upon the observation that performance information is often not used. Several theories can explain why performance information is not always functional for management and policy. Besides insufficient quality of performance information, psychological, cultural and institutional barriers may inhibit use.

Chapter 9 discusses the effects of performance measurement; does performance measurement perform? Both the functional and dysfunctional effects are treated. The chapter concludes with some strategies to cope with dysfunctional effects of measurement effects.

Chapter 10 is titled 'The future of performance management'. Some slightly provocative statements are put forward in order to challenge thinking about performance management while using the concepts of the book. The chapter first outlines some paradoxes in measurement, after which a number of potential improvements in implementation are taken into consideration. Finally, three more fundamental departures from the current practice of performance management are discussed.

9 CONCLUSION

This introductory chapter has sketched the subject of the book in broad outlines. It is argued that performance is pivotal in contemporary public management. Performance permeates management, public sector reform and public policy. However, performance is not only a concept; it also suggests an agenda of change and improvement. As a result, performance is also heavily contested as being too one-sided. The core of the critique is a neglect of other values such as equity, openness, integrity, etc.

Much of the controversy is about performance as an agenda (propagated by a performance movement) and not as much about performance as a concept. Chapter 3 deals with the history of performance movements which propagated often contested performance agendas. Chapter 2 seeks more conceptual precision and suggests a framework to reconcile the performance concept and the concept of public values. This book further builds on the concepts, and not the controversy around the performance agenda.

DISCUSSION QUESTIONS

1   What does it mean when somebody claims an organization (e.g. a railway company, a municipality, a police department) is performing?
2   Is performance the 'holy grail' of public administration? In that case why is it contested?

REFERENCES

Bouckaert, G. and Halligan, J. (2008) *Managing Performance: International Comparisons*. London, Routledge.

Bouckaert, G. and Peters, B. G. (2002) Performance measurement and management: the Achilles' heel in administrative modernization. *Public Performance & Management Review*, 25, 4, 359–62.

Calmette, J. F. (2006) La loi organique relative aux lois de finances (LOLF): un texte, un esprit, une pratique. *Revue française d'administration publique*, 117, 43–55.

De Lancer Julnes, P. and Holzer, M. (2008) *Performance Measurement: Building Theory, Improving Practice*. Armonk, NY, M. E. Sharpe.

Dubnick, M. (2005) Accountability and the promise of performance: in search of mechanisms. *Public Performance & Management Review*, 28, 376–417.

Dunleavy, P. (1986) Explaining the privatization boom: public choice versus radical approaches. *Public Administration*, 64, 13–34.

Flynn, N. (2007) *Public Sector Management*. Thousand Oaks, Sage.

Gore, A. (1993) *From Red Tape to Results: Creating a Government That Works Better & Costs Less*. Report of the National Performance Review. Washington, DC, US Government Printing Office.

Hatry, H. P. (1999) *Performance Measurement: Getting Results*. Washington, DC, Urban Institute Press.

Hood, C. (2007) Public service management by numbers: Why does it vary? Where has it come from? What are the gaps and the puzzles? *Public Money and Management*, 27, 95–102.

Ingraham, P. W. (2005) Performance: promises to keep and miles to go. *Public Administration*, 65, 390–95.

Ingraham, P. W., Joyce, P. G. and Donahue, A. K. (2003) *Government Performance: Why Management Matters*. Baltimore, Johns Hopkins University Press.

KPMG (2008) *Holy Grail or Achievable Quest? International Perspectives on Public Sector Performance Management*. Ottawa, CAPAM.

Maxwell School of Citizenship and Public Affairs (2002) *Paths to Performance in State and Local Government: A Final Assessment of the Maxwell School of Citizenship and Public Affairs*. Syracuse, Maxwell School of Citizenship and Public Affairs.

McDavid, J. C. and Hawthorn, L. R. L. (2006) *Program Evaluation and Performance Measurement: An Introduction to Practice*. Thousand Oaks, Sage.

Moynihan, D. P. (2008) *The Dynamics of Performance Management: Constructing Information and Reform*, Washington, DC, Georgetown University Press.

Naschold, F. and Bogumil, J. (2000) *Modernisierung des Staates: New public management in deutscher und internationaler Perspektive*. Leverkusen, Leske & Budrich.

OECD (2009) *Measuring Government Activity*. Paris, OECD.

Osborne, D. and Gaebler, T. (1993) *Reinventing Government: How the Entrepreneurial Spirit is Transforming the Public Sector from Schoolhouse to State House, City Hall to Pentagon*. Boston, MA, Addison Wesley.

Pollitt, C. (1993) *Managerialism and the Public Services: Cuts or Cultural Change in the 1990s?* Oxford, Blackwell.

Pollitt, C. and Bouckaert, G. (2004) *Public Management Reform: A Comparative Analysis*. Oxford, Oxford University Press.

Premfors, R. (1998) Reshaping the democratic state: Swedish experiences in international perspective. *Public Administration,* 76, 141–59.

Radin, B. A. (2006) *Challenging the Performance Movement: Accountability, Complexity, and Democratic Values*. Washington, DC, Georgetown University Press.

Rossi, R. J. and Gilmartin, K. J. (1980) *The Handbook of Social Indicators: Sources, Characteristics, and Analysis*. New York, Garland STPM Press.

Tanner, L. (2008) *Operation Sunlight: Enhancing Budget Transparency*. Canberra, ALP.

Weiss, C. H. (1998) Have we learned anything about the use of evaluation? *American Journal of Evaluation,* 19, 23–33.

Wholey, J. S., Hatry, H. P. and Newcomer, K. E. (2004) *Handbook of Practical Program Evaluation*. San Francisco, Jossey-Bass.

FURTHER READING

A good start to situate the performance concepts is Dubnick's (2005) article on accountability and the promise of performance. Ingraham (2005) and Bouckaert and Halligan (2008) provide an overview of the performance agenda: where it came from, what it promised and where it is going. A good introduction to the state of the art of performance research is *Performance Measurement: Building Theory, Improving Practice* by De Lancer Julnes and Holzer (2008). The controversy around performance management is best described by Radin's book *Challenging the Performance Movement* (Radin 2006). It may also be useful to critically revise some of the texts that advocate performance management, e.g. Gore's National Performance Review (1993), and Osborne and Gaebler's *Reinventing Government* (1993).

Chapter 2

Defining the concepts

LEARNING OBJECTIVES

- To have a precise understanding of the distinct concepts of performance, performance measurement and performance management.
- To be able to recognize differences in measurability.
- To situate performance management vis-à-vis other management types.

KEY POINTS

- Performance can be operationalized using a production logic. A substantial definition of performance can build on public value theory.
- The unique characteristics of public sector performance compared to the private sector warrants a distinct public administration approach.
- Performance measurement has to take measurability of organizations and issues into account.
- Performance management does not exist in its pure form; public management is always a mixture of ideal typical management types.

Performance management has accumulated many meanings. Since virtually all NPM flavoured public administration practices are associated with performance management, the utility of the concept for analysis diminishes. In debates on performance management, people often feel they are talking at cross-purposes. In order to avoid such ambiguity in this text, more definitional precision is required. This chapter develops the definitions that will be used in further chapters.

Performance is the great unknown. Performance can be made operational as outputs and outcomes, but also as public values. *Performance measurement* is the bundle of activities aimed at obtaining information on performance. Besides traditional measurement, other more qualitative resources such as focus groups with citizens, expert advice, and privileged witnesses may yield performance information. Besides this explicit information, people usually also have *tacit knowledge* of government performance built up through personal experience. As we will discuss in chapter 8, tacit knowledge and prior experience may play a vital role in explaining non-use. *Performance management* is a type of management that incorporates and uses performance information for decision-making.

1 PERFORMANCE

The conventional definition of performance uses the metaphor of the production process. Performances are the outputs and outcomes of activities. An alternative view sees performance as the realization of public values.

1.1 *Performance as a the result of a production process*

The most widely used conception of performance follows a production logic. A basic model, derived from the private sector, only looks at inputs, activities and outputs. A growing awareness of the inadequacies of this simple model for public and non-profit activities led several public administration scholars to redefine the model (see for instance Hatry 1999, Poister 2003 and Pollitt and Bouckaert 2004). Policy evaluators generally use the same logic to assess programme performance (McDavid and Hawthorn 2006). Figure 2.1 includes the most important elements of the extended production model of performance. Performance management can cover the whole chain from input to outcome. Bouckaert and Halligan (2008) refer to this dimension as the 'span of performance'.

Problems, needs and relevance

The starting point is the socio-economic situation. Socio-economic issues (No. 1 on Figure 2.1) induce a need for action by the public sector (2). In accordance with the traditional politics–administration dichotomy, politicians are expected to define the societal needs. Agenda-setting research however demonstrates that not only politicians are involved in translating issues to problems and problems to policies. Civil servants, interest groups, media and chance events also play a role in formulating needs. The political system however has the unique role of filtering issues and determining priorities. These priorities are, following the model, translated into objectives (3) of the organization or programme under review. The confrontation of the objectives of a policy with the needs allows the assessing of the relevance (7) of the pursued policies.

17

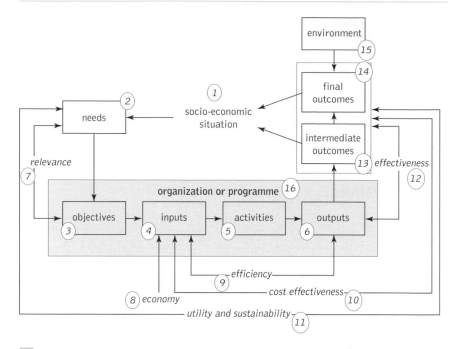

Figure 2.1 *The production model of performance*

Outputs and efficiency

Inputs (such as financial and human resources) (4) are allocated to organizations and programmes in order to stage activities (5) that yield outputs (6). Economy (8) is the ratio of a monetary input over another input (e.g. the cost of a computer). The ratio of the input over the outputs is efficiency (9).

It should be noted that economists usually employ a more narrow definition of efficiency. In economics, efficiency has two dimensions: technical and allocative efficiency. *Economic (or cost) efficiency* requires both. *Technical or operational* efficiency refers to the output–input ratio compared to a standard ratio, which is considered optimal or ideal (and so can never exceed 100 per cent). Both output- and input-oriented efficiency can be defined. Output efficiency focuses on the maximization of output for a given set of inputs, or alternatively, input orientation aims at the minimizations of inputs for a given set outputs. *Allocative* efficiency refers to the use of inputs in optimal proportions given their respective prices and production technology. For example, allocative efficiency in input selection involves selecting the mix of inputs (e.g. labour and capital) which produce a given quantity of output at minimum costs, based on prevailing input prices.

Figure 2.2 gives a graphical representation of input and output efficiency. The figure depicts the isoquants, i.e. the bundles of inputs that produce the same level of output and the bundles of output that require the same level of inputs. It also includes the isocost

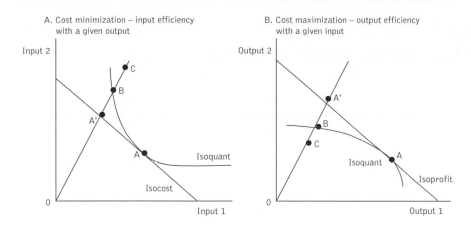

Figure 2.2 *Allocative and technical efficiency for input and output efficiency*

Source: based on De Borger and Kerstens 1995

curve that gives bundles of input that can be obtained with identical costs. The isoprofit curve gives bundles of output that yield identical profits. Costs are minimal in the point where the isocost curve touches the isoquant. Profits are maximized where the isoprofit curve touches the isoquant.

Point A is technically and allocative efficient, and thus economic efficient. Point B is technically efficient but allocatively inefficient. The distance BA' in scenario A represents the costs that could be saved when the optimal input mix (point A) would be selected. In scenario B, the distance BA' represents the lost profits. Point C is both allocative and technically inefficient.

Maximization of financial profit is not normally an objective of public sector organizations. However, public sector organizations should also evaluate their output mix. They should also consider whether they provide the right bundle of services. This assessment is intrinsically more complicated in the public sector. First, the definition of output in itself is more complex. The number of transactions between producers and consumers is not a valid way of defining public sector output. We need to consider the volume of services *provided*. For more information on the provision versus the transaction approach, see Box 2.1. Second, the criterion for determining optimal output levels should be societal profit instead of financial profit. A hospital that is routinely taking X-rays of all its patients is maximizing its output and in all probability will become technically efficient. However, it will not be allocatively efficient.

Performance is thus, in economic parlance, about maximizing profit for society. Yet, it is far from clear what profit for society actually means. A complex and dynamic system of political representation, fuelled by interests, power, ideology and political judgement, is determining what society values. As a result, there is no such thing as a single and definite allocative optimum for public services. There is a constant tension between increasing or decreasing public service provision and interference of government in

19

BOX 2.1 OUTPUT AS TRANSACTION OR AS PROVISION

An important technical distinction is between output measures that capture transactions, and those that reflect the provision of services. These approaches reflect the perspectives used traditionally in economics and public administration respectively.

In the economic notion, output is counted when the transaction is complete, i.e. when the output is consumed. This transaction approach is used in many existing direct output measures of public services, e.g. number of pupils, prisoners, crimes, number of fires attended, etc. The Atkinson review (2005) provides an elaborate discussion of the uses and limitations of this approach. This is the approach proposed by the System of National Accounts, UK.

The provision (public administration) approach sees output as products or services that come out of the production process, regardless of whether they are consumed or not. Instead of the number of pupils or prisoners, the number of teaching hours or the number of cells are defined as the outputs. This approach is more common in public administration because of the potential use of the data for holding people or entities to account. Public organizations that are providing services often have no impact on the level of consumption. For example, prisons cannot reasonably be held accountable for the low level of consumption of their services if, fortuitously, criminality decreases.

OECD 2009

the private sphere. Hence, economic models for understanding public administration sometimes appear to be deceitfully simple.

Outputs and efficiency are adequate conceptualizations of performance in the private sector but are unsatisfactory in the public sector. Both in public and private organizations, outputs are expected to have effects in society. In the private sector, this effect is determined and valued by each individual consumption decision. When a customer buys a car, he or she devotes a significant share of income to the purchase and thus values it. The difference between sales price and production costs is the added value of the product. The aggregation of these individual added values is the main component of the total profit of the firm, and thus its outcome in society. Financial analysts speak of the bottom line of a firm.

It should be noted that public/private distinction is not black and white. Also in the private sector, there has been a debate on its social role beyond individual consumption. The United Nations, for instance, has defined a triple bottom line (TBL), which is an expanded spectrum of values and criteria for measuring organizational success: profits, people and planet. The *people* concept refers to fair and beneficial business practices towards labour and the community in which a firm conducts its business. The *planet* concept refers to sustainable environmental practices. *Profit*, in the TBL definition, is the economic benefit of economic activity for society. It is the lasting economic impact the organization has on its economic environment. The TBL definition of profit is clearly broader than the conventional definition of internal profit discussed above. It remains to be seen whether efforts of private companies to reflect upon their social role imply a converging trend between public and private concerns, or whether TBL and other efforts are mainly cosmetic. The response of private corporations to the financial crisis may be a test; which bottom line will come under greatest pressure?

Outcomes and effectiveness

The outcomes of public services are either collective, or consist of externalities that are not taken into account by individual consumers. There is no direct determination of added value by citizens. Rather, and only in democratic societies, there is a remote and indirect assessment through elections. For public services, elections are by no means sufficient to assess their impact in society. As a result, defining outcomes of public services becomes the subject of much research and practice.

Public administration scholars have disentangled the outcome concept. Outcomes can be *intermediate* (usually in the short term) (13 in Figure 2.1) or *final* (usually in the long term) (14). The final outcomes in particular are influenced by the *environment* (15) on which the organization or the programme has a limited or no impact. Such environmental factors can encompass socio-economic or ecological trends, but also policy measures from other governments. Agencies in European Union member states for instance are restrained by European regulation. The ratio of output over effect is the *effectiveness* (12). The ratio of the input over the effects is the *cost-effectiveness* (10). The outcomes of a programme or an organization have to address the needs of society. The confrontation of needs and outcomes allows assessment of the *sustainability and utility* (11) of the programme or the organization (see Box 2.2).

The metaphor of a production process is currently the dominant perspective on performance. It was initially launched by systems theorists such as David Easton (1965). Public administration in his view is an open system which converts inputs (demands as well as support) into outputs. Outputs of different other systems within (intrasocietal environment) and outside (extrasocietal environment) society are inputs for the political system. Outputs of the political system in turn influence the environment. In public administration practice, systems thinking was a defining element of major reform packages such as Planning Programming and Budgeting System (PPBS) (Schick 1966). In order to provide more insight into performance, budgeting systems had to systematically account for planned outputs and outcomes instead of the traditional report on inputs spent.

BOX 2.2 PRODUCTION MODEL OF PERFORMANCE APPLIED TO THE ISSUE OF TRAFFIC CASUALTIES

As an example, we apply the model to the issue of traffic casualties. Suppose that politicians formulate the need to reduce the number of casualties in traffic. Typically, several interest groups and the (perceived) pressure from their constituencies influence politicians. The issue is also particularly vulnerable to chance events such as accidents with children that put it all at once at the top of the agenda. A potential objective is to reduce the number of casualties to a number comparable to other developed countries. In order to attain this goal, the government will use (financial and other) resources to build cycle tracks, to reconstruct crossroads, to install speed traps, etc. The outputs then are the kilometres of new tracks, the new crossroads constructed and the number of vehicles controlled. To this point, the government has a good grip on the chain of events. The decisive test however is the outcome in society. In the short run, it may be that more children cycle to school and that fewer drivers violate the speed limits. These are intermediate outcomes. The government, however, wants to reduce the number of casualties. The question then is whether the immediate outcomes lead to the final outcomes? Undoubtedly, environmental factors will interfere. For instance, a reduction in the number of casualties may be the result of bad weather conditions. In cold and rainy weather, there are usually fewer cyclists and pedestrians, and therefore fewer potential victims. Yet, driving conditions are worse, and therefore there is a higher chance of accidents.

1.2 Performance as the realization of public values

The definition of performance as a production process leaves an important question unanswered: what are the defining characteristics of performance? Besides the process of getting to performance, we also need to conceptualize the substance of performance. In the performance measurement and management literature, little conceptual work has been done to describe the substance of performance. This lacuna may be filled by the literature on public sector values (see Box 2.3).

- Hood (1991) distinguishes between three types of public values (see also Voets *et al*. 2008 for an application on network performance).
- A first set of values allege to keep it lean and purposeful – to match resources to defined tasks. Thus, frugality of resource use in relation to given goals is the criterion of success, while failure is counted in terms of instances of avoidable waste and incompetence (Hood 1991: 12). Good value implies the efficient and

BOX 2.3 INVENTORIES OF PUBLIC VALUES

Several studies attempted to sort out the concept of public value.

Moore (1995) draws a parallel with the private sector. Public value in the public and non-profit sector is the analogue of shareholder and user value in the private sector. Public value refers to the value created by government through services, laws, regulation and other actions. The public value concept is also received in practice. The UK Cabinet Office published a study on the concept (Kelly and Muers 2002).

Jørgensen and Bozeman (2002) list 13 public values. Among others, they mention political accountability, equal treatment, *Rechtstaat* ('rule of law'), regime stability, social cohesion and local self governance as typically public values.

Further research on the 'public values universe' led them to a list of about 80 public values (Jørgensen and Bozeman 2007) related to seven themes: (1) the public sector's contribution to society, (2) the transformation of interests to decisions, (3) the relationship between public administrators and politicians, (4) the relationship between public administrators and their environment, (5) intra-organizational aspects of public administration, (6) the behaviour of public sector employees, and (7) the relationship between public administration and the citizens.

effective production of high-quality goods and services – hence the label '*product*' values.

■ A second set of values intend to keep government fair and honest. Government has to pursue honesty, fairness and mutuality through the prevention of distortion, inequity, bias and abuse of office (Hood 1991: 13). These values are institutionalized in appeal mechanisms, public reporting requirements and ethical codes. Good value implies the open and honest processes – hence the label '*process*' values.

■ A third set of values are set to keep the public sector robust and resilient. Government has to keep operating even in adverse 'worst case' conditions and to adapt rapidly in a crisis (Hood 1991: 14). Reliability is often an argument for choosing public production instead of private production. Good value implies the assurance of strong regimes to fall back on – hence the label '*regime*' values.

Two visions of how public values and public performance conceptually relate to each other can be developed. Performance can be seen as one value among others in the public values universe (Vision A in Figure 2.3). In Hood's framework, performance would roughly be equivalent to the first set of values. This approach builds on the

23

Vision A:
Performance as a subset of the public value universe

Product: efficiency and effectiveness
Process: openness, integrity and participation
Regime: robustness, reliance and innovation

Vision B:
Performance as the realization of public values

	group 1 'product'	group 2 'process'	group 3 'regime'
Performance			
Values			

Figure 2.3 *Two visions of the relation between public values and public performance*

controversy around the performance movement; performance defined as efficiency and effectiveness goes at the expense of other values. Alternatively, performance is seen as the realization of public values. In this view, values and performance are distinct concepts (Vision B in Figure 2.3). Approach B is less controversial, since all public values can lead to performance. Besides efficiency and effectiveness, successful practices of, for instance, participation or innovation could also be seen as dimensions of performance.

Vision A is, for example, taken in Beryl Radin's challenge to the performance movement (Radin 2006). This book critiques a set of public values that is promoted by actors in academia, government and society (i.e. the performance movement) that are promoting values such as efficiency, effectiveness and accountability. Radin argues among others that the performance movement forgets about the context, interferes with professionalism, is not concerned with equity and is apolitical. She argues that the performance movement stresses too much the product subset of public values and too little the process and regime values.

Vision B considers performance to be an analytical concept rather than a label for a set of values. Values are the frame of reference for the assessment of performance. Values and performance ask different questions about the same issue – the public interest.

■ A performance assessment will analyse to what extent public organizations and programmes further the general interest. Are public services provided in an efficient and effective way? What are the impacts of a programme on equity? Have sufficient measures been taken to guarantee the functioning of the public sector, even in the wake of disastrous events?

■ A value assessment will ask questions about the values that prevail, whether they are in conflict or whether they complement. In order to make this assessment of dominant values in the public sector, a researcher may want to have a look at behaviour. One can study intentional behaviour that is aimed at the fulfilment of the general interest (performance). A researcher could also look at non-intentional behaviour.

1.3 Micro, meso and macro performance

Performance has a potentially broad stretch. It includes micro, meso and macro levels. Bouckaert and Halligan (2008) call this the 'depth of performance' (p.18), indicating that performance can be discussed at different levels. Three levels of analysis can be distinguished. The *macro level* typically includes general discussions on the performance of a country, but it also encompasses performance of supra-national governments (the Euro zone, OECD countries) as well as local and regional governments. The key element of macro performance is its government-wide character, regardless of the tier of government. *Micro performance* is defined at the level of an individual organization and its interface with citizens and other organizations. In between macro and micro, *meso performance* refers to either the performance of a policy sector (e.g. education) or the performance of governing a chain of events (e.g. the food chain) or networks (e.g. an urban development project).

Macro, meso and micro performance are a nested configuration. Like Russian dolls, the meso level fits into the macro, and the micro fits into the meso level. This image however is deceitfully simple. In reality, the configuration is more complex for different reasons. First, policy sectors, chains and networks cut across each other. The food safety chain, for instance, involves education (policy sector: education) as well as (judicial) punishments for non-compliance (policy sector: justice). Second, individual organizations regularly are involved in a multitude of policy sectors. A prison for instance primarily belongs to the sector of justice, but has also dealings with other sectors such as mental health, job reintegration and education. Third, organizations may also be involved in governing different chains and networks. An environmental inspectorate intervenes in chains that lead to the conservation of nature as well in economic value creation. Finally, reality is even more complex than this suggests, because chains and networks are not always entirely contained by the performance of the macro level entity – they literally go out of the box. Immigration for instance is a phenomenon that does not respect national borders. As a result, the performance of a single country is relative to the performance of others (see Figure 2.4).

2 PERFORMANCE MEASUREMENT

Performance measurement is the bundle of deliberate activities of quantifying performance. The result of these activities is performance information.

This definition of performance measurement follows quite naturally from the discussion of performance. When we talk about performance information in this book and unless indicated otherwise, we mean quantitative performance information. The definition also emphasizes that performance measurement is a bundle of tangible activities that can observed in organizations. We identify five activities: defining a measurement object, the formulation of indicators, data collection, data analysis and reporting. In chapter 4, we describe those activities in more detail. Finally, the definition highlights

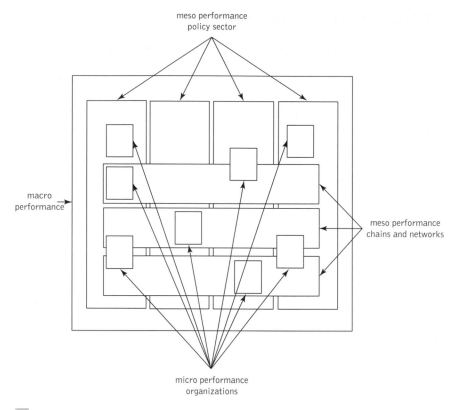

Figure 2.4 *Macro, meso and micro performance in a complex nested configuration*

that performance measurement is a deliberate, intentional activity. As we argued above, tacit knowledge is excluded. This is not to say that performance measurement does not have unintended consequences. In chapter 9, we discuss the behavioural consequences of measurement.

Particularly because performance information has become a central tenet of contemporary accountability schemes, measurability has become an important discussion in the performance measurement literature. Some activities, outputs and outcomes, it is argued, are easier to measure by nature. Ouchi (1977), for instance, argued that output controls are only feasible in organizations that have measurable outputs. If that is not the case, behavioural or clan control are more appropriate. NPM reforms have strongly promoted the use of performance information for accountability purposes. Organizations regularly claim that low measurability makes it impossible for them to account for quantified performance. This complaint is often heard in organizations that have a role in policy advice (see Box 2.4).

Several authors have attempted to define the operational characteristics of measurability (Bouckaert 1996). We review some key frameworks that help us understand measurability. In the 1960s, Downs (1967) identified eight structural aspects of bureaus,

BOX 2.4 MEASURING THE QUALITY OF POLICY ADVICE

Policy advice comprises many activities, including research, data analysis, proposal development, consultation with stakeholders, formulation of advice for decision-makers, guiding policy through governmental and parliamentary processes, and the subsequent evaluation of the outcomes of the policy (Gregory and Lonti 2008). According to Nicholson (1996), performance of policy advice can be measured based on whether advice has accurate, comprehensive, up-to-date information and is responsive to client needs. Other criteria are clarity, practicality, appropriateness, fairness, cost-effectiveness and consultation with interested parties.

Gregory and Lonti (2008) assessed the measurement of policy advice in the New Zealand public sector. Their main critique was the inadequacy of performance measures to accurately reflect the political nature of policy advice. A former British cabinet minister, Roy Hattersley, is quoted as saying that 'a disgruntled civil servant noticed that my policy advisor's main task was to give a spurious intellectual justification to my prejudices . . . but you could say that his job was to demonstrate the fundamental wisdom of my beliefs' (quoted on p.848). It is concluded that although policy advice can be genuinely and meaningfully gauged from a number of different perspectives – including those of ministers, parliament, policy stakeholders, and the public at large – the performance measures that are being used seem to reflect a narrower managerialist predisposition to count what can most easily be counted (p. 852).

which each can be used to assess measurability of an organization. All but the last are matters of degree (see Table 2.1). Behind the criteria lay two opposite images of organization; organizations as machines versus organizations as transformation and flux (Morgan 1997). Measurement is believed to be more straightforward in the former. Similar arguments can be developed from contingency theorists such as Thompson (1967).

Wilson (1989) developed a well-known scheme, which is related to the second structural dimension of Downs. He distinguishes between measurability of output and outcome and combines these two dimensions in order to distinguish four types of organizations: production, procedural, craft and coping (see Table 2.2). Both the output and the outcome of *production organizations* are observable, for example. Examples include mail services or routine tax collection. Performance measurement and management is possible. *Craft organizations* have observable outcomes, but their output is not visible – the results can be observed, not the processes. Park rangers are an example of this type of organization. It is noticed when the number of poachers is reduced, but we do not know precisely which activities the park rangers have performed. Many other examples

Table 2.1 *Downs' structural characteristics of bureaus and the implications for measurability*

	Profile for highly measurable organizations	Profile for hardly measurable organizations
The clarity with which the functions of the bureaus can be defined	High ◄————►	Low
The ease with which the results of bureau actions can be perceived and their effectiveness evaluated	High ◄————►	Low
The stability of the bureau's internal technological environment over time	High ◄————►	Low
The stability of the bureau's external environment over time	High ◄————►	Low
The operational interdependence of its various functions	Low ◄————►	High
The complexity of its functions	Low ◄————►	High
The scope of its functions, that is, the breadth of the different activities those functions encompass	Low ◄————►	High
The power setting of the bureau in its environment; that is, the nature of its institutional surroundings	Nominal variable	

are found in the health profession. We know when people are getting better, but most of us do not have an understanding of what doctors have done in order to attain this result. *Procedural organizations* have outputs that are observable and outcomes that are less well defined. Many counselling services fall under this category. An extreme example is mental health – generally, discussions with psychiatrists are understandable, but whether mental health actually improves is hard to observe. Finally, *coping organizations* have problems in observing both output and outcome; diplomatic efforts by embassies are an example. Diplomatic activities and outcomes are diverse and hard to define. Moreover, outcomes are contingent upon many other variables besides the diplomatic intervention.

The use of the typologies risks provoking a rather stereotypical image of the organizations, based on a limited number of activities. Organizations however usually capture an extensive bundle of goods and services. Residential care, for example, entails a complex package of services including the provision of meals, infrastructure, nursing and psychological support. Even a typical coping organization such as an embassy will have some routine production activities – for instance the issuing of passports. The apparent ease of measurement of the aggregate package might conceal significant difficulties in measurement within some of the constituent components. Therefore, the typologies are mainly useful to typify activities and not organizations or programmes.

Table 2.2 *Wilson's (1989) typology of organizations*

		Outcomes observable	
		Yes	No
Outputs observable	Yes	Production organizations Examples: mail services, tax collection, sanitation, vehicle registration, revenue collection	Procedural organizations Examples: mental health, counselling, military (peacetime), youth penitentiary
	No	Craft organizations Examples: field inspections, military (wartime), doctors, forest rangers	Coping organizations Examples: diplomacy, intelligence, research

Hackman and Oldham (1980) developed a scheme at a micro-analytical level. They distinguish between task routine and task ambiguity. Routine refers to whether a task is repeated while ambiguity refers to whether the course of action is clear or not. Measurement becomes increasingly difficult when routine lowers and ambiguity rises (see Figure 2.5).

1 Measurement of activities with high ambiguity and a low routine is most challenging. Typical examples would be interest representation in embassies or creative work in cultural institutions. The measurement base in these cases is progress.
2 Activities with average routine and ambiguity have group and human relations as a measurement base. Typical examples are the many social services where client characteristics introduce a certain level of ambiguity and break the routine.
3 Finally, high routine and low ambiguity are typically found in administrative processes such as registering vehicles, processing standard tax forms, payroll administration. The measurement base is time.

Blankart (1987) finally also touches on the measurability of services when he discusses the limits of privatization. He assumes that only those goods and services of which the quality of the output is measurable are liable for privatization (see Table 2.3). He distinguishes between three types of consumption technology. *Inspection goods* (raw materials, stationery) can be privatized easily because quality is tangible and measurable. *Experience goods* (e.g. advice, debt collection) can also be privatized. Although quality is more difficult to measure here compared to inspection goods, an assessment can be made based on the extrapolation of experiences and the accumulation of goodwill by clients. In this way, quality becomes predictable. Finally, *trust goods* (courts, police, general public administration) are difficult to privatize, because they are hard to evaluate, even through experience. Measurement of quality in the latter cases is very difficult.

Figure 2.5 *Hackman and Oldham's (1980) analysis of measurability*

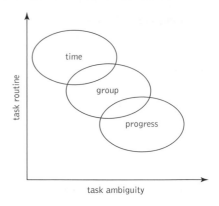

Table 2.3 *Blankart's (1987) clusters of services*

	Inspection	Experience	Trust
Criteria	Quality is tangible	Quality is predictable	Quality is intangible

However useful these schemes may be, in practice, most people find their own organization and policy sector hard to measure. An outsider may judge the work of a fire patrol to be easy to measure – i.e. extinguishing fires as quickly as possible. Firemen however will see the complexity of a big conflagration, the risk of flashovers and back-draft, and the importance of choosing the right extinguisher. Therefore, they will often oppose counting fires as if they are all alike. Similar reactions will be heard by teachers, doctors and road construction workers. Just because we know our own situation better, we often believe it is more complex, interconnected and ambiguous and thus less apt for measurement. This observation does not invalidate the empirical search for differences in measurability, but rather serves as a warning sign for not jumping to conclusions when assessing measurability from outside.

3 PERFORMANCE MANAGEMENT: WHAT IT IS AND WHAT IT ISN'T

In the previous paragraphs, we suggested three ways to make sense of performance: performance measurement, performance judgement and tacit knowledge and discussed measurability of organizations. The next question is how this relates to performance management. The answer is relatively straightforward: performance management is a type of management that incorporates and uses performance information for decision-making. As we will discuss later, incorporation is about integrating performance information into policy and management cycles of among others policy-making, budgeting and contract management. The uses are grouped in three clusters of decisions: learning, steering & control, and account giving (see Table 2.4).

Notions such as management-by-objective, strategic management, performance budgeting, managing for results, results-based management and entrepreneurial budgeting all share a common logic that public organizations should produce performance information and use this information to inform decision-making (Moynihan 2008). We follow this relatively down-to-earth approach to performance management – which is broad but precise and analytical rather than normative.

This definition contrasts with a rather narrow and linear conception of so-called performance management which is sometimes found in practitioners' literature. These definitions are often disconnected from the definition of performance as such, and it is an ultimate reduction of performance management to one of the managerial functions. Another is the National Performance Review's 'process of assessing progress toward achieving predetermined goals' (quoted in Blalock and Barnow 2001: 489). According to an OECD definition, performance management more generally 'covers corporate management, performance information, evaluation, performance monitoring, assessment and performance reporting'. A stricter definition is also provided to reflect the context of the current performance trend, as 'a management cycle under which programme performance objectives and targets are determined, managers have flexibility to achieve them, actual performance is measured and reported, and this information feeds into decisions about programme funding, design, operations and rewards or penalties' (Curristine 2005: 131).

A not uncommon practice in the literature is the equation of performance management and performance measurement. Under the heading performance management, discussions mainly focus on performance measurement without further clarification (Bovaird and Gregory 1996; De Bruijn 2002). This text will make a clear distinction between performance measurement and performance management, which is needed for a better insight in the functioning of performance management systems.

Table 2.4 *Three clusters of performance management*

	To learn	To steer & control	To give account
Key question	How to improve policy or management?	How to steer & control activities?	How to communicate performance?
Focus	Internal	Internal	External
Orientation	Change/future	Control/present	Survival/past
Exemplary instruments	Strategic planning, benchmarking, risk analysis, business process reengineering	Monitors and management scorecards, performance pay, performance budgeting	League tables, citizen charters and annual reporting, performance contracts

Since the performance jargon sounds so familiar and commonsensical, it may be useful to end by asking what the alternative for performance management would be. Talbot (2005) notes that discussions of performance have existed as long as government itself. Elections are fought over both future performance and past performance. Although a focus on performance seems to be ingrained in government, performance management is considered a relatively new phenomenon (say post-World War II). To newcomers to public administration, this may come as a surprise.

Performance management is a late-bloomer in public administration. Statistical systems and the development of administrative nomenclature have been essential to the development of the modern state. The development of these information systems was, however, driven by a need to *administer* the state with the tax system as one of the prime fields of innovation (Desrosières 1998). It seems that only in the last half of the previous century, did governments feel the need to systematically introduce performance information into *management* (see also chapter 3). This trend has been leveraged by a culture of modernity that strongly values rational and factual approaches to management and policy (Van de Walle and Roberts 2008).

The question we set out above, however, remains. On what else than performance could management be based? Since an essay on management traditions is clearly outside of the scope of a textbook, we limit ourselves to a categorization of management traditions by one of the founding fathers of the discipline: Max Weber. Weber's discussion of the bases of authority laid the groundwork for a theory of bureaucracy. The related management practices – although Weber did not use the word – can be differentiated from performance management. Weber identified three types of authority, which can be transposed to three sources of management capacity (Fry and Raadschelders 2008). None of the three approaches particularly focuses on results, and thus they are distinct from performance management (see Table 2.5).

The Weberian ideal-typical approaches to public management are still relevant today, although the relative importance may have shifted. The implication is that public management is always a blend of ideal-types. Performance management in its pure form does not exist. Cultural theory should be the first candidate in order to better understand which configuration is functional in which conditions (Schedler and Proeller 2007).

4 CONCLUSION

This chapter laid the conceptual groundwork for the book. Performance, performance measurement and performance management were treated as separate and well defined concepts. Performance is defined as the realization of public values such as efficiency, effectiveness, equity, robustness, openness and transparency. Performance measurement is the process of acquiring performance information. Measurability of activities is a key concern. Performance management is the incorporation and use of performance information in decision-making.

Table 2.5 *Max Weber's types of authority as alternatives to performance management*

Weber's authority types	Type of management
Charismatic authority. The personal qualities of the leader/manager determine legitimacy. Weber speaks of the belief of ordinary man in the exceptional powers and heroism of the leader. The leader demands obedience by virtue of his mission. In keeping with the transient nature of charisma, charismatic *administration* is loose and unstable. Weber, writing during the second industrial revolution in Germany (1870–1914), saw charismatic authority to be on the wane. The contemporary leadership literature however seems to re-establish some of the virtues of charismatic leadership. According to Van Wart (2003), while reviewing the leadership literature, leaders are nowadays required to be visionary, entrepreneurial and charismatic.	Charismatic management is about building goodwill, creating a sense of mission and developing a cult around managers. The Richard Bransons and Steve Jobs from this world are witnesses to the enduring appeal of this management style. Performance can be instrumental in developing this cult, since it can be assumed that it radiates from charisma. Yet, in contrast to performance management, it remains peripheral.
Traditional authority. Here, too, personal qualities of the manager determine legitimacy, but the qualities are founded on respect for traditions and routines; Weber speaks of the eternal past. In contrast to charismatic authority, traditional authority is stable. People obey persons rather than rules and the development of rational regulations is impeded. Normative institutionalists have continued to study the constraints that routines and norms enforce on rational agency (Scott 2001).	Traditional management is about establishing and institutionalizing routines. Although performance may be at play when routines are developed, it typically is no longer taken into consideration when those routines become institutions; in Selznick's words, when they become infused with value (1957). All organizations need routines and a sense of institutional integrity that needs to be guarded, rather than challenged based on performance arguments (Selznick 1957).
Legal authority. Legitimacy of managers is based on them acting in accordance with their duties as established by a code of rational rules and regulations. Managers are a 'trustee' of an impersonal, compulsory institution. Weber abstains from suggesting an evolutionary, linear progress towards legal authority. Although he sees a general trend towards legal domination, it is punctuated by bursts of charisma and regressions towards tradition (Fry and Raadschelders 2008).	Bureaucratic management, finally, is about coordination and directing within and based on the rules that are set out. It is assumed that these rules are rational, which means that they are means to a political end (Weber 1948). Performance may be a consideration when rules are developed. Good managers, however, operate within this regulatory framework, which is not to be challenged.

DISCUSSION QUESTIONS

1 Apply the production model of performance to a policy field: higher education, urban renewal, mobility, etc. (and experience the confusion of applying a straightforward model).
2 Are economic models useful for discussing public sector performance?
3 Which public services are easy to measure, which are not?
4 What is the dominant management type in your organization, university, municipality, administration?

REFERENCES

Atkinson, A. B. (2005) *Atkinson Review: Final Report: Measurement of Government Output and Productivity for the National Accounts.* London, Palgrave Macmillan.

Blalock, A. B. and Barnow, B. S. (2001) Is the new obsession with performance management masking the truth about social programmes? In Forsythe, D. (ed.) *Quicker, Better, Cheaper?: Managing Performance in American Government.* New York, Rockefeller Institute Press.

Blankart, C. B. (1987) Limits to privatization. *European Economic Review,* 31, 346–51.

Bouckaert, G. and Halachmi, A. (1995) The range of performance indicators in the public sector: Theory vs. practice. In Halachmi, A. and Grant, D. (eds.) *Reengineering and Performance Measurement in Criminal Justice and Social Programmes.* Perth, Western Australia, IIAS Ministry of Justice 1996, 91–106.

Bouckaert, G. and Halligan, J. (2008) *Managing Performance: International Comparisons.* London, Routledge.

Bovaird, T. and Gregory, D. (1996) *Performance Indicators: The British Experience.* Westport, CT, Quorum Books.

Coelli, T. and Rao, P. (1998) *An Introduction to Efficiency and Productivity Analysis.* Boston, Kluwer.

Curristine, T. (2005) Government performance: lessons and challenges. *OECD Journal on Budgeting,* 5, 127–51.

De Borger, B. and Kerstens, K. (1995) Produktiviteit en efficiëntie in de Belgische publieke sector: situering van recent empirisch onderzoek. *Tijdschrift voor Economie en Management,* 40, 101–31.

De Bruijn, H. (2002) *Managing Performance in the Public Sector.* London, Routledge.

Desrosières, A. (1998) *The Politics of Large Numbers: A History of Statistical Reasoning.* Cambridge, Harvard University Press.

Downs, A. (1967) *Inside Bureaucracy*. Boston, Little, Brown and Company.

Easton, D. (1965) *A Systems Analysis of Political Life*. New York, Wiley.

Fry, B. R. and Raadschelders, J. C. N. (2008) *Mastering Public Administration: From Max Weber to Dwight Waldo*. Washington, DC, CQpress.

Gregory, R. and Lonti, Z. (2008) Chasing shadows? Performance measurement of policy advice in the New Zealand government departments. *Public Administration, 86*, 837–56.

Hackman, J. and Oldham, G. R. (1980) *Work Redesign*. Reading, MA, Addison-Wesley.

Hatry, H. P. (1999) *Performance Measurement: Getting Results*. Washington, DC, Urban Institute Press.

Hood, C. (1991) A public management for all seasons. *Public Administration, 69*, 3–19.

Jørgensen, T. B. and Bozeman, B. (2002) Public values lost? Comparing cases on contracting out from Denmark and the United States. *Public Management Review, 4*, 63–81.

Jørgensen, T. B. and Bozeman, B. (2007) Public values: an inventory. *Administration & Society, 39*, 354–81.

Kelly, G. and Muers, S. (2002) *Creating Public Value*. London, Strategy Unit, Cabinet Office.

McDavid, J. C. and Hawthorn, L. R. L. (2006) *Program Evaluation and Performance Measurement: An Introduction to Practice*. Thousand Oaks, Sage.

Moore, M. H. (1995) *Creating Public Value*. Cambridge, MA, Harvard University Press.

Morgan, G. (1997) *Images of Organization*. Thousand Oaks, Sage.

Moynihan, D. P. (2008) *The Dynamics of Performance Management: Constructing Information and Reform*. Washington, DC, Georgetown University Press.

Nicholson, J. (1996) Measures for monitoring policy advice. In Uhr, J. and Mackay, K. (eds.) *Evaluating Policy Advice: Learning from Commonwealth Experience*. Canberra, Federalism Research Centre.

OECD (2009) *Measuring Government Activity*. Paris, OECD.

Ouchi, W. G. (1977) The relationship between organizational structure and organizational control. *Administrative Science Quarterly, 22*, 95–113.

Poister, T. H. (2003) *Measuring Performance in Public and Nonprofit Organizations*. San Fransisco, Jossey-Bass.

Pollitt, C. and Bouckaert, G. (2004) *Public Management Reform: A Comparative Analysis*. Oxford, Oxford University Press.

Radin, B. A. (2006) *Challenging the Performance Movement: Accountability, Complexity, and Democratic Values*. Washington, DC, Georgetown University Press.

Schedler, K. and Proeller, I. (2007) *Cultural Aspects of Public Management Reform*. Amsterdam, Elsevier.

Schick, A. (1966) The road to PPB: the stages of budget reform. *Public Administration Review, 26*, 243–58.

Scott, W. R. (2001) *Institutions and Organizations.* Thousand Oaks, Sage Publications.

Selznick, P. (1957) *Leadership in Administration.* New York, Harper Row.

Talbot, C. (2005) Performance management. In Ferlie, E., Lynn, L. E. and Pollitt, C. (eds.) *The Oxford Handbook of Public Management.* Oxford, Oxford University Press.

Thompson, J. D. (1967) *Organizations in Action: Social Science Bases of Administrative Theory.* New York, McGraw-Hill.

Van de Walle, S. and Roberts, A. (2008) Publishing performance information: an illusion of control? In Van Dooren, W. and Van de Walle, S. (eds.) *Performance Information in the Public Sector: How It Is Used.* Basingstoke, Palgrave: Macmillan.

Van Wart, M. (2003) Public-sector leadership theory: an assessment. *Public Administration Review,* 63, 214–28.

Voets, J., Van Dooren, W. and De Rynck, F. (2008) A framework for assessing the performance of policy networks. *Public Management Review,* 10, 773–790.

Weber, M. (1948) Politics as a vocation. In Kegan, P., Gerth, H. and Mills, C. (eds.) *From Max Weber.* London, Routledge.

Wilson, J. Q. (1989) *Bureaucracy: What Government Agencies Do and Why They Do It.* New York, Basic Books.

FURTHER READING

The OECD (2009) recently published a volume titled *Measuring Government Activity* which discusses some of the conceptual debates in the field. It is based on the technical papers supporting the 'government at a glance' initiative. The production logic of performance is discussed in several contributions: Pollitt and Bouckaert's *Public Management Reform* (2004) and Hatry's Performance Measurement: Getting Results (1999) are a good starting point. McDavid and Hawthorn are a reference from the evaluation literature (2006). An overview of econometric performance methods is provided by Coelli and Rao (1998). A seminal article outlining the different values underpinning public management is Hood's 'A public management for all seasons' (Hood 1991). Jørgensen and Bozeman (2007) undertook recent research on public values. The distinctiveness of the public sector, including the measurability of activities, is described in a lucid way by Wilson (1989). Finally, Fry and Raadschelders (2008) provide a good overview of the work of old masters such as Max Weber. These works often are a good sparring partner for contemporary performance research.

Chapter 3

The history of performance management

LEARNING OBJECTIVES

■ To understand the contingency between the political and social environment on the one hand, and the rise and fall of performance movements, on the other.
■ To develop a historical consciousness with regard to performance management.

KEY POINTS

■ Performance has been on the agenda at several points in time; it is not a NPM invention.
■ Most performance movements share a stable set of concepts (i.e. the production model).
■ What has changed is the intensity and pervasiveness of the use of the performance information.

Performance ideas have been around for a hundred years or more. Historical consciousness on the issue, however, is generally low. It is often forgotten that long-term trends have supported the ascendancy of performance ideas as a central force in public management internationally. The antecedents to contemporary performance measurement and management have a long lineage.

The observation that performance measurement and management extends well beyond NPM has been made on several occasions. Williams (2003) for instance analysed management practices in early twentieth-century New York, and found many of the features of contemporary performance measurement (see also Stivers 2000). These analyses paint a somewhat sobering picture – they seem to suggest that a whole century of study and practice of performance management led mainly to stagnation. Moreover, they run counter to observations on the increasing influence of performance measurement and management (Bouckaert and Halligan 2008; Radin 2006). The central question of this chapter is in what respect performance management changed, in order for it to have an impact that it never had before.

In order to answer this question, we need to analyse in what respect performance management has changed or has *not* changed. We will argue that it is mainly changes in use that account for the impact of the contemporary performance movements. The most striking feature of performance management is its expansion in public sectors over the last two decades, making this current period its most influential. First, however, we briefly discuss the most important performance movements in the twentieth century (Van Dooren 2008).

1 PERFORMANCE MOVEMENTS IN THE TWENTIETH CENTURY

The chapter is organized around a number of performance movements. The concept of 'movement' is analogous to the sociological term 'social movement'. Unlike other forms of organization, movements are informally organized around a set of thoughts and practices that form the glue. Members of a performance movement share an agenda of change with a particular vision on performance, its measurement and management.

We discuss eight movements that have propagated performance management. They are clustered into three time segments: (a) pre-World War II, (b) the 1950s–1970s, which roughly parallels the development of the welfare state and the related growth of government, and (c) the 1980s onwards, when welfare states came under pressure from a variety of sources.

In the list of movements, a distinction between policy movements and management movements can be made. Policy movements mainly focus on performance in terms of the *outcomes* of organizations and public programmes. Management movements have more of an internal focus on *outputs* and efficiency. Yet, there is a grey zone with management movements taking into account some elements of outcome and vice versa.

1.1 1900–1940s

Three performance movements developed at the end of the nineteenth century and the beginning of the twentieth century: (a) the social survey movement, (b) scientific management and the science of administration, and (c) cost accounting. These movements emanated from different milieus, respectively social reformers, engineers and specialist administrators, and large corporations. Yet, all three movements were a response to the social context of industrialization, poverty and social unrest, and governments plagued by corruption. The performance movements of the day sought the answer to these societal issues through rationalization and quantification of policy and administration.

The *social survey movement* was a movement of social reformers who needed facts about social problems (Bulmer *et al.* 1991). The best-known work of the social survey movement is Charles Booth's study on the *Life and Labour of the People in London* (1886–1903) (Linsley and Linsley 1993). Booth believed that the poverty debate was underdeveloped because three questions were unanswered: how many people were poor, why were they poor and what should be done to alleviate poverty? These questions not only demonstrate the performance dimension of the social survey movement, but also that measurement was an instrument to influence a policy agenda.

While the social survey movement mainly targeted the social inequalities, the driver behind the second movement, *scientific management* and *the science of administration* (see Box 3.1 for a treatment of the common ground in these movements) was a response to the need for infrastructure and resource mobilization that ensued from industrialization (Rose 1976). Corruption and adhocracy plaguing government stood in the way of the development of large infrastructures such as national railways or sanitation works. According to Ridley and Simon (1938: 1) a 'generation ago a municipal government was considered commendable if it was honest. Today we demand a great more of our public

BOX 3.1 THE SCIENCE OF ADMINISTRATION AND SCIENTIFIC MANAGEMENT

There is some debate about the differences between scientific management and the science of administration. Williams (2004) pointed to some discrepancies. Scientific management for instance supported distributed management, while the science of administration advocated a hierarchical executive branch. Although the concrete practices they developed were sometimes contradictory, the movements share a number of important principles. Mosher (1968:72–3) summarized this common ground of two sub-movements in six points (see also Sayre 1958).

(1) Rationality: the applicability of the rule of reason.
(2) Planning: the forward projection of needs and objectives.
(3) Specialization: of materials, tools and machines, products, workers and organizations.
(4) Quantitative measurement: applied as far as possible to all elements of operations.
(5) 'One best way': there is one single best method, tool, material and type of worker.
(6) Standards and standardization: the 'one best', once discovered, must be made the standard.

39

service. It must be not only honest but efficient as well'. Government institutions therefore needed a professional workforce and rational, Weberian-style regulation. Administration was now seen as a profession and a science in its own right.

A third evolution in the early twentieth century was the development of *cost accounting*, which was a joint venture of the public and the private sector. Claims of control and openness echoed in both the public and private sector (Previts and Merino 1979; Rivenbark 2005). In addition, stronger information systems were needed in order to manage the increasingly large and complex organizations and corporations. Cost accounting is in essence the process of tracking, recording and analysing costs associated with the activity of an organization. Through cost accounting, output indicators are incorporated into the financial system. Cost accounting has become institutionalized in the private sector. In the public sector, it is still considered innovative in most OECD countries (Pollitt and Bouckaert 2004).

The New York Bureau of Municipal Research (NYBMR) was a synthesis of scientific management, cost accounting and the social survey (Schachter 1989; Stivers 2000). The Bureau put into practice many of the performance measurement concepts that are in use today (Williams 2003). Data collection was embedded in accounting practices. Record keeping efforts such as time sheets and work plans, as well as output and outcome indicators, were developed. These indicators were supplemented by social indicators. The fact that this integration of ideas was conceivable in practice points to a common trend in all three movements: the rationalization and de-personification of management and policy.

Gulick and Urwick (1937: 44–5) recorded the accomplishments of the Bureau of Municipal Research in New York state and city:

> the development of efficiency surveys and reorganization programs; the organization of other bureaus of government research in the United States, and Canada, and abroad, and the growing attention which has been directed to administrative reforms, the factual study of government and principals of administration are all a vindication of the unique experiment which was set in motion . . . when the Bureau of Municipal Research was established.

This best practice spread to other cities that created their own bureaus of efficiency. The initial decades of the twentieth century resulted in many institutions focusing mostly on municipal efficiency. Many ideas were taken national, however, and several institutions emerged: the Institute for Government Research (the predecessor of the Brookings Institution, 1916), a Bureau of Efficiency (1912, abolished in 1933), the Bureau of the Budget (the predecessor of the Office of Management and the Budget, 1921) and the General Accounting Office (1921) (Van Riper 1983).

1.2 1950s–1970s

A second generation of performance measurement activity emerged with post-World War II experiments. The mission statement of the next performance movement, *performance budgeting*, was found in the report of the first Hoover Commission (1947–9), officially named the Commission on Organization of the Executive Branch of the Government. The fifth finding stated that 'the budgetary processes of the Government need improvement, in order to express the objectives of the Government in terms of the work to be done rather than in mere classification of expenditure' (the Hoover Commission report in Shafritz and Hyde 2004: 162).

Performance budgeting became well established in the 1960s with the introduction of the Planning Programming Budgeting Systems (PPBS). New programme expenditures had to be weighed against the marginal benefits of each programme in a systemic way. PPBS inspired subsequent initiatives such as Management by Objectives (MBO) and Zero Based Budgeting (ZBB) (see Table 3.1). Performance budgeting was found in other countries as well. Great Britain introduced it in the Ministry of Defence in the late 1960s and then extended it to other departments, particularly in education and science. The French PPBS variant, RCB (*rationalisation des choix budgétaires*), was first applied 1968 in the Ministry of Defence and then in sectors of energy, town planning, postal services and telegraph. By the early 1970s, PPBS had become an integral tool of national economic planning. PPBS practices were also implemented in among others Australia, Austria, Belgium, Canada, Ireland and Japan (Novick 1973).

The consensus however is that PPBS, MBO and ZBB failed. PPBS is judged to be a success in the Ministry of Defence where it is still in use today (McAffery and Jones 2004), but the transfer to other departments was problematic. The dominance of system thinking, attempting to link everything together in a large scheme, left its mark on the management tools of the day. PPBS overcommitted itself to this systemic dimension, which eventually led to its collapse. Among others, Aaron Wildavsky (1969) cogently attacked the system, arguing that in particular the fixation on the programme structure is pernicious. There is not sufficient analytical capacity to provide a meaningful programme structure for all the activities, to explore causality and to develop a sensible weighing scheme. Further, he points to the conflict between analysis by analysts and the value judgements of politicians. The former cannot resolve the problems of the latter. With his criticism, Wildavsky does not only attack PPBS, but also the holistic system approach to public administration.

In 1966, Bauer branded the social indicators movement, publishing a book on the social side effects of the NASA space investment programmes (Bauer 1966). After almost two decades of economic growth and prosperity, the limits of economic growth were felt, and the development of the welfare state triggered the demand for social data (De Neufville 1975). The social indicators movement sought to construct such standard measures of the state of health, crime, well-being, education and many other social characteristics of a population and living environments. The movement conjured up visions of 'social engineering', which again fitted well into the prominence of system thinking.

The economic crises of the second half of the 1970s and the cutback management of the 1980s explain why the movement ran out of steam (Bulmer 2001). The social indicators movement, however, did have a manifest impact. The statistical apparatus

Table 3.1 *US performance budgeting initiatives*

Acronym		
PPBS	Planning Programming Budgeting System	PPBS assumed that different levels and types of performance could be arrayed, quantified and analysed to make the best budgetary decisions. In essence, PPBS introduced a decision-making framework to the executive branch budget formulation process by presenting and analysing choices among long-term policy objectives and alternative ways of achieving them. (Initiated in 1965 by President Johnson.)
MBO	Management by Objectives	MBO sought to link agencies' stated objectives to their budget requests. MBO is a process to hold agency managers responsible for achieving agreed-upon outputs and outcomes. Agency heads would be accountable for achieving presidential objectives of national importance; managers within an agency would be held accountable for objectives set jointly by supervisors and subordinates. Performance was primarily defined as agency outputs and processes, but efforts were also made to define performance as the results of federal spending – what would today be called 'outcomes'. (Initiated in 1973 by President Nixon.)
ZBB	Zero-Based Budgeting	ZBB proposed to develop budgets from scratch, rather than to build them incrementally. In practice, agencies were expected to set priorities based on the programme results that could be achieved at alternative spending levels, one of which was to be below current funding. In developing budget proposals, these alternatives were to be ranked against each other sequentially from the lowest level organizations up through the department and without reference to a past budgetary base. In concept, ZBB sought a clear and precise link between budgetary resources. (Initiated in 1977 by President Carter.)

Source: based on General Accounting Office 1997

of governments was expanded to cover more phenomena, and new time series were developed. Moreover, the extended statistics on the social condition of the population allowed performance measurement systems to cover the outcomes of government action better. We still see the impact of this movement in contemporary social indicators on quality of life, happiness or sustainable development (Eckersley 1998).

1.3 1980s–2000s

In the 1980s, fiscal hardship led to considerable pressure on government, which was reinforced by the ascent of New Right ideologies. A number of countries, notably New

Zealand, Australia and the UK, responded to this pressure by experimentation with managerial approaches. In the 1980s, savings were the prime focus. Under Reagan, the President's Private Sector Survey on Cost Control, the Grace Commission, estimated potential yearly savings of US$3 billion. Performance management at that time was cutback management. Performance measurement became a growth industry in the UK as well following the launching of the Financial Management Initiative in 1982, which was designed to focus on objectives and to measure outputs and performance. A significant component of the approach was the use of performance indicators (PIs). Prime Minister Thatcher, for instance, proclaimed 'that a thousand PIs should flourish' (Carter *et al.* 1992: 2). By 1987, departments had 1800 PIs (Pollitt 1993).

Managerialism in the 1980s resulted in a diffuse set of management reforms that spread globally in the 1990s and became known as the New Public Management (NPM). Under the colours of NPM resides a broad array of management tools, of which the compatibility is often contested (Williams 2000). Notwithstanding the internal variation, the NPM doctrine has all the characteristics of a performance movement (Hood 1991). It prescribes that public agencies should be subdivided into small policy units and larger performance-based managed organizations for service delivery. The latter organizations were to compete with private sector organizations. Performance was to be the criterion to evaluate agencies, and this required measurement in an all-inclusive way. The use of performance information is not restricted to policy advice, as for social indicators, or budget and planning documents, as for performance budgeting. Performance information is incorporated in almost all management functions. In chapter 5 on incorporation, we will discuss finance, contract management and policy.

Notwithstanding its apparent failure in previous decades, performance budgeting made a remarkable comeback in NPM, with a clear lineage between preceding and contemporary performance budgeting efforts (Kelly and Rivenbark 2003; Robinson and Brumby 2005). In the USA, the Government Performance and Results Act (GPRA) and the Program Assessment Rating tool are the main proponents of current performance budgeting (General Accounting Office 1997, 2004). Other countries also undertook performance budgeting initiatives; the output-purchase budgeting systems of New Zealand and Australia, the British Financial Management Initiative Public Service Agreements (PSA), the French 'Loi Organique Relative Aux Lors de Finances' (LOLF) (see Schick 1990 for an overview).

From the vantage point of the end of the decade, a range of international observers agreed that something special was happening around the world in the 1990s. A UK specialist noted that 'the 1980s and especially the 1990s saw the rise and rise of "performance" as an issue in public sector theory and practice' (Talbot 1999). Similarly a US expert reports that 'if there is a single theme that characterises the public sector in the 1990s, it is the demand for performance. A mantra has emerged in this decade, heard at all levels of government, that calls for documentation of performance and explicit outcomes of government action' (Radin 2000: 168). These trends continue into the 2000s, and there is no indication that they are abating. 'If you can't measure it, you can't manage it' has become a familiar refrain. Pollitt and Bouckaert (2004) demonstrate how measurement gradually becomes more extensive, more intensive and more external.

New Public Management has an interesting place in these developments. Originally derided by many OECD members (generally those who had not accepted its precepts), the take-up of NPM elements that involve performance (much less so market aspects) has spread almost universally across Europe. While NPM has been partly superseded in first generation countries, performance management has been further institutionalized in countries such as Australia and the United Kingdom. The language of NPM has become more prevalent now in late reforming countries.

The most recent performance movement is evidence-based policy (EBP). If we accept that outcomes of programmes are key in performance and performance management, EBP does fit the description of a performance movement. EBP prescribes that facts and figures on outcomes should inform policy decisions rather than ideologies or opinions of the day. EBP has a predominantly British origin (Solesbury 2001) and was initially mainly pursued in the medical and public health sector (Davies *et al.* 2000). By the end of the 1990s, EBP had spread to virtually all policy sectors.

Solesbury (2001) identifies three conditions that furthered the EBP movement in the UK. First, there has been a utilitarian turn in research funding. Research should not only improve understanding, it should also offer guidance. Second, he observes a decline in confidence in the professions; a 'retreat from priesthood', he calls it (p.6). Third, New Labour propagated the replacement of ideology by pragmatism. As such, EBP seemed to fit in well into Third Way politics of UK prime minister Tony Blair and US president Clinton, but also of Bob Hawke and Paul Keating in Australia, Jean Chrétien in Canada, and Gerhard Schröder's 'Neue Mitte' in Germany. Burnham (2001) typifies this strategy as 'the politics of depoliticisation'.

In a sense, EBP echoes some of the promises of social engineering in the social indicator movement. Critique on EBP reiterates some of the critiques on social indicators as well. The belief that evidence can overcome political conflict is seen as naïve at best. Some radical political scientists such as Mouffe (2000) even consider these trends dangerous for democracy. On a more mundane level, the House of Commons warns that the government 'should certainly not seek selectively to pick pieces of evidence which support an already agreed policy, or even commission research in order to produce a justification for policy: so-called "policy-based evidence making"' (House of Commons Science and Technology Committee 2006: 164).

2 CHANGE AND CONTINUITY IN THE PERFORMANCE MOVEMENTS

There have been at least eight performance movements in the twentieth century: social surveys, scientific management and the science of administration, cost accounting, performance budgeting, social indicators, NPM and evidence-based policy (see Table 3.2). Notwithstanding the withering away of some of these performance movements, quantification of government activity has been a recurring tendency. As a consequence, observers may have a been-there-done-that reflex. In what follows, we paint a more nuanced picture of change and continuity in the history of the performance movements.

2.1 Continuity

The eight performance movements resemble each other in some remarkable ways. Probably the most striking similarity is the conceptual stability (1). The performance mindset did not change dramatically throughout time. Other elements of constancy are the co-existence of policy and management movements (2), the political nature of the movements (3), the homogeneity of the sets of carriers for performance ideas (4) and the existence of deliberate strategies to diffuse practices to other administrations and countries (5).

Table 3.2 *Performance movements in the twentieth century*

Performance movement	Timescale	Characterization
Social survey movement	1900s–1940s	Social reformers needed facts about social problems.
Scientific management and the science of administration	1900s–1940s	Government needed a scientific approach as opposed to adhocracy.
Cost accounting	1900s–1940s	Large corporations and government needed insight in costs of products and services for management and transparency.
Bureaus of Municipal Research and its offspring		Synthesis in practice of previous three movements.
Performance budgeting	1950s–1970s	Shift attention in the budgetary process from inputs to outputs and objectives. Coincides often with an agenda of executive control.
Social indicators	1960s–1970s	Social engineering of the welfare state.
New Public Management (2nd generation performance budgeting)	1980s–2000s	Public sectors worldwide are under pressure and adopt performance strategies.
Evidence-based policy	1990s–2000s	Research and indicators rather than ideology and opinion have to undergird policy. Fits into Third Way politics.

(1) Conceptual stability

Concepts are the intellectual artefacts we use to comprehend reality. Williams (2003) demonstrated that most of the concepts we use today to make sense of the very broad concept of performance were already used by the New York Bureau of Municipal Research. He argues that by 1912, performance measurement exhibited many of the features associated with the contemporary practice: measuring of input, output and results; attempting to make government more productive; making reports comparable among communities; and focusing on allocation and accountability (p.643). The conceptual framework that sees government intervention as a process of turning inputs into outputs that subsequently should have outcomes in society is a returning feature of all performance movements. Although more refined models have been developed since its conception, the performance mindset did not change fundamentally throughout time.

(2) Management and policy movements; coexistence, not a pendulum

Each performance movement has either a policy or a management orientation. Some performance movements were mainly concerned with output and efficiency, while others focused on outcomes and effectiveness. The social survey, the social indicator and the evidence-based policy movements were mainly policy movements. Scientific management, cost accounting, PPBS, and the New Public Management were predominantly management movements.

But how do policy and management movements relate to each other? Is there a pendulum that swings from management to policy and back, or do policy and management movements coexist? The pendulum hypothesis seems attractive, since the deficiencies of an overly strong focus on management might be remedied by a stronger focus on policy, and vice versa. Yet, this does not seem to have been the case. Movements coexist. Social surveying, cost accounting and scientific management ran parallel in the early twentieth century. The NY Bureau of Municipal Research integrated elements from all three movements (Stivers 2000). A similar pattern of coexistence is found in the 1970s with the performance budgeting and social indicator movements running parallel and in the 1990s with the evidence-based policy movement and NPM.

This is a noteworthy observation. In the twentieth century, new impetuses to performance measurement for policy and management occurred every few decades. The coexistence of performance movements in policy and management may point to a *Zeitgeist* that values quantification as indication of both rational policy-making and rational management. This is in line with Feldman and March's (1981) argument that the use of information symbolizes a commitment to rationality. Adopting performance measurement, being the symbol of rationality, reaffirms the importance of this social value. The mere activity of measurement as such defines managerial performance or successful policy-making.

(3) All performance movements are political

All performance movements are political in the sense that they all have a power dimension. Agendas, hidden or not, are always an ingredient of the movement. Performance movements have been the subject of tactical manoeuvres between legislatures, and executives, between politics and administration, between horizontal and vertical departments, and between political parties. The early twentieth-century attempts to separate politics from administration purposed a power shift from political appointees to administrators. The agenda of performance budgeting reforms in the USA and Australia in the 1990s was to reinforce executive control over the departments and the agencies (Sterck 2007). PPBS was, besides a planning system, an attempt by the executive to get a grip on a fragmented public sector. In 1930s, the New Deal programmes addressing the Great Depression were mainly executed through new organizational structures such as the Tennessee Valley Authority. These organizations and agencies were deliberately held out of the realm of the traditional Washington bureaucracies. This has led to a disintegration of the executive branch of government. Performance budgeting was expected to re-establish executive control through a clear line of executive authority (Kelly and Rivenbark 2003).

(4) Performance movements have a similar set of carriers for performance ideas

We defined movements as informally organized around a set of ideas. Since ideas are what holds the movement together, ideas need to be able to float. Therefore, performance ideas need carriers. A common set of carriers can be found in most movements.

(a) Movements need some main proponents, or heroes, that symbolize the movement. Names such as Frederick Taylor (scientific management), Woodrow Wilson (science of administration), or Vice President Al Gore (NPM) are emblematic for their respective movements. Performance heroes need however not to be persons. Often, cases – labelled best practices – serve the same heroic function. The New York Bureau of Municipal Research, PPBS in the American army and NPM in New Zealand and Australia are some examples. These figures and cases make movements identifiable throughout place and time.

(b) Movements need to be endorsed by organizations and associations promoting the ideas of the movement. The International City/County Management Association for instance had a long history in disseminating performance measurement in the local public sector. A more recent example is the Public Management Section (PUMA) of the OECD, which promoted NPM concepts in its member countries. Premfors (1998) speaks of the OECD story of management reform.

(c) Movements need their biblical texts, academically flavoured and typically written by the main figures of a movement. Such key texts are used for research, training and advocacy. One of the key texts of the NPM movement for instance has been Osborne and Gaebler's *Reinventing Government* (1993). It is well-written and persuasive. Although the book is practice-oriented, it is larded with scientific argumentation. Other movements have had similar key texts. Bauer's (1966) assessment of the side effects of the NASA space programme has a similar function for the social indicator movement.

(d) Movements need to influence the curricula of the universities. Almost all twentieth-century movements set up courses, academic conferences and even their own journals such as social indicators research and a host of journals for evidence-based practices in among others healthcare, social work, schools, nursing and mental health.

(5) The export of practices has been a deliberate policy

In the twentieth century, the export of performance practices has become a deliberate strategy of actors that confess to a performance movement. The NYBMR intentionally exported its work to other communities through the provision of services and through contacts with agencies and officials. The PPBS system too was intentionally promoted in other countries as well as in the private sector. The same applies to NPM. In the late 1990s, many international delegations visited the NPM champions such as New Zealand and the United Kingdom. German local officials travelled to the city of Tilburg in the Netherlands – an acknowledged NPM champion. It led a Dutch academic to conclude that everyone seemed to be applying the Tilburg model, apart from Tilburg itself. While the city was hiring an external consultant to organize the reception of delegations, the city itself was already changing its course (Kickert 2003).

2.2 Change

Despite the continuities, there are some remarkable changes too. First, there has been a technological revolution that has revitalized old concepts. Second, and most importantly, the intensity of the use of performance information has changed.

(1) Technological evolution enables the reinvention of old concepts

The technological infrastructure for measuring performance has improved significantly. The most relevant evolutions have been the unparalleled increase in processing power of computers and the development of networks. Information technology enables better generation, display and analysis of the performance information, and performance data can be generated more easily thanks to the automation of administrative record keeping. This is in particular the case for collecting output data and less so for outcome measures. The latter usually are not embedded in the administrative information systems and therefore remain notoriously difficult to collect.

These technological evolutions allow reviving of old concepts. Geographic Information Systems (GIS) are a good illustration (Goodchild and Janelle 2004). In essence, GIS provides knowledge about *what* is happening *where* and *when*. The modern concept of building a spatial data infrastructure is not conceptually different from Charles Booth's attempts to build a social map of London where social characteristics were attributed to spatial data (the location of the houses). Modern techniques however have expanded the amount of data that can be linked to the reference map. Different layers of data can be combined, for instance linking up crime, unemployment, traffic congestion and air quality in the neighbourhoods of a city.

(2) Institutionalization, professionalization and specialization of use

Probably the most important change in the subsequent performance movements is the nature of the use of performance information (Bouckaert 1990). Performance management has become (a) more institutionalized and (b) more professional.

(a) The use of performance information has gradually become institutionalized. Early twentieth-century movements such as the social survey and the NYBMR mostly operated in the periphery of government. Although these movements were innovative and influential, the impact on the government of the day should not be overrated. Davidson *et al.* (1991) concluded from a historical analysis that although senior researchers of the social survey movement were appointed to positions in the British government, there is little evidence of their impact (p. 360). Similarly, it took scientific management and the science of administration several decades to penetrate the core of the US government. Arguably, this only happened with the mandatory adoption of PPBS in the federal administration (Schick 1966). By that time, the science of administration was included in the curricula of the most important schools (Williams 2003).

Nowadays, performance measurement has become a focal part of management that is often laid down in management scorecards and management information systems. Increasingly, performance management is seen as part of the job of the contemporary manager. We argued before that a commitment to measurement can also be of a symbolic nature: a commitment to rationality. Yet, since contemporary performance movements such as NPM are furthering the performance discourse, it becomes real in its consequences.

(b) Parallel with institutionalization, there has been an increasing professionalization of measurement. This trend has two dimensions.

On the supply side of information, professionalization implies that measurement has become a profession with a mounting number of measurement professionals: management accountants, management consultants, policy advisors in think-tanks,

49

analysts in statistical offices, etc. This management profession may run counter to traditional professions that experience measurement to be an intrusion upon their autonomy (Johnsen 2008).

On the demand side of information, there is a more professional dealing with information. The most important trend seems to be that performance information has gradually become embedded in systems of accountability between the executive and top managers, between tiers of government, between institutions (schools, hospitals) and central departments, and between employees and their supervisors. These systems of accountability may run counter to the use of performance information.

3 CONCLUSION

It is sometimes suggested that most change is superficial spin while the bottom line remains untouched. Mintzberg (1994) for instance, in an article on strategic planning, argued that it is always our own age that is turbulent and that therefore turbulence is normalcy. Does this apply to measurement in and of the public sector too? Are recent measurement efforts normalcy rather than change? We do not think so. Although there are tides of reform, every performance movement leaves some sediment which is acquired for future movements. The mapping of poverty was something novel in the late nineteenth and early twentieth century. Nowadays, poverty indicators are an institutionalized means of assessing government performance in the provision and redistribution of prosperity.

One of the most notable evolutions in the twentieth-century performance movements was the ever-increasing integration of measurement in the core of the public sector. The quantification of government started at the periphery of government. The twentieth century witnessed a growing integration of measurement within and by the public sector itself. Quantitative approaches to policy and management became an inclusive part of government.

NPM was the first movement that introduced performance information in public management on a government-wide scale, on an international scale and in all management functions. However, NPM did not come out of the blue. It was conceptually conceived in the early twentieth century. Only after a long incubation period does the performance mindset seem to have reached the fibres of government, for better and worse.

DISCUSSION QUESTIONS

1   Is performance management new wine in old bottles? Is NPM Taylor revisited?
2   Why does performance management revive every decade?
3   What is the difference between social indicators and evidence-based policy?

REFERENCES

Bauer, R. A. (1966) *Social Indicators.* Cambridge, MIT Press.

Bouckaert, G. (1990) The history of the productivity movement. *Public Productivity & Management Review,* 14, 53–89.

Bouckaert, G. and Halligan, J. (2008) *Managing Performance: International Comparisons.* London, Routledge.

Bulmer, M. (2001) Social measurement: what stands in its way? *Social Research,* 68, 455–80.

Bulmer, M., Bales, K. and Sklar, K. K. (1991) *The Social Survey in Historical Perspective, 1880–1940.* Cambridge, Cambridge University Press.

Burnham, P. (2001) New Labour and the politics of depoliticisation. *British Journal of Politics and International Relations,* 3, 127–49.

Carter, N., Klein, R. and Day, P. (1992) *How Organizations Measure Success: The Use of Performance Indicators in Government.* London, Routledge.

Davidson, P., Bulmer, M., Bales, K. and Sklar, K. K. (1991) The Social Survey in Historical Perspective: a governmental perspective. *The social survey in historical perspective: 1880–1940.* Cambridge, Cambridge University Press.

Davies, H. T. O., Nutley, S. M. and Smith, P. C. (2000) *What Works?: Evidence-based Policy and Practice in Public Services.* London, Policy Press.

De Neufville, J. I. (1975) *Social Indicators and Public Policy: Interactive Processes of Design and Application.* Amsterdam, Elsevier.

Eckersley, R. (1998) *Measuring Progress: Is Life Getting Better?* Collingwood, CSIRO Publishing.

Feldman, M. S. and March, J. G. (1981) Information in organizations as signal and symbol. *Administrative Science Quarterly,* 26, 171–186.

General Accounting Office (1997) *Performance Budgeting: Past Initiatives Offer Insights for GPRA Implementation* (GAO/AIMD-97-46). Washington, DC, GAO.

General Accounting Office (2004) *Performance Budgeting: OMB's Program Assessment Rating Tool Presents Opportunities and Challenges for Budget and Performance Integration.* GAO-04-439T. Washington, DC, GAO.

Goodchild, M. F. and Janelle, D. G. (2004) *Spatially Integrated Social Science.* Oxford, Oxford University Press.

Gulick, L. and Urwick, L. (1937) Notes on the theory of organizations. With special reference to government. In *Papers on the Science of Administration.* New York, A.M. Kelley.

Hood, C. (1991) A public management for all seasons. *Public Administration,* 69, 3–19.

House of Commons Science and Technology Committee (2006) *Scientific Advice, Risk, and Evidence Based Policy Making.* London, Stationery Office.

Johnsen, A. (2008) Performance information and educational policy making. In Van Dooren, W. and Van de Walle, S. (eds.) *Performance Information in the Public Sector: How It Is Used.* Basingstoke, Palgrave Macmillan.

51

Kelly, J. M. and Rivenbark, W. C. (2003) *Performance Budgeting for State and Local Government.* Armonk, NY, M. E. Sharpe.

Kickert, W. (2003) Beyond public management. *Public Management Review,* 5, 377–99.

Linsley, C. A. and Linsley, C. L. (1993) Booth, Rowntree, and Llewelyn Smith: a reassessment of interwar poverty. *Economic History Review,* 46, 88–104.

McAffery, J. L. and Jones, L. R. (2004) *Budgeting and Financial Management for National Defence.* Greenwich, CT, Information Age Publishers.

Mintzberg, H. (1994) The fall and rise of strategic planning. *Harvard Business Review,* 72, 107–14.

Mosher, F. C. (1968) *Democracy and the Civil Service.* New York, Oxford University Press.

Mouffe, C. (2000) *The Democratic Paradox.* London, Verso Books.

Novick, D. (1973) *Current Practice in Program Budgeting (PPBS): Analysis and Case Studies Covering Government and Business.* London, Heinemann.

Osborne, D. and Gaebler, T. (1993) *Reinventing Government: How the Entrepreneurial Spirit Is Transforming the Public Sector.* Boston, MA, Addison Wesley.

Pollitt, C. (1993) *Managerialism and the Public Services: Cuts or Cultural Change in the 1990s?* Oxford, Blackwell.

Pollitt, C. and Bouckaert, G. (2004) *Public Management Reform: A Comparative Analysis.* Oxford, Oxford University Press.

Premfors, R. (1998) Reshaping the democratic state: Swedish experiences in international perspective. *Public Administration,* 76, 141–59.

Previts, G. J. and Merino, B. D. (1979) *A History of Accounting in America: An Historical Interpretation of the Cultural Significance of Accounting.* New York, Wiley.

Radin, B. A. (2000) The Government Performance and Results Act and the tradition of federal management reform: square pegs in round holes. *Journal of Public Administration: Research and Theory,* 10, 111–35.

Radin, B. A. (2006) *Challenging the Performance Movement: Accountability, Complexity, and Democratic Values.* Washington, DC, Georgetown University Press.

Ridley, C. E. and Simon, H. (1938) *Measuring Municipal Activities: A Survey of Suggested Criteria and Reporting Forms for Appraising Administration.* Chicago, IL, International City Managers' Association.

Rivenbark, W. C. (2005) A historical overview of cost accounting in local government. *State and Local Government Review,* 37, 217–27.

Robinson, M. and Brumby, J. (2005) *Does Performance Budgeting Work? An Analytical Review of the Empirical Literature.* IMF *Working Paper.* Washington, DC, IMF.

Rose, R. (1976) On the priorities of government: a developmental analysis of public policies. *European Journal of Political Research,* 4, 247–89.

Sayre, W. S. (1958) Premises of public administration: past and emerging. *Public Administration Review,* 18, 102–5.

Schachter, H. L. (1989) *Frederick Taylor and the Public Administration Community: A Reevaluation.* New York, State University of New York.

Schick, A. (1966) The road to PPB: the stages of budget reform. *Public Administration Review,* 26, 243–58.

Schick, A. (1990) Budgeting for results: recent developments in five industrialized countries. *Public Administration Review,* 50, 26–34.

Shafritz, J. M. and Hyde, A. C. (2004) *Classics of Public Administration.* Harcourt, Brace College Publishers.

Solesbury, W. (2001) *Evidence Based Policy: Whence It Came and Where It's Going.* London, ESRC UK Centre for Evidence Based Policy and Practice.

Sterck, M. (2007) The impact of performance budgeting on the role of the legislature: a four-country study. *International Review of Administrative Sciences,* 73, 189–203.

Stivers, C. (2000) *Bureau Men, Settlement Women: Constructing Public Administration in the Progressive Era.* Kansas, University Press of Kansas.

Talbot, C. (1999) Public performance – towards a new model? *Public Policy and Administration,* 14, 15–34.

Van Dooren, W. (2008) Nothing new under the sun? Change and continuity in the 20th century performance movements. In Van Dooren, W. and Van de Walle, S. (eds.) *Performance Information in the Public Sector: How It Is Used.* Basingstoke, Palgrave Macmillan.

Van Riper, P. P. (1983) The American administrative state: Wilson and the founders – an unorthodox view. *Public Administration Review,* 43, 477–90.

Wildavsky, A. (1969) Rescuing policy analysis from PPBS. *Public Administration Review,* 29, 189–202.

Williams, D. W. (2000) Reinventing the proverbs of government. *Public Administration Review,* 60, 522–34.

Williams, D. W. (2003) Measuring government in the early twentieth century. *Public Administration Review,* 63, 643–59.

Williams, D. W. (2004) Evolution of performance measurement until 1930. *Administration Society,* 36, 131–65.

FURTHER READING

This chapter is based on a book chapter 'Nothing new under the sun? Change and continuity in the twentieth century performance movements' (Van Dooren 2008). Another historical overview of performance movements is Bouckaert's history of the productivity movement (1990). Williams published several articles of performance measurement in the early twentieth century (Williams 2003, 2004). Schachter (1989) pointed to the relevance of Taylor for public administration (and for performance management). Bulmer *et al.* describe the social survey movement (1991). Kelly and Rivenbark (2003) documented the historical roots of performance budgeting.

Chapter 4

Performance measurement

LEARNING OBJECTIVES

- To identify the main steps and the design parameters in the measurement process.
- To understand variation in the potential measurement designs.

KEY POINTS

- Performance measurement is a process in five steps: targeting, indicator selection, data collection, analysis and reporting.
- Quality is a point of attention in each of these steps.
- Each step involves a range of choices, which should be made based on the envisaged used of performance information.

Wordnet, an online dictionary at Princeton, defines measurement in general terms as *the act or process of assigning numbers to phenomena according to a rule* (Miller 2009). This chapter discusses the process of assigning numbers to the phenomenon of public sector performance. According to the definition, the assignment of numbers should follow a rule. The formulation of the performance indicators can be conceived as the measurement rule for public sector performance.

Performance measurement is conceived as a *process* in five steps (see Figure 4.1). The first step is about targeting the measurement efforts. The question what will be measured needs to be answered. Next, indicators need to be selected. Subsequently, data needs to be collected and results need to be analysed. Finally, findings need to be reported. Throughout the process, quality of measurement is an important point of attention.

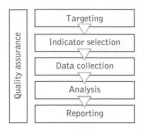

Figure 4.1 *An ideal-typical model of the performance measurement process*

We use the stages as an ideal-typical representation of the measurement process. To depict measurement as an orderly process of distinct and chronological steps may, however, not necessarily correspond to reality. It is for instance a quite common practice to select only those indicators for which data are available. Data collection in this case precedes and determines indicator selection and, as a result, measurement may be biased towards measureable dimensions. The description of the ideal type, however, is useful for identifying such deviations from a pure measurement model.

1 STEP 1: TARGETING MEASUREMENT EFFORTS

The first phase in the measurement process is about targeting measurement efforts. The question is: targeting on what? Wide-ranging terms like performance, management, organization, programme or policy do not usually give a precise clue. Through interaction, however, people develop mental maps that make sense and define these terms (Weick 1995). Implicit and partially shared definitions are codified at several occasions, e.g. when an organization draws up a new organization chart, a policy programme sets out its objectives, or a minister drafts a policy brief. In order to target measurement efforts, the implicit mental picture of the organization, programme or sector needs to be exposed. These frameworks *in* which and *through* which we can think about management, policy and performance are of vital importance for measurement efforts.

When people employ a framework, they are imposing a way of thinking about the world. 'Two doctors in search of the truth to Mona Lisa's smile said in Lyon yesterday that the person posing for the portrait suffered from muscular atrophy' (*Guardian*, 26 April 1991, quoted in Parsons 1995: 58). To which Parsons observes that 'no doubt had they been chiropodists they would have diagnosed athlete's foot!' (p.59). All too often, as this quotation demonstrates, people do not critically reflect upon the frameworks in use – we see what we are looking for. This may lead to what could be called the implicit targeting of measurement efforts – although implicit *attribution* might be a better term since there is no intentionality or deliberation in selecting the indicators. As a result, indicators risk reconfirming and even reinforcing preconceived standpoints, rather than providing an account of performance. Etzioni and Lehman (1967) explain by means of the example of the IQ tests how a complex concept such as intelligence is reduced to its operational definition in the test (see Box 4.1).

55

BOX 4.1 THE RISK OF CONCEPT REDUCTION

The risk of concept reduction occurs when a solution for the problem of fractional measurement is to define the social concept as only that which is measured by the operational definition. This is, according to Etzioni and Lehman, more apparent than a real solution, since concepts have an established content, institutionalized either in common parlance or in technical, theoretical formulations – and occasionally in both. To act as if an operational definition were automatically the same as the underlying concept is a questionable procedure, and it is also likely to have important negative consequences in the realm of policy-making, they argue.

Etzioni and Lehman discuss the example of intelligence tests, which were initially assumed to measure native intelligence. However, as data have accumulated, it has become apparent that such factors as cultural background, social class, past learning experiences, and the like, influence performance on these tests. They argue that concept reduction, here stating that intellectual capacity is whatever intelligence quotient (IQ) tests measure, is harmful for two reasons: first, because people told that they have a low IQ will continue to interpret this statement as if they lack intellectual capabilities and, second, because denying the significant residue in the concept, the road towards better IQ tests and more encompassing measurements is blocked.

As a solution, Etzioni and Lehman (1967) point to the importance of mapping the dimensions of concepts. They argue that 'the concept of mental health implies more than the avoidance of psychiatric hospitalisation; the quality of a society's educational system cannot be gauged solely by the number of PhDs it produces; and a man's satisfaction with his job involves more than satisfaction with his income' (p.3). Similarly, the measurement of performance of a public agency requires a careful analysis of the dimensions of performance as well as the dimensions of the agency.

Etzioni and Lehman 1967: 8–9

Three issues are thus of importance when discussing the mental maps that are used for measurement.

1 What is the mental picture or map of the organization, programme or policy?
2 What are the targets for the measurement effort?
3 What is the argumentation for a selecting a target?

(1) In order to decide what to measure, we first need an understanding of what we are measuring. A representation of the organization, programme or policy field is needed.

As we argued above, such representations or models are quite common in everyday situations. We need a menu to decide what to eat, a map to decide where to go, and a travel guide to decide where to take our vacation. Similarly, we need a representation of the organization, programme or policy field in order to decide what to measure. Such a representation can be conceived in different ways.

(a) One of the most common representations of an organization is the *organizational chart* which visually depicts the division of tasks and responsibilities. The chart defines the structure of the organization and hence it is a codification of the organization. Is it a bureaucratic, divisional, functional or matrix organization?

(b) *Management models* such as the Balanced Scorecard, the Common Assessment Framework, the EFQM (European Foundation for Quality Management) model and the ISO (International Organization for Standards) model provide managers with an overview of the dimensions of good management (see Bovaird and Lœffler 2003 for an overview).

(c) *Trees of objectives.* Strategic planning processes prescribe the development of a logically consistent tree of objectives. Starting from a mission statement, organizations have to develop strategic goals from which operational goals are derived. The operational objectives guide the use of resources.

(d) *Stakeholder analysis* can provide an impression of the external relations of the organization (see Mitchell, Agle and Wood 1997 for an overview of stakeholder theory). Measurement can be targeted to the concerns of those stakeholders that matter most.

(e) A *programme logic* specifies the inputs and components of a programme, as well as short-term and long-term outcomes, along with the assumed linkages. Programme logic models help to identify the outputs and outcomes of organizations and programmes. They are seen as a necessary step preceding the selection of indicators for policy programmes (Hatry 1999).

(f) There is a substantial literature on *programme theory*. A programme logic rarely outlines the underlying mechanisms that are presumed to be responsible for the linkages between outputs and outcomes (Rogers *et al.* 2000). These underlying mechanisms need to be reconstructed. Leeuw (2003) regroups the methods for reconstruction in a policy scientific cluster, a strategic assessment cluster and an elicitation cluster.

(2) Once we have gained an understanding of the organization, programme or policy, it is possible to target measurement efforts. As we argued, it is unrealistic to pursue a measurement system that perfectly mirrors every aspect of the organization or programme, its policies and environment. Complexity and multi-dimensionality of public management and policy make it practically impossible to measure everything.

It could even be argued that it is epistemologically inconceivable to measure every-thing. Performance measurement possesses the dialectic nature of knowledge creation; the more we know, the more we become aware of what we do not know. Bouckaert

57

(1993) describes a study by mathematician Mandelbrot, who demonstrated that the length of the British coastline approaches infinity when more measurement points are introduced (see Figure 4.2). With the introduction of more detail in measurement, more bays, inlets and peninsulas are uncovered and included in its measurement. Similarly, while probing the performance concept, every indicator will generate new questions and uncover new dimensions that are not yet measured. For example, quantification of performance in the academic world through international publications, citation indices and impact factors led to a renewed debate on the quality of research and the failure of many performance indicators to accurately grasp these dimensions (Merton 1988).

If it is assumed that it is impossible to measure everything, a choice has to be made on what to measure and what not to measure. Table 4.1 suggests different cut-outs for which measurement can be developed. The measurement object can be delineated by selecting a part of the organization or programme (internal focus) and/or by selecting a set of policy variables (external focus). The appropriate approach will depend on what the performance information is needed for (see chapter 6 on use).

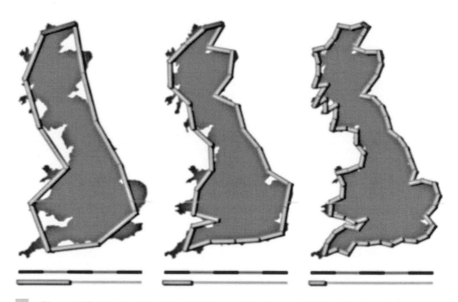

Figure 4.2 *The length of the British coastline (source Wikipedia, GNU licence)*

Table 4.1 *Definition of the measurement object*

Which part of the organization or programme will be measured?
Which part of the organization chart? All the divisions or only a selection?
Which input? Which entries of the budget? Which staff members?
Which activities? Which processes?
Which outputs? Which products of the organizations (goods and services) are being measured?

Table 4.1 *continued*

Which part of the policy objectives is being measured?
Which intermediate ends? Which target groups? Which geographical circumscriptions?
Which outcomes? Only the intended outcomes, or also the side effects and cross-cutting
impacts?
Which contextual factors are taken into account?

(3) Finally, we turn to the argumentations for targeting measurement efforts. These are often mutually exclusive. Moreover, there are no generally right or wrong argumentations. Measurement prioritization depends, again, on the (planned) use of performance information (see chapter 6).

(a) *Indications of problems*. Measurement can be initiated when there are indications of problems through symptoms such as complaints or waiting lists. It is assumed that measurement is needed to get a better grip on the problems at hand.

(b) *Financial importance*. In many organizations, a small amount of the activities accounts for the majority of the budget. By measuring these activities, the organization has a good coverage of the budget. Similarly, by measuring a limited amount of activities, most of the personnel may be comprised in the measurement system.

(c) *Societal visibility*. Some activities, which may not have a high financial impact, may still have a high societal visibility. Theories of issue salience and agenda-setting have demonstrated that media, politicians and civil society have a selective interest in particular activities (see for instance Galtung and Ruge 1965 for media salience, and Baumgartner and Jones 1993 for a model of agenda-setting). By measuring these activities, the organization may be able to respond to most of the issues that those actors bring up.

(d) *Feasibility*. Some processes or outcomes are easier to measure than others (see chapter 2). Feasibility of the measurement effort is a valid criterion from a developmental perspective. In order to overcome resistance and to make people accustomed to measurement, some quick wins from measurement may be beneficial.

(e) *Diffusion*. Measurement efforts can be dispersed throughout the organization, programme or policy field. The strategy to have some measurement for many rather than doing an intense measurement for some may for instance be prompted by the desire to introduce a results-oriented culture in the whole organization. The plea of many practitioner's texts for a limited set of Key Performance Indicators (KPIs) fits into this line of reasoning. Kaplan and Norton's (1996) book on the Balanced Scorecard is a good example.

(f) *Cost of measurement*. Measurement can be a costly activity and in some cases the potential benefits of measurement do not weigh up against the costs. It should

59

be noted that benefits of measurement are usually much more difficult to observe than the costs of measurement.

(g) *Predetermined*. Often, there is no choice on what to measure. This is for instance the case for international reporting obligations. Within the European Union, the Lisbon criteria are an example of a predetermined indicator set that is imposed upon member states.

2 STEP 2: SELECTION OF THE INDICATORS

The second step deals with the selection of the indicators. After deciding *what* to measure, one needs to determine *how* to measure. The selection of indicators largely depends on the specialized expertise in organizations or policy domains. Obviously, performance indicators will differ in a cultural programme, a fiscal administration, or an environmental agency. In this section, we do not discuss the substance of developing indicators, but focus on indicators in general terms.

The production model of performance, represented in chapter 2, is a widely shared base for defining indicators. This model guides the development of single and ratio indicators that combine the dimensions of the model (see Table 4.2). The choice of the indicators depends on how performance information will be used (see chapter 6).

Several criteria for good indicators circulate; see for instance HM Treasury (2001), Hatry (1999), United Way of America (1999) and Broom (1998). First, good indicators are *sensitive to change*. For instance, a measure which relies on a yes/no question for customer satisfaction will fail to register the difference between someone being just

Table 4.2 *Single and ratio indicators*

Single indicators	
Indicators on input	What goes into the system? Which resources are used?
Indicators on output	Which products and services are delivered? What is the quality of these products and services?
Indicators on intermediate outcomes	What are the immediate impacts of the output?
Indicators on final outcomes	What are the ultimate outcomes achieved that are significantly attributable to the output?
Indicators on the environment	What are the contextual variables that influence intermediate and final outcomes?
Ratio indicators	
Efficiency	Cost/output
Productivity	Output/input
Effectiveness	Output/outcome (intermediate or final)
Cost-effectiveness	Input/outcome (intermediate or final)

satisfied and very satisfied. Indicators should also be *precisely defined*. There needs to be an unambiguous understanding of the indicator. Building such understanding among experts in an organization is often a lengthy process that results in quite detailed indicator descriptions. Another requirement however posits that indicators should be *understandable for users*. The definition of an indicator that is both easy to understand and precise is a balancing act (see Box 4.2). A fourth requirement is that indicators are *documented*. This implies the development of meta-documentation that includes the definition of the indicator, the measurement unit, the data sources, the time series, possible breaks in the time series, the responsibilities for administering the indicator, etc. Documentation is important to assure that the measurement processes can be verified, for instance by external auditors. Fifth, indicators need to be *relevant*. They should reflect important dimensions of the concept that is being measured. For indicators to be relevant for decision-making, they also need to be *timely*. Next, data collection and reporting needs to be *feasible*. For instance, attempts to integrate output measures in the national accounts system, as proposed by the UK Atkinson review, have been critiqued for (among other criticisms) the insurmountable data collection effort it would require (Atkinson 2005; Van Dooren 2009). Finally, indicators should *comply with coordinated data processes and definitions*. The dual trend of increasing specialization/fragmentation on the one hand and coordination/interdependence on the other also reflects on performance measurement. Many performance indicators will only be useful when they can be compared with results of other organizations or when joint analyses can be made. Compliance to definitions is a *sine qua non*.

BOX 4.2 INDICATORS NEED TO BE PRECISELY DEFINED AND EASY TO UNDERSTAND – A BALANCING ACT

The OECD, in a publication called *Pensions at a Glance,* defines the indicator of the Net Pensions Replacement Rate. It seems a straightforward concept: what percentage of a pre-retirement income is acquired through a retirement allowance? Nonetheless, several clarifications are needed to attain an acceptable level of precision.

'The net replacement rate is defined as the individual net pension entitlement divided by net pre-retirement earnings, taking account of personal income taxes and social security contributions paid by workers and pensioners. Otherwise, the definition and measurement of the net replacement rates are the same as for the gross replacement rate [. . .] The results again cover full-career workers with median earnings and with 0.5, 0.75, 1, 1.5 and 2 times average (mean) earnings' (OECD 2006:34).

3 STEP 3: DATA COLLECTION

Data collection procedures and sources are vital. Each method has different strengths and weaknesses (Hatry 1999). A first distinction is whether organizations use internal or external data sources. Internal data is produced by the organization itself while external data is purchased or obtained from outside. Internal data is usually cheaper and more readily available than external information. However, in principal agent relationships, the principal (e.g. a department) may not trust information produced by the agent (e.g. an executive agency). Therefore, third parties may be asked to collect the data or, at least, to audit the data provided by the agent.

A further refinement of the data sources is represented in Table 4.3, which also assesses the advantages and disadvantages of different data sources (Hatry 1999; United Way of America 1999; Weiss 1998).

Most organizations have administrative registration systems of their activities: project planning and monitoring, dossier tracking systems, time registration systems, client databases, etc. Such *existing registration systems* have several advantages. The data is usually cheap, readily available, uninterrupted and well understood (see also Pollitt's (2000) article on institutional amnesia for an appreciation of administrative registration systems). The main disadvantage is their path dependent character. These systems are gradually built over time and past decisions may strongly affect future options for registration. Administrative registration, for instance, does usually not focus on outcomes and does not have data on drop-out cases or target groups that are not reached by policies.

Nonetheless, it seems useful to look at existing administrative registration systems first as a default data source. Only when administrative registrations cannot provide the data, as will be often the case, should other data sources be considered. We briefly sketch the alternatives.

(1) First, *extra registrations* could be added to existing registrations. For instance, in the context of gender programmes, counter clerks could be asked for gender registration of the applicants for social benefits. The main cost of extra registration is the staff time invested. This cost is less visible compared to the financial costs of outsourced data-gathering. Additional registrations will yield data more quickly when the typical dossier of the organization has a short processing cycle. An employment counselling service for instance will have extra data more swiftly compared to a fiscal administration (with typically a one-year cycle) or an organization that deals with foreign investment projects (with a multi-year cycle).

(2) A second option is to conduct a *survey* of customers or citizens. Often, surveys are the only way of obtaining outcome information, for instance in order to address changes in attitudes or knowledge. The main disadvantages are the costs of a survey and the growing difficulty of obtaining adequate response rates. Polling may yield data in a shorter time compared to a full-fledged survey, albeit often at the expense of validity and/or reliability.

Table 4.3 *Advantages and disadvantages of different data sources*

Data source	Advantages	Disadvantages
Existing registrations	Continuity (time series) Low cost In house, good insight into quality and content Readily available	Path dependent focus No drop-out data Less focus on outcome
Additional registrations	Continuity In-house, good insight into quality and content	'Hidden' costs Medium- to long-term availability
Surveys	Suitable for outcome information	High cost Medium-term availability Response rate issue
Self-assessments	Low cost Combination of quantitative and qualitative approaches Linked to operations	Perceptual Risk of gaming
Technical measurement	Non-obtrusive	Limited applicability to human services Risk of technocracy
External observers	Limited obtrusiveness Observers are not involved	High costs for specialized observers Medium- to long-term availability
Other public organizations	Usually low cost Short-term availability	Confidentiality and privacy issues may interfere with data exchange Less insight into quality and content (definitions)
Statistical, international, and research institutions	Good quality Authoritativeness Readily available Moderate costs Continuity	Not directly tailored to organization's needs Only outcomes

(3) Third, *self assessments* have the advantage of combining measurement with qualitative assessments. A limitation is the perceptual nature of a self assessment. Self assessments are also vulnerable for strategic behaviour (gaming), in particular when an outsider (media, principals) is known to be watching over the shoulder of the self assessors.

(4) Fourth, the main advantage of *technical measurement* is its non-intrusive character. Applications may be found in the environmental sector (e.g. air quality, water quality), in housing (e.g. level of humidity as an element of housing quality) and in public health (e.g. toxic substances in the population). The main

disadvantage is its inapplicability to the majority of public service provision (i.e. virtually all human services). Moreover, technical measurement may lead to technocratic measurement that is not understood by policy-makers and managers and as such violate the quality criterion of intelligibility mentioned above.

(5) Fifth, *external observers* may provide a neutral opinion on performance in a relatively unobtrusive way. US cities for instance used observers to assess the cleanliness of the streets. Disadvantages are the high costs (unless the external observers are volunteers) and the medium-term availability (given the time needed to train the observers).

(6) Sixth, *administrative registrations of other organizations* may be useful. Ecological awareness programmes for instance could use the vehicle registration databases to assess their success in promoting environment-friendly cars. Privacy issues and an inadequate understanding of definitions and methods may complicate the use of other organizations' data.

(7) Finally, *statistical institutions* (internationally and nationally) may provide good quality data. This data however is seldom sufficiently specific to fulfil the organization's needs. Moreover, these statistics mainly cover outcomes.

Sometimes it may appear that authoritativeness of statistical institutions is used as a substitute for data quality – in particular in the international institutions. A review of the European Central Bank data on public sector efficiency, World Bank data on government effectiveness, World Economic Forum data on public institutions and IMD business school data on government efficiency shows serious weaknesses in all four rankings (Arndt and Oman 2006; Van de Walle 2006).

4 STEP 4: ANALYSIS

Since numbers rarely speak for themselves, data needs to be analysed. In essence, the purpose is to transform *data* into *information* which may lead to decisions. We distinguish three interpretative strategies: norm and target setting, breakouts and causal analysis.

(a) A first strategy is to confront a result with a norm (Weiss 1998). When a norm is set in advance, it is called a target. While norms and targets often are plain numbers, more sophisticated variants take into account margins of error (Rubenstein *et al.* 2003). In some cases, there seems to be no conscious deliberation at all about the norm setting. Yet, behind this appearance of arbitrariness, implicit frames of reference may be at play.

There are several frames of reference for norms and targets. First, targets can be based on the *time-dimension*. The norm then usually is to do at least as well as last year. In order to mitigate exceptional variation over time, a moving average may be suitable.

Second, norms can be based on *comparisons with other organizations*; within the sector, outside the sector, or in other jurisdictions or countries. Within organizations, divisions may be compared. The norm can be the average, the top quartile or the best performing parts. Third, *scientists* can calculate the norms. Tolerance levels of harmful substances in food and the living environment are examples. Fourth, norms may have a *political* foundation with mainly a symbolic function (see Table 4.4). Absolute norms such as a zero tolerance for integrity breaches or traffic casualties are utopian. However, for symbolic reasons, they are maintained. The message is that government should not rest on its laurels, when for instance a 95 per cent target is attained.

(b) A second interpretative strategy is to break out data in order to understand *where*, *when* and for *whom* (e.g. for which target groups) performance is manifesting. This will require the breaking out or aggregation of the data to the appropriate level. For some purposes, more detailed information will be needed (e.g. for cost accounting). For other purposes, the information may have to be more general and consolidated (e.g. for reporting to parliament). Different purposes will require different aggregation levels. Breaking out and aggregation can be directed at the measurement objects or at the indicators.

(1) The breaking out and the consolidation of information may be oriented towards the measurement *object*, such as regions or target groups. The indicator 'traffic casualties' for instance can be broken out for different regions or even different roads, or can be consolidated on a national level. The indicator of educational achievement can be broken out for gender, ethnicity, socio-economic background of the pupils, or can be aggregated.

(2) Second, the breaking out and consolidation may be oriented towards different *indicators* that say something about a single measurement object. An example is the composition of a quality of life index for a neighbourhood. Indicators may for instance reflect the average surface of the houses; the number of crimes per capita; population density; amount of traffic; availability of parks, etc. The level of aggregation thus may range from a single indicator to an index of indicators on the one hand and from a single unit to a multitude of observations on the other hand (see Table 4.5).

The methodology for breaking out and consolidation should be revealed. Composite indicators are often suspicious, in particular when the methodology is not stated (Best 2001). On the one hand, positive results can be sought for by breaking out for the right categories. For instance, in order to mollify the perception of youth unemployment as being problematic, an employment agency may search for the optimal age brackets for breaking out unemployment statistics. On the other hand, negative data can be presented in a much nicer way by diluting them in a composed measure. Problems with a waiting list for hearing devices, for instance, can be hidden in an overall index of waiting lists for services for the disabled.

Table 4.4 *Foundations for targets*

Fundament	Assessment	Example
Time	− fit for unique policy initiatives − fit for organizations that have no counterpart − fit for confidential information − contextual variables may cause disturbance − risk of stagnation, no innovative impulses from the outside	− trends in the number of youth in special care
Other organizations within the sector	− fit for comparing results of policies − learning effects through confrontation with other practices − controls for contextual variables	− the stress-index for personnel of different organizations in the public sector − the crime figures of one big city compared to another big city
Other organizations outside the sector	− fit to compare management results − learning effects through confrontation with other practices − comparability is harder to achieve	− sick leave in the private sector versus the public sector
Other countries	− fit for monopolists that have no national counterparts − learning effects through confrontation with other practices − difficulty of overcoming cultural and structural differences	− comparison of the educational achievement through the OECD's 'education at a glance' reports
Scientific standards	− well funded, less debatable − technical, risk for technocracy	− the vaccination level of the population that should be attained in order to eradicate a disease
Political and ideological norms	− embedded in the system, higher acceptance of the whole measurement system − not always realistic (but not necessary unrealistic)	− a zero norm for traffic casualties

Table 4.5 *An illustration of breakouts and aggregation of data*

Direction Subject	Direction indicator			
	Indicator Oxygen	Indicator Fish stock	Indicator Nitrogen	Σ indicators
Measurement subject River 1	Oxygen in river 1	Fish stock in river 1	Nitrogen in river 1	Water quality in river 1
Measurement subject River X	Oxygen in river X	Fish stock in river X	Nitrogen in river X	Water quality in river X
Measurement subject River Xn	Oxygen in river Xn	Fish stock in river Xn	Nitrogen in river Xn	Water quality in river Xn
Σ measurement subjects	Oxygen in all rivers	Fish stock in all rivers	Nitrogen in all rivers	Water quality in all rivers

Three conditions need to be met before a meaningful aggregate index of diverse indicators can be compiled (Innes 1990). First, there needs to be a *conceptual model* that provides meaning to the addition of elements. The index should correspond to an idea we can understand. For instance, the Consumer Price Index and the Gross Domestic Product are comprehensible concepts – respectively the price of a basket of goods and services and the value of production of the nation. Second, there needs to be a reasonable method to transform unlike things to a *common scale*. Economic indicators have money as a common unit of measurement. Many indices of non-economic phenomena such as quality of life struggle to meet this condition (Rossi and Gilmartin 1980). How to combine for instance noise nuisance (measured in decibels) with proximity to shops and public services (measured in kilometres) in a single quality of life index? Third, indices often give different *weights* to the composing indicators. Since such weights are usually highly debatable and sometimes even necessarily arbitrary, the opportunities for embellishing performance are substantial. The weighing at least should be made explicit. Box 4.3 represents an extended list of criteria as defined by the OECD.

(c) A third interpretative strategy is to search for causes of (under-)performance. This approach is not wholly disconnected from breaking out data. The choice of the breakout categories is often based on (often implicit) hypotheses about the explanatory variables. When for instance absenteeism statistics are broken out for gender, it may be assumed that women are more often absent from work because of family affairs. However, when absenteeism data are broken out for commuting distances of staff, it is implicitly assumed that long travel times may be the cause of absenteeism.

67

BOX 4.3 OECD CRITERIA FOR CONSTRUCTING COMPOSITE INDICATORS

The OECD formulated a number of criteria for constructing composite indicators. Many recommendations boil down to the disclosure of methodologies and theories or, in other words, exposing the mental map that underpins the index.

1. Clear theoretical framework
2. Indicators selected on the basis of their quality and relevance
3. The methodological choice in weighting and aggregation exposed
4. Different approaches for imputing missing values exposed
5. Indicators normalized to make them comparable
6. Indicators aggregated and weighted according to the underlying theoretical framework
7. Explicit assessments made of the robustness of the composite indicator
8. Composite indicator correlated with other data
9. Presentation should clarify, not mislead
10. Underlying indicators or values should be readily available.

OECD 2009

The search for causes of performance however is substantially more far reaching than the simple breaking out of data. The relations are usually also tested in statistical analyses. In many cases however the statistical analysis will not be sufficient. In order to get a more profound insight into the causes, qualitative research (e.g. interviews, focus groups, etc.) may be undertaken.

Attribution is an endemic debate in the performance literature. Often, it is very difficult to ascribe performance to the intervention of a particular programme or organization. The main reason is usually sought in the interference of socio-economic factors such as economic growth, demographics, or ecological trends that lie beyond the scope of individual organizations or programmes. However, noise in attribution analysis is not only caused by socio-economic variables – often it stems from other public programmes and organizations. The failure of a trade agency to attract foreign investment may be caused by failure of the agency, but also by fiscal policies imposing new taxes or by patent registration becoming more complex. Joined-up government (JUG) programmes, including JUG indicators, have been devised to overcome the negative effects of public programme interference (Bogdanor 2005).

Attribution is important because indicators are often used to hold organizations accountable for their performance (see chapter 6). It would be unfair to judge

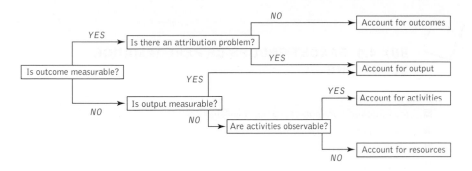

Figure 4.3 *Outcomes in accountability relations*

Source: translated from Bouckaert, Van Dooren and Sterck 2003

organizations on outcome indicators when it is acknowledged that these measures are inadequate. Similarly, it is unreasonable to hold an organization responsible for success or failure when the outcomes can only be partly attributed to the programme or organization. In these cases, it would be better to account for output. Sometimes, when output is not measurable either, accountability can be based on activities/efforts. When even efforts are not observable, for instance in many diplomatic services, the only option will be to account for input. Figure 4.3 represents this accountability scheme based on the measurability of outcome and output, attribution of outcomes to an organization or public programme and the extent to which activities are observable.

5 STEP 5: REPORTING

The last step in the process of measuring performance is reporting. The main point here is that format should be appropriate for the target group (Hendricks 1994; Rossi and Gilmartin 1980). Obviously, the reporting of performance information to top management will require other reporting formats than for media or interest groups. Two questions thus should be answered.

Who is consuming the information? The most important target groups of performance information are represented in Box 4.4. The first category, the general public, is the proposed target group of many initiatives. In reality, it is hard to reach a significant part of the general public. The most evident way to reach the general public is through the mass media (for instance by buying publicity, releasing press statements). Other target groups may be interest groups, advisory boards, international institutions and other governments, for which performance information will have to be more specialized and detailed. The same detail is usually not expected by politicians – who want snapshot information. Managers usually prefer scorecard reporting which can be quickly

BOX 4.4 TARGET GROUPS OF PERFORMANCE REPORTING

- the general public
- mass media: newspapers, radio, television
- interest groups
- advisory boards
- international institutions
- other governments
- executive politicians
- parliament
- the board of the organization
- top management
- middle management

BOX 4.5 FORMATS OF PERFORMANCE REPORTING

- annual reports and annual plans
- financial documents: budget and accounts
- specific publications in hard copy and/or on a website
- interactive information on a website
- oral witnesses
- news flashes
- publicity
- scorecards

confronted with professional judgement (see chapter 7 for a discussion on the users of performance information).

What is the right format? Different formats for reporting performance information exist. Box 4.5 gives the main options. Annual reporting, for instance, will be a good instrument for reporting to stakeholders and interest groups. It should be noted that annual reports are for specialists. It is improbable that they have a direct impact on the public in general. Oral communications will be suitable for reporting to the middle and top management, together with scorecards. News flashes and publicity are instruments to reach the general public through the mass media.

6 QUALITY OF PERFORMANCE MEASUREMENT

There are good reasons not to disregard the quality of performance information. First, when users of information learn about the weaknesses of performance information, the chances are that they disregard it. Non-use of performance information is a waste of resources. Moreover, it will be hard to regain trust in performance measurement. Second, and even more perniciously, poor quality information may nonetheless be used, which consequently may lead to wrong decisions and actions (Etzioni and Lehman 1967). Users of information (decision-makers, politicians, media) often lack the time and/or competences to assess the quality of performance information. Chapter 8 includes a more elaborate, theoretical discussion of the non-use of performance information.

The organization of quality assurance ideally parallels the control pyramid of auditors. The first level is the internal control system of the organization itself which is performing the controls in order to obtain reasonable assurance about the operations of the organization. The COSO model (see pages 78, 81) is a well-known framework for internal control processes. The second level is the internal audit that controls the control processes and assesses the risks. The internal audit reports to the management of the organization. Third, the external audit reviews the quality independently from the organization. For what financial information is concerned, this system is well established. Non-financial information is seldom included in the audit systems (Wholey 1999).

Quality should not be confined to statistical quality. Quality should be an issue in the whole production process of performance information, where the quality of a preceding step is a necessary condition for the next step. Indicator development can only be done properly when the subject of measurement is well-targeted within an explicit mental framework of the programme or organization. Focused data collection has to be based on well-defined indicators. Meaningful analyses are only possible with high quality data and reporting is only feasible based on appropriate analyses.

Bouckaert (1993) identifies three aspects of quality. First, quality implies the *functionality* of the measurement system. Measurement should be fit for use. There are two gradations of non-conformity to the functionality requirement: non-functionality and dysfunctionality. Non-functionality implies that the information is disregarded while dysfunctionality implies that there are negative effects due to measurement. The organization, in that case, is worse off than before (see chapter 9 for a developed discussion on the effects of performance measurement).

Second, quality implies indicators that are *valid and reliable*, which are established notions in social scientific research. Measurement is valid when a study is measuring what it is supposed to measure. It is about the accuracy of measurement. In performance measurement, the selection of the indicators defines the validity of measurement. Reliability is the consistency of measurement, or the degree to which an instrument measures the same way each time it is used under the same condition with the same subjects. Reliability is the repeatability of measurement. Indicators can be valid, but not reliable as well as reliable but not valid. A thermometer put in boiling water should

Table 4.6 *Reliability and validity*

	High validity	Low validity
High reliability	Right	Precisely wrong
Low reliability	Roughly right	Wrong

measure 100°C. When it measures 90°C at repeated attempts, measurement is reliable but invalid. When it measures 100°C at first attempt, 110° at the second and 90° at the third, the first measurement is valid, but not reliable. Validity is the more important quality criterion, given that it is better to be roughly right than precisely wrong (see Table 4.6).

The third quality dimension is legitimacy of a measurement system. In an ideal scenario, all organization members support the measurement system. Manipulation and gaming with performance information are less likely when ownership is high. Only when unobtrusive indicators exist, ownership may be less vital for the measurement effort.

7 CONCLUSION

This chapter described the design parameters of an ideal-typical measurement process. The five-step model starts with the decision of what to measure, which is followed by the identification of the indicators and the collection of data. The fourth step is the analysis of the data and, finally, performance information needs to be reported, with the right format for the right target group.

There is no one best way to do performance measurement. The design of the measurement system needs to be conditioned by the envisaged use of the performance information. This chapter has described the choices that have to be made. In chapter 6, the contingency with the foreseen uses is further explored. For now, the main lesson is that a simple how-to-do guide is insufficient for successful measurement.

DISCUSSION QUESTION

1   Consider a set of indicators (for instance in an annual report or reported in a newspaper). What is the mental framework behind the indicators? How relevant are indicators for the framework? What are the motivations behind the targeting of the indicators? Are the indicators data driven or not? What are the data

sources? What is the level of analysis? What is the quality of the set (validity, reliability, functionality, legitimacy)?

REFERENCES

Arndt, C. and Oman, C. (2006) *Uses and Abuses of Governance Indicators.* Paris, Organisation for Economic Co-operation and Development.

Atkinson, A. B. (2005) *Atkinson Review: Final Report: Measurement of Government Output and Productivity for the National Accounts.* London, Palgrave Macmillan.

Audit Commission (2000) *On Target: The Practice of Performance Measurement.* London, Audit Commission.

Baumgartner, F. R. and Jones, B. D. (1993) *Agendas and Instability in American Politics.* Chicago, University of Chicago Press.

Best, J. (2001) *Damned Lies and Statistics: Untangling Numbers from the Media, Politicians, and Activists.* Berkeley, CA, University of California Press.

Bogdanor, V. (2005) *Joined-Up Government.* Oxford, Oxford University Press.

Bouckaert, G. (1993) Measurement and meaningful management. *Public Productivity and Management Review,* 17, 31–43.

Bouckaert, G., Van Dooren, W. and Sterck, M. (2003) *Prestaties Meten in de Vlaamse Overheid: Een Verkennende Studie.* Leuven, Public Management Institute.

Bovaird, T. and Lœffler, E. (2003) Evaluating the quality of public governance: indicators, models and methodologies. *International Review of Administrative Sciences,* 69, 313–28.

Broom, C. (1998) *Performance Measurement Concepts and Techniques.* Washington, DC, American Society for Public Administration.

De Lancer Julnes, P., Aristigueta, M., Yang, K. and Berry, F. S. (2007) *International Handbook of Practice-based Performance Management.* Thousand Oaks, Sage Publications.

Etzioni, A. and Lehman, E. W. (1967) Some dangers in 'valid' social measurement. *Annals of the American Academy of Political and Social Science,* 373, 1–15.

European Institute Of Public Administration (2008) *European Primer on Customer Satisfaction Management.* Maastricht, EIPA.

Galtung, J. and Ruge, M. H. (1965) The structure of foreign news: the presentation of the Congo, Cuba and Cyprus crises in four Norwegian newspapers. *Journal of Peace Research,* 2, 64–90.

Hatry, H. P. (1999) *Performance Measurement: Getting Results.* Washington, DC, Urban Institute Press.

Hendricks, M. (1994) Making a splash: reporting evaluation results effectively. In Hatry, H. P., Wholey, J. S. and Newcomer, K. (eds.) *Handbook of Practical Program Evaluation*. San Fransisco, Jossey Bass.

Innes, J. E. (1990) *Knowledge and Public Policy: The Search for Meaningful Indicators*. New Brunswick, Transaction Publishers.

Kaplan, R. S. and Norton, D. P. (1996) *The Balanced Scorecard: Translating Strategy into Action*. Boston, MA, Harvard Business School Press.

Leeuw, F. L. (2003) Reconstructing program theories: methods available and problems to be solved. *American Journal of Evaluation,* 24, 5–20.

Liner, B., Hatry, H., Vinson, E., Allen, R., Dusenbery, P., Byrant, S. and Snell, R. (2001) *Making Results-based State Government Work.,* Washington, DC, Urban Institute.

Merton, R. K. (1988) The Matthew effect in science, II: Cumulative advantage and the symbolism of intellectual property. *Isis,* 79, 606–23.

Miller, G. A. (2009) *Wordnet*. Princeton, Trustees of Princeton University.

Mitchell, R. K., Agle, B. R. and Wood, D. J. (1997) Toward a theory of stakeholder identification and salience: defining the principle of who and what really counts. *Academy of Management Review,* 22, 853–86.

National Audit Office (2001) *Measuring the Performance of Government Departments*. London, NAO.

OECD (2006) *Pensions at a Glance*. Paris, OECD.

OECD (2009) *Measuring Government Activity*. Paris, OECD.

Parsons, W. (1995) *Public Policy: An Introduction to the Theory and Practice of Policy Analysis*. Northampton, MA, Edward Elgar.

Pollitt, C. (2000) Institutional amnesia: a paradox of the 'information age'? *Prometheus,* 18, 5–16.

Rogers, P. J., Hacsi, T. A., Petrosino, A. and Huebner, T. A. (2000) *Program Theory in Evaluation: Challenges and Opportunities*. San Francisco, Jossey-Bass.

Rossi, R. J. and Gilmartin, K. J. (1980) *The Handbook of Social Indicators: Sources, Characteristics, and Analysis*. New York, Garland STPM Press.

Rubenstein, R., Schwartz, A. E. and Stiefel, L. (2003) Better than raw: a guide to measuring organizational performance with adjusted performance measures. *Public Administration Review,* 63, 607–15.

Treasury, H. M. (2001) *Choosing the Right Fabric: A Framework for Performance Information*. London, H.M. Treasury.

United Way of America (1999) *Achieving and Measuring Community Outcomes: Challenges, Issues, Some Approaches*. United Way of America.

Van de Walle, S. (2006) The state of the world's bureaucracies. *Journal of Comparative Policy Analysis: Research and Practice,* 8, 437–48.

Van Dooren, W. (2009) A Politico-administrative agenda for progress in social measurement: reforming the calculation of government's contribution to GDP. *Journal of Comparative Policy Analysis,* 11: 3, 309–26.

Weick, K. E. (1995) *Sensemaking in Organizations.* Thousand Oaks, Sage Publications.

Weiss, C. H. (1998) Have we learned anything about the use of evaluation? *American Journal of Evaluation,* 19, 13–21.

Wholey, J. S. (1999) Performance Based Management: responding to challenges. *Public Poductivity & Management Review,* 22: 3, 288–307.

FURTHER READING

One of the most clearly structured and practical handbooks on how to measure performance was developed by Hatry (1999) at the Urban Institute. A case book from the state level in the USA was published a few years later (Liner *et al.* 2001). One of the most thoughtful guides on customer satisfaction measurement is provided by the European Institute of Public Administration (EIPA) (2008). A combination of case studies and theoretically grounded practical guidance is De Lancer Julnes *et al.*'s (2007) *International Handbook of Practice-based Performance Management.* One of best critiques on measurement is Etzioni and Lehman's article on the dangers of social measurement (1967). Innes (1990) analyses the institutionalization of indicators. By far the most thorough critique on the quality of governance indicators is offered by Arndt and Oman (2006). The quality criteria they use to assess governance indicators could easily be transferred to other contexts. Bouckaert (1993) also provides a useful model to assess quality using three criteria; validity, functionality and legitimacy. Finally, it may be worthwhile to critically assess the performance measurement guides provided by oversight agencies such as the UK Audit Commission (Audit Commission 2000), or the National Audit Office (2001).

Chapter 5

Incorporation of performance information

LEARNING OBJECTIVES

- To know what incorporation of performance information means.
- To understand the requirements of good incorporation.
- To understand why good incorporation is a condition for using performance information.

KEY POINTS

- Using performance information assumes not only measurement but also incorporation.
- Incorporation should be coherent and systematic; policy, financial, and contract cycles are coherent systems for incorporation.
- The better the incorporation, the higher the chances of using performance information.

Measuring performance (chapter 4) is necessary but not sufficient to manage performance. In order to manage, performance information should be used (chapters 6 and 7). Yet, use does not just happen. Deliberate action is needed to incorporate performance information into the organization. Therefore, measured performance needs to be incorporated into the management and policy system (Bouckaert and Halligan 2008) (see Box 5.1 for a related discussion). This chapter focuses on ways to do this. The emphasis will be on incorporation in the policy, financial and contract cycles, and not so much on incorporation in personnel management and HRM.

BOX 5.1 INCORPORATION AND USE AND THE RELATED CONCEPTS OF ADOPTION AND IMPLEMENTATION

Several recent studies have used a conceptually comparable distinction in order to assess the use of performance information. Instead of talking about incorporation and use, these studies speak of adoption and implementation. The idea that performance information first needs to be integrated into the management systems before it can be used, however, remains. We opt for the notions of incorporation and use since in particular the concept of implementation lacks precision. It is usually connoted with the policy implementation literature.

The distinction was first introduced by Beyer and Trice in a study of knowledge utilization (Beyer and Trice 1982). De Lancer Julnes and Holzer (2001) applied the framework on performance information. Adoption is the development of a capacity to act based on performance information while implementation reflects the actual use of this capacity in decision-making. They found that rational-technical factors were important for adoption while political-cultural factors better explain the level of implementation. Yang and Hsieh (2007) made the distinction between adoption and managerial effectiveness of performance information. They pointed to the significance of politics.

It is important to note that in this framework both adoption and implementation can be high or low (see Table 5.1). Some organizations score high on adoption and low on implementation. Measurement in these organizations is predominantly outward oriented. They measure because they have to or because they see promotional opportunities in presenting performance data. These may be the window-dressing cases, which have many measurement initiatives on the shelf, but do not use it in operations. Some organizations score low on adoption and high on implementation. These organizations do not have many formal initiatives, but the ones that are in place are being used internally for management. We can suspect that these measurement systems are better geared towards the organization's needs.

The reasons for and the way of embedding measured performance are crucial for using performance information effectively. A first issue is what kind of performance information should or could be included and incorporated. Chapter 2 gives an overview of the different elements of performance information that could be incorporated in different stages of managing organizations and policies. The whole range of inputs, activities, outputs, outcomes and objectives could or could not be incorporated.

Table 5.1 *Adoption and implementation: four profiles*

	Low adoption	High adoption
Low implementation	No performance management	Outward oriented PM
High implementation	Inward oriented PM	Full performance management

Source: Van Dooren 2005

This chapter first discusses what controlling means. Management systems are the infrastructure in which performance information is integrated. Hence, a good understanding of how performance can be managed is crucial. Next, three cycles that are eligible for management control are taken into consideration: the policy cycle, the financial cycle and the contract cycle. To illustrate the models, some real-life examples of incorporation are presented.

1 CONTROLLING ORGANIZATIONS

Controlling is defined as a process to provide reasonable assurance regarding the achievement of objectives (COSO 2008). To the extent that being in control is crucial, four key questions need to be answered in all organizations (see Box 5.2). Management cycles have to contribute to this aim of reasonable assurance. In other words, management capacity is in essence about building the capacity to ask and to answer these key questions in a regular way. This section first outlines four key questions that organizations should ask. Next, the role of cycles in building management capacity is dealt with.

First, there is an *ex ante question* in which the future performance of a system is reflected upon and ultimately determined: What shall we do next year (or in subsequent years)? The answer to this prospective question needs to be authorized by a legitimate institution. For instance, an executive office should offer an answer to the legislative branch which discusses, approves or amends. Within the executive office there could also be a range of often contradictory debates between finance and line departments, between ministries and agencies, between central and local government, etc.

In all these cases, the answers to the prospective question need to be documented with data and information. The richness of the information can vary. As discussed in Table 5.2, a minimalistic answer only refers to input and cash. The answer to the question 'What will happen next year?' is to say: 'next year we will expend this amount of money on personnel, operating costs, transfers and capital'. What actually happens with this input is unknown. On the other hand, a maximalist answer to the prospective question could be: 'Next year we will spend this amount of money (in cash and in cost) to deliver these outputs (quantity and quality) in the context of these outcomes.'

BOX 5.2 BEING IN CONTROL: THE METAPHOR OF DRIVING A CAR

The analogy of being in control of your car may be helpful to understand controlling in organizations. If we drive from A to B, we want reasonable assurance of arriving on time. Hence, different controlling issues can be identified. The *first issue* is about where we want to go – we have to define B. We have to look to the road ahead in terms of where we want to arrive. We thus have to determine the road to be taken. Nowadays many people rely on Global Positioning Systems to make these practical decisions. While driving a car we constantly switch our attention from the road ahead of us to the screen in front of us which shows all kinds of useful performance information on the behaviour of our car during the implementation of our scheduled trajectory: speed, temperature, oil pressure, time, etc. This is the *second issue*; what is happening now? We permanently adjust our behaviour to the various indicators of what is happening. Good controlling does not rely on only one source of information. Over-reliance on GPS as a monitoring system may, for instance, have dramatic effects. One driver once drove his car down a public stairway in an old Italian town while following the instructions on the GPS. In a similar way, another chauffeur steered his car into a supermarket. Monitoring systems are not reality. As some American car mirrors mention, objects look different in reality and could be closer than perceived. Once we have arrived with our car in B, we look at the clock to check whether we are on time. This is the *third issue*; performance is evaluated. Could we have taken a faster, or more agreeable route? What were the causes of delay? The way in which we arrived is also important. Did we get tickets for driving too fast? Or could we have driven in a more ecological way? Next time, undoubtedly, we will take these experiences into account. This is the fourth controlling issue of feed-forward into an new cycle. With our car, we may have to go back to A for another trip to B, or we may want to go to C and take the A-B trip experience into account. Or maybe we will take the train.

Second, once it is known and approved what needs to be done, there is an *ex nunc* question of what is happening during implementation. This requires a monitoring system that allows making corrective actions during implementation. This stage also needs to be documented with data and information. Again, there could be a minimalistic position exposing the amount of money received and expended, or a maximalist position that reveals not only the current cash position (receipts and expenses), but also benefits and costs.

Third, once the implementation stage is over, there is a need to compare results with what was planned, and to assess this result *(ex post)*. This is a retrospective question. Goal

Table 5.2 *Four key questions and the capacity to provide answers*

	Input and cash driven systems	Output/outcome and accrual driven systems
Ex ante: prospective perspective: What will be done?	Next year we will expend this amount of money for personnel, operating costs, transfers and capital	Next year we will spend this amount of money (in cash and in cost) to deliver these outputs (quantity and quality) in the context of these outcomes
Ex nunc: real time perspective: What is happening?	Up to this moment we have received so much money, and we have expended so much money	At this moment the cash position (receipts and expenses) is evolving in this direction; at this moment benefits and costs are evolving in this direction
Ex post: retrospective perspective; What has happened?	We have been compliant, and all financial figures are correct	We have been compliant, all financial figures are correct, and we performed in an economic, efficient and effective way
Feed forward: What will change?	We used the above information to write the next budget	We used the above information to change our strategy, our performance based budgets, and our contracts

attainment should be discussed taking other criteria such as economy, efficiency, openness, transparency, etc. into account (see chapter 2). The minimalistic version of a controlling system provides information on compliance and correctness of financial figures. A maximalist version yields insights on economy, efficiency and effectiveness in addition to compliance and correctness of financial figures.

Fourth, it is necessary to feed this information forward into the next cycle and to use information on the past for improving the future way of managing performance. In the minimalist design, information can be used to write the next budget in an incremental way. The maximalist design may trigger a change in strategy, inform performance-based budgets and renegotiating contracts, as summarized in Table 5.2.

The capacity to answer these questions largely derives from the management and policy information systems in the organisation. Box 5.3 proposes some key issues in assessing controlling capacity. Table 5.2 suggests that this capacity can be minimalistic and input based or maximalist and output/outcome based. This has consequences for the degree of incorporation of performance information. Incorporating just input information results in less control. The incorporation of information on the whole span of performance (input, activities, outputs and outcomes) yields a richer, but also more costly controlling system.

In conclusion, measuring performance is necessary but not sufficient for performance management. Performance information needs to be incorporated into the management

BOX 5.3 ASSESSING CONTROLLING CAPACITY

Some quite detailed models exist to assess the quality of the control systems. The most well-known in probably the COSO model (COSO 2008). Hence, some key questions stand out:

- Who asks and who answers the questions in Table 5.2?
- What documents provide answers to these questions?
- Are there any missing documents, or stages in the organization?
- What is the quality of the information across the whole system?
- What is the coherence of the documents available which incorporate performance information?

system for it to be 'in control' – i.e. for it to provide reasonable assurance about the attainment of objectives. In a minimal version, only inputs are incorporated while in a maximalist version, information on outputs and outcomes is also integrated. A maximalist version will enable organizations to better answer four key control questions: what will be done, what is happening, what happened and what does this mean for the future?

2 FROM ANSWERING KEY QUESTIONS TO MANAGING THREE CYCLES

The sequence of these four questions is cyclical with corresponding documents in each stage. There are three cycles which are relevant to manage performance in the public sector:

- the policy cycle: policy preparation, monitoring, policy evaluation and feedback
- the financial cycle: budgeting, accounting and auditing
- the contract cycle: negotiation, monitoring and evaluation.

From an analytical perspective, there is a hierarchy between the cycles. Policies set out the priorities, which are then translated into budgets. Only then, does the question of which agency will perform which task arise. This is the subject of contract negotiations. The policy cycle should thus determine the financial cycle, which then should determine the contract cycle.

In reality, the timing as well as the hierarchical relations between the cycles is much more complicated. Literature on incrementalism demonstrates the importance of past budgets and past task allocations in developing new policies (Lindblom 1959; Wildavsky and Hammond 1965). Documents often combine content which could belong to different cycles. In some countries, the contracts are fully part of the financial cycle and budgets and contracts become the same document (Pollitt and Bouckaert 2004).

Figure 5.1 shows how performance information will be incorporated in the *policy cycle*. There is a (strategic) plan which includes major objectives and targets for resources, activities, outputs and outcomes. These plans need to be implemented and monitored. Monitoring arrangements, such as Balanced Scorecard (BSC), EFQM (European Foundation for Quality Management), the official European CAF (Common Assessment Framework) or the Canadian MAF (Management Accountability Framework) are models which can be used as mental maps to guide incorporation. Policy sectors may in addition develop other more specialized monitoring instruments: crime monitors (see for instance the Compstat movement (O'Connell 2001)), air quality monitors, neighbourhood monitors, quality of life monitors, etc. The next stage is evaluation, which incorporates performance information for the purpose of assessing past performance. Evaluation reports, which incorporate performance information, are fed forward into the next strategic plan. This evaluation stage could also include comparisons and benchmarks, based on surveys of users and citizens. Hence, there are three sets of documents that incorporate performance information: planning, monitoring and evaluation documents.

The *financial cycle* is analytically embedded in the policy cycle. This is shown in Figure 5.2. Budgets should be the corresponding documents to strategic plans, or at least their annual slice. Budgets should incorporate the same information from the strategic plan in a different way, and for different purposes. The budget authorizes expenses during implementation. A limited authorization involves input budgets that allow (and oblige) spending a certain budget on a line item. A higher density of incorporation of performance information is found in output budgets that authorize to spend resources to attain specified output levels. Some empirical evidence on output budgeting can be found in an OECD publication (Curristine 2005).

Implementation is monitored through the accounting system. Again, there are more limited systems, i.e. cash accounting, to answer the question of what is happening, or more developed systems, i.e. full accrual accounting, which allows for extensive cost calculations and comparisons. This also shows the varying density of incorporation of performance information. It could vary from simple cash information to sophisticated direct or full cost information. Box 5.4 discusses the pros and cons of accrual accounting and cost accounting in the public sector.

Figure 5.1
Incorporating performance information: the policy cycle

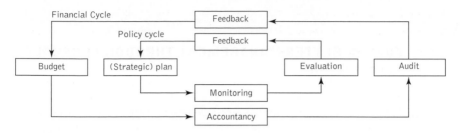

Figure 5.2 *Incorporating performance information: policy and control cycle, and financial cycle*

The third stage in the financial cycle is audit. Performance audits gain importance over compliance and financial audits and consequently they are an important avenue for incorporating performance information (Raaum and Morgan 2001). Performance audit reports are, in most cases, publicly available. Ideally, these performance audit reports feed into the policy and budget debates for the next year. The result are three sets of documents; budgets, accounts and audits.

The contract cycle is embedded or at least derived from the financial cycle. This is shown in Figure 5.3. Contracts are concrete documents that define agreements between key actors or organizations in a policy field which incorporate essential performance information. In return for an envelope of money, a contract states what is expected in terms of activities, outputs or (contributions to) outcomes from outputs provided. There should be a monitoring system for contract implementation, which includes reporting. These reporting and monitoring documents incorporate major performance information which in many countries are called KPIs or Key Performance Indicators. Contract implementation is evaluated in an accountability context. The responsibility defined and granted in the contract is confronted with the results. Finally, the evaluation which contains the degree of realization (or not, and why) will feed forward into the next contract cycle. In some cases this may include changing those in charge for not having delivered. In that case, there is an element of personnel evaluation of the top managers as an autonomous unit. Pollitt (2008), for instance, points to the dismissal of hospital managers in England after negative evaluations.

The contracting cycle typically produces three sets of documents which incorporate performance information: contracts or agreements, their monitoring and their evaluation documents.

Three sets of documents in three cycles could, in principle, result in nine (sets of) documents. It will be a challenge to connect these, or even better, to merge these documents so that they have different functions according to the different cycles. This is not just necessary to prevent controlling leading to red tape rather than control. It is also indispensable to avoid all kinds of contradictions between performance information in all these documents.

BOX 5.4 BETTER MANAGEMENT THROUGH ACCRUAL ACCOUNTING?

The UK Public Audit Forum (2002) strongly believes in the benefits of accrual accounting. They argue that accrual accounting means better management. No organization should hesitate, in their view, to incorporate performance information into the accounting system. The benefits of accruals accounting are:

- Completeness – accruals-based accounts are more complete than cash accounts. The need to include transactions in the period in which they occur reduces the potential for manipulation of accounts and improves comparability between periods and organizations.
- Better planning, management and decision-making – accurate and objective financial and management information is essential for good management, decision-making and better resource planning and allocation.
- Ability to change behaviours – better management is possible with accruals accounting, but it is not automatic. Achieving some changes may also require policy changes or financial incentives.
- Performance management – good performance management needs effective performance measures. Performance measures, or indicators, have to be calculated on the basis of comprehensive and consistent financial and operational data. Accruals accounting is therefore an essential component of better performance management.
- Assessing financial resilience – one of the purposes of published financial statements is to enable the user to predict future cash flows and assess resilience or risk. Financial statements cannot foretell the future with complete accuracy but the aim can at least be to give a fair and balanced picture of the past and some signposts to future performance.

More critical sounds are heard among academics studying Australian and New Zealand accrual accounting initiatives (Carlin 2006). Accrual accounting requires massive amounts of output information. Moreover, the complexity of the system is not always understood by politicians who are supposed to exert control (see also Paulson 2006 for the Swedish case).

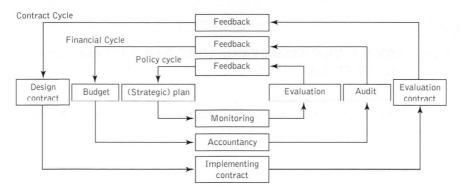

Figure 5.3 *Incorporating performance information: policy, financial and contract cycle*

3 FROM MODELS TO REALITY: SOME EXAMPLES OF INCORPORATION

In this section, some real-life examples of incorporation are described (Boxes 5.5, 5.6 and 5.7). The examples are from museums and reflect how strategy and plans, budgets and contracts incorporate performance information.

Box 5.5 shows what a resource agreement between a line department and the Treasury looks like. Starting from a general 'Government Goal', 'desired outcomes' are defined which should be realized by implementing seven 'services' or outputs. There are dollars allocated to these services, as well as full-time equivalents (FTEs) for the personnel side of these services.

Box 5.6 shows how a UK department is funding an agreement with a museum. From the beginning there is a requirement for the museum to contribute to the general objectives of the government. It is also clear from the beginning (*ex ante*) what indicators will be used, which targets are set, and how this will be monitored (*ex nunc*). Finally, a delivery plan is provided to demonstrate how these strategic objectives will be realized, through primary activities, deliverables and outcomes. Although the terminology of Box 5.6 is a bit different from Box 5.5, there is a similarity in the way of incorporating and connecting performance information.

Box 5.7 is an Australian budget (whereas Boxes 5.5 and 5.6 were agreements or contracts). Here the logic is very linear: outputs are resulting in outcomes. This is made visible using KPIs.

Examples of monitoring schemes during implementation could be found in standardized 'quality models'. The Common Assessment Framework was developed specifically for the public sector in Europe, and allows for improvement strategies in all fields covered by the model. In many cases these models are also used for planning purposes. Finally, the number of performance audits is growing. Box 5.8 gives examples of some recent performance audits in Australia, the UK and the USA.

85

BOX 5.5 THE CASE OF CULTURE AND ARTS IN WESTERN AUSTRALIA: RESOURCE AGREEMENT

The following performance information (financial and non-financial) is the subject of a Resource Agreement signed by the Minister, Accountable Authority and the Treasurer under Part 3, Division 5 of the Financial Management Act 2006.

Government goal

Enhancing the quality of life and well-being of all people throughout Western Australia by providing high quality, accessible services

Desired outcomes

Outcome 1 A creative, sustainable and accessible culture and arts sector

Services

1   Arts Industry Support
2   Screen Production Industry Support
3   Venue Management Services

Outcome 2 Western Australia's natural, cultural and documentary collections are preserved, accessible and sustainable

Services

4   Art Gallery Services
5   Library and Information Services
6   Museum Services
7   Government Recordkeeping and Archival Services

Outcome 1: A creative, sustainable and accessible culture and arts sector:

■   Proportion of funding applicants satisfied with the key elements of the 'creative' funding programs:
    2006–07 estimated: 82%; 2007–08 target: 82%
■   Perceived values of culture and arts to the Western Australian community:
    2006–07 estimated: 80%; 2007–08 target: 80%
■   Proportion of triennially funded organizations within the culture and arts sector regarded as financially healthy:
    2006–07 estimated: 27%; 2007–08 target: 28%

Service 4: Art Gallery Services

■ Delivery of the State Art Collection and access to art gallery services and programmes through visual arts advocacy, collection development, facilities and services. Services ensure that primary access to art, heritage and ideas locally, regionally and internationally are preserved and displayed for future generations.

■ This includes indicators such as: total and net cost of services, key efficiency indicators (average cost of art gallery services per Art Gallery access), full time equivalent (FTEs)

BOX 5.6 THE CASE OF THE UK BRITISH MUSEUM: FUNDING AGREEMENT

Funding Agreement between the British Museum and the Department for Culture, Media and Sport (DCMS) 2005/06–2007/08

This agreement:

■ summarizes the Museum's whole mission, strategic priorities, rationale, programme, planned output and delivery partners as set out in the Delivery Plan Summary;

■ sets out the contribution that the Museum will make towards the delivery of key DCMS objectives, Efficiency Public Service Agreement PSA 3 and public value, in the context of its overall mission;

■ explains how the benefits of DCMS investments will be spread geographically, in particular by delivery through the Museum's regional partners;

■ confirms the commitment of DCMS to the Museum in terms of funding and other support;

■ shows how delivery will be measured and monitored by reference to a set of key targets and performance indicators agreed with the Museum and by such other quantitative and qualitative measures that the Museum wishes to use to assess its performance and the achievement of public value in the context of their wider activities;

■ provides an assessment of the risks and how they will be managed.

The British Museum's contribution to the delivery of Government objectives

'. . . the Museum is uniquely placed to demonstrate the continuity and importance of cultural diversity . . .'

Performance monitoring

This Funding Agreement will be monitored by:

(a) Assessment of the achievement of the agreed Funding Agreement targets in the table below;
(b) Assessment of the effectiveness of projects which support PSA 3;
(c) Reference to the Key Performance Indicators;
(d) Performance against the British Museum's Delivery Plans and related measures; and
(e) Performance against delivering efficiencies.

The figures for each Funding Agreement target will be negotiated and agreed individually between DCMS and the British Museum. The targets are as follows:

Key Funding Agreement Targets (2005–06 – 2006–07 – 2007–08)
■ Total number of visits to the Museum (excluding virtual visits): 4,300,000; 4,500,000; 4,700,000;
■ Number of unique users visiting the website: 7,600,000; 7,800,000; 8,000,000;
■ Number of UK adults aged 16 and over from lower socio-economic groups attending the Museum: 183,250; 192,700; 200,000;
■ Number of children aged 15 and under visiting the Museum: 860,000; 900,000; 940,000;
■ Number of children aged 15 and under in on- and off-site organized educational sessions: 180,000; 900,000; 940,000;
■ Net income from trading (including corporate hiring): £1,260,000; £1,375,000; £1,500,000;
■ Efficiency savings: £7,137,000; £7,633,000; £8,181,000;

Museum/Gallery Delivery Plan Summary (some examples):
■ Stewardship (examples)
   Strategic Objective: Care of the collection
   Primary Activities: Acquisition strategy
   Deliverables/Outcomes: Enriched and contextualized collection

- Scholarship and Research (examples)
  Strategic Objective: Electronic publication of academic research
  Primary Activities: Develop web-based publishing
  Deliverables/Outcomes: Open access; cost efficiency
- Access, Education and Communities (examples)
  Strategic Objective: Public Programme
  Primary Activities: Define three-year programme of exhibitions, events and lectures
  Deliverables/Outcomes: An attractive, financially sound and critically acclaimed programme
- Business Excellence and Efficiency (examples)
  Strategic Objective: Resource efficiency
  Primary Activities: Organizational development: senior management team in place, training and development plans for all staff
  Deliverables/Outcomes: Effective teamworking; higher output

BOX 5.7 THE CASE OF THE NATIONAL GALLERY OF AUSTRALIA: BUDGET OUTCOMES AND PERFORMANCE INFORMATION

The Australian Government requires agencies to measure their intended and actual performance in terms of outcomes. Government outcomes are the results, impacts or consequences of actions by the Government on the Australian community. Agencies are required to identify the outputs which demonstrate their contribution to Government outcomes over the coming year.

Each outcome is described below by outputs, specifying the performance indicators and targets used to assess and monitor the performance of the National Gallery of Australia (NGA) in achieving Government outcomes.

Outcome 1

Encourage understanding, knowledge and enjoyment of the visual arts by providing access to, and information about, works of art locally, nationally and internationally.

Output 1.1: Collection Development (Total estimated available resources in $000)

Components of output 1.1: The NGA aims to build a collection of works of art of outstanding quality through acquisition, gift and bequest, and through disposal.

Key Performance Indicators (2008–09 Target)
- Percentage of works of art acquired in accordance with the endorsed Acquisition strategy: 100%
- Percentage of works of art acquired researched and documented: 100%
- Number of works of art deaccessioned during the year: 5

Output 1.2: Collection Management: pro memoria.

Output 1.3: Access to and promotion of works of art

The NGA provides access to works of art by displaying, exhibiting and lending its collection, as well as borrowing works from other sources. Access to works from the collection which are not on display is also provided. The NGA enhances the understanding, knowledge and enjoyment of art by providing information about and promoting the benefits of works of art through visitor services, education, and public programmes and through multimedia. The NGA seeks to achieve the widest possible audience both in attracting visitors to the Gallery and by sending works of art around Australia and oversees thereby improving access to works of art and providing information about them.

Key Performance Indicators (2008–09 Target)
- Number of people visiting the NGA as well as accessing the national art collection through travelling exhibitions and loans: 3,000,000
- Percentage of NGA visitors surveyed satisfied with displays and exhibitions: 85%
- Number of people who accessed information via the NGA's research library, collection study room and website: 1,000,000
- Number of works of art from the national collection loaned nationally and internationally: 1200
- Percentage of attendees satisfied with NGA events: 85%

BOX 5.8 EXAMPLES OF PERFORMANCE AUDITS

From the ANAO (Australian National Audit Office), Australia (2008–09) (www.anao.gov.au)

- *Business Continuity Management and Emergency Management in Centrelink*: This audit assessed the capacity of Centrelink, an agency that ensures social security payments, to avoid business outage. This is an example of assessing the robustness of the system. In terms of the dimensions of performance defined in chapter 2, this is regime performance.
- Funding for Non-governmental Schools: The audit assessed the effectiveness of the Department of Education's administration of general recurrent grants for non-government schools. It thus assessed the product performance of the department of education.
- Planning and Allocating Aged Care Places and Capital Grants: The objective of the audit was to assess the effectiveness of Department of Health and Ageing's management of the planning and allocation of aged care places and capital grants (product performance).

From the NAO (National Audit Office), UK (2009) (www.nao.org.uk)

- *Measuring up: How good are the Government's data systems for monitoring performance against Public Service Agreements?* The aim of the audit was to assure that departments are operating sound data systems for the purposes of monitoring and reporting progress against their Public Service Agreements (regime performance).
- *Partnering for school improvement.* This report evaluates the extent and nature of partnering with other schools in secondary schools, and assesses its impact on the attainment and behaviour of 11–14 year olds (product and process performance).
- *The Department for Transport: The failure of Metronet.* This audit assesses risk management in the Department of Transport. It is a follow-up on other reports on the London Underground PPPs (regime performance).

From GAO (Government Accountability Office), USA (2009) (www.gao.gov)

- Aviation Weather: FAA and the National Weather Service are considering plans to consolidate weather service offices, but face significant challenges. This audit evaluated agency plans for the restructuring and for establishing performance measures. Hence, it is a study of incorporation.

■ Metropolitan Planning Organizations: Options exist to enhance transportation planning capacity and federal oversight. Metropolitan planning organizations are responsible for transportation planning in metropolitan areas; however, little is known about what has been achieved by the planning efforts (product performance).

■ Social Security Disability: Additional performance measures and better cost estimates could help improve SSA's efforts to eliminate its hearings backlog. GAO (1) examined the Plan's potential to eliminate the hearings-level backlog, (2) determined the extent to which the Plan included components of sound planning, and (3) identified potential unintended effects of the Plan on hearings-level operations and other aspects of the disability process (regime and product performance).

4 CONTROLLING SYSTEMS AND MANAGING CYCLES: A NECESSARY COMBINATION FOR INCORPORATION

Figure 5.4 shows that all stages of the cycles are present simultaneously, but refer to different years. The dynamics of incorporating performance information implies that in 2011 we are evaluating and auditing the reality of 2010 which was planned, budgeted and contracted in 2009. In 2011 we are monitoring and accounting for plans, budgets and contracts generated in 2010. Finally, in 2011 we are planning, budgeting and contracting for the year 2012. Figure 5.4 shows that incorporation implies that in each year there are three simultaneous exercises which refer to three different years of activity. Incorporation is therefore linked to the three stages of each cycle, which are connected.

Figure 5.4 *The dynamics of incorporating performance information*

The whole incorporation exercise of performance information requires automatically a time series of at least three years to be useful, coherent and systematic. Hence, stability over time of incorporation efforts becomes more important. Changing performance information over time complicates the way it will be incorporated. This will have a serious negative impact on the use. For that reason it is crucial to consider measurement in the perspective of incorporation and potential use.

5 ORGANIZATIONAL READINESS

There are several 'organizational readiness for performance' checklists (see for instance Broom 1998). Organizational readiness checklists should not be used as a 0/1 total index. Rather, they reflect degrees of readiness that allow for levels of less or more complex systems to manage performance. According to Niven there are 10 criteria to evaluate an organization's readiness to deploy and sustain a performance management system (based on Niven 2003):

1   A clearly defined strategy
2   Strong, committed sponsorship
3   A clear and urgent need
4   The support of mid-level managers
5   The appropriate scale and scope
6   A strong team and available resources
7   A culture of measurement
8   Alignment between business and IT
9   Trustworthy and available data
10   A solid technical infrastructure.

To manage performance it is necessary to measure performance, but it is not sufficient. It is also necessary to incorporate. The possibility to incorporate depends therefore on the practice of measuring performance as well as on the important question of how to organize incorporation. Is this a top-down or a bottom-up exercise? Do we need a legal framework or is a voluntarism-based culture and atmosphere more appropriate? Is this necessarily a big bang exercise or is a more incremental approach, including increasing levels of coverage, possible? There is no general answer to these questions, but there is a need to have a clear vision on how to guide the incorporation process.

CONCLUSION

This chapter discussed the incorporation of performance information into key policy and management cycles: the policy cycle, the financial cycle and the contracting cycle.

The purpose of management is to control the organization i.e. to provide reasonable assurance about goal attainment. By incorporating performance information, the capacity of organizations to control their goal attainment should be enhanced. In this sense, incorporation is almost literally a bridge between measurement and use.

DISCUSSION QUESTIONS

1   What does the budget of a public sector organization look like? How does it incorporate information on inputs, activities, outputs, outcomes, objectives or targets (or not)? When you read the budget, are you able to understand what will happen next year?

2   Download a strategic plan and an evaluation/performance audit report of the same organization. Look for the general objectives/targets of the organization and the related KPIs. Try to assess, through the performance audit or the evaluation, whether the objectives were reached.

REFERENCES

Beyer, J. M. and Trice, H. M. (1982) The utilization process: a conceptual framework and synthesis of empirical findings. *Administrative Science Quarterly,* 27, 591–622.

Bouckaert, G. and Halligan, J. (2008) *Managing Performance: International Comparisons.* London, Routledge.

Broom, C. (1998) *Performance Measurement Concepts and Techniques.* Washington, DC, American Society for Public Administration.

Carlin, T. M. (2006) Victoria's accrual output based budgeting system – delivering as promised? Some empirical evidence. *Financial Accountability & Management,* 22, 1–19.

COSO (2008) Website of the Committee of Sponsoring Organizations of the Treadway Commission. Available from www.coso.org/resources.htm [cited 01/09/2009].

Curristine, T. (2005) Performance information in the budget process: results of OECD 2005 questionnaire. *OECD Journal on Budgeting,* 5:2, 87–131.

De Lancer Julnes, P. and Holzer, M. (2001) Promoting the utilization of performance measures in public organizations: an empirical study of factors affecting adoption and implementation. *Public Administration Review,* 61, 693–708.

Lindblom, C. E. (1959) The science of 'muddling through'. *Public Administration Review,* 19, 79–88.

Niven, P. (2003) *Balanced Scorecard Step by Step For Governement and Nonprofit Agencies.* Hoboken, NJ, John Wiley & Sons.

O'Connell, P. E. (2001) Using performance data for accountability: the New York City Police Department's CompStat Model of Police Management. Washington, DC, PricewaterhouseCoopers.

Paulson, G. (2006) Accrual accounting in the public sector: experiences from the central government in Sweden. *Financial Accountability & Management, 22,* 47–62.

Pollitt, C. (2008) *Time, Policy, Management: Governing with the Past.* Oxford, Oxford University Press.

Pollitt, C. and Bouckaert, G. (2004) *Public Management Reform: A Comparative Analysis.* Oxford, Oxford University Press.

Public Audit Forum (2002) *The Whole Truth: Or Why Accruals Accounting Means Better Management.* London, National Audit Office.

Raaum, R. B. and Morgan, S. L. (2001) *Performance Auditing: A Measurement Approach.* Altamonte Springs, FL, Institute of Internal Auditors.

Van Dooren, W. (2005) What makes organisations measure? Hypotheses on the causes and conditions for performance measurement. *Financial Accountability & Management, 21,* 363–83.

Wildavsky, A. and Hammond, A. (1965) Comprehensive versus incremental budgeting in the Department of Agriculture. *Administrative Science Quarterly, 10,* 321–46.

Yang, K. and Hsieh, J. Y. (2007) Managerial effectiveness of government performance measurement: testing a middle-range model. *Public Administration Review, 67,* 861–79.

FURTHER READING

Bouckaert and Halligan (2008) further elaborate incorporation in their book *Managing Performance: International Comparisons*. De Lancer Julnes and Holzer (2001) published one of the most cited articles on the related concepts of implementation and use (see also Beyer and Trice 1982; Van Dooren 2005).

Many cases of incorporation can be found on websites of Supreme Audit Institutions and oversight agencies. Performance contracts are often available through the websites of the contracted agencies. Parliaments usually publish the budget online, which allows for assessing incorporation into the financial cycle.

Chapter 6

The use of performance information

LEARNING OBJECTIVES

- To distinguish the three categories of uses of performance information and their defining characteristics.
- To understand the implications of use for the design of a performance measurement system.

KEY POINTS

- The use of performance information ranges from soft to hard. Learning is generally softer than steering & control, which is in turn softer than use for accountability.
- The use determines the design of the measurement system.
- Building a sound data-infrastructure may overcome the difficulties of multifunctional measurement systems.

The use of information is often conceived in a bipolar way; it is either used or not. This view assumes a direct 1:1 relation between performance information and managerial or policy decisions. Bipolar thinking is fed by a somewhat technocratic hope that performance information will tell univocally how to allocate resources, how to hold organizations and managers to account, and which employees to reward for excellent performance. Performance measurement systems almost never can do that. Often, these unfulfilled expectations provoke a categorical rejection by users of performance information. A more nuanced perspective on use is needed.

Use has many faces, and it is important to be clear about the exact way in which performance information is used (Hatry 2008). Hence, this book allots a lot of attention to the use of performance information. This chapter discusses *the uses* of performance information. In the next chapter, the perspective of the potential *users* of performance information is explored. The reasons for *non-use* are discussed in chapter 8.

The analysis of the uses of performance information starts with a practical perspective in section 1. The uses in practice are manifold, and not surprisingly scholars have attempted to make categorizations. The most fundamental categorization, however, is how performance information will be used, which can range from soft to hard (section 2). The decision on how to use performance information will have ramifications for the design of the whole measurement process. Section 3 reiterates the steps in the measurement process and indicates for each step the variation that follows from the distinction between soft and hard use. It is thus assumed that intended use should determine the design of the measurement system and not vice versa. The chapter ends with a brief comment on multifunctional measurement systems.

1 USE IN PRACTICE

Forty-four potential uses of performance information can be identified (Van Dooren 2006). The practices mentioned in Table 6.1 are traditional management practices that are redefined by incorporating performance information. Allocation of resources, for instance, allegedly can be more focused if based on performance information instead of on last year's budget. For grantor reporting, it is assumed that grantors will be more interested in results than in whether the grantee has spent the budget. Similarly, the use of performance information in auditing may enrich the findings of the auditors. Note that this list of potential uses does not say anything about the breadth and the intensity of use in organizations (see Table 6.1).

Although the list of uses demonstrates the variation in practice, the distinction between the 44 uses is not always clear-cut. Performance budgeting, output budgeting and outcome budgeting are for instance closely related. In order to study use in organizations, scholars have developed classifications of uses into broader categories with similar features. Behn (2003) proposes a categorization of eight managerial uses.

1 *To evaluate.* How well is the organization performing? Almost all indicators can and will be used for evaluation purposes. The question is whether the indicators allow for such an evaluation. Is performance information providing a fair representation of the activities under review?

2 *To control.* How can managers ensure that subordinates are doing the right thing? Or, how can supervisory bodies ensure that executive agencies are delivering what they are supposed to deliver? Performance information can be used to control behaviour. In this sense, it has a similar function to traditional regulation.

3 *To budget.* On which programmes, people or projects should the organization spend money? The general idea is to invest in the most cost-effective activities. Two factors curb this strategy. First, budget decisions are to a large extent an expression

Table 6.1 *The uses of performance information in policy and management practice*

Potential uses of performance information

1. allocation of resources
2. enable consumers to make informed choices
3. changing work processes/more efficiency
4. improving responsiveness to customers
5. formulation and monitoring of licensed or contracted privatized services
6. creditor reporting
7. rewarding staff/monetary incentives/performance pay
8. grantor reporting
9. strategic planning
10. output budgeting: pay per output (price x quality)
11. communication with the public to build trust
12. outcome budgeting: pay per outcome
13. reporting and monitoring
14. changing appropriation levels
15. accountability to elected officials
16. performance budgeting: alongside budget figures
17. accountability to the public
18. cost accounting
19. results-based budgeting: budget documents
20. performance auditing
21. results-based budgeting: justify budget requests
22. capital management
23. motivation rewards for groups, organizations
24. managerial incentive schemes
25. evaluation of outcomes and effectiveness
26. management by objectives
27. reducing duplication of services/delivery alternatives (incl. privatization)
28. staff motivation/non-monetary incentives
29. adopting new programme approaches/changing strategies
30. strategic HRM
31. setting programme priorities
32. clarifying objectives
33. communication with the legislature and the legislative staff
34. quality models (TQM)
35. cost saving
36. sanctioning prolonged low performance
37. performance budgeting: information
38. allocating discretionary funds to high performance agencies or programs
39. setting individual job expectations/staff performance plans
40. communication between managers
41. cost benefit analysis
42. organizational development
43. trigger for further investigation and action
44. coordination of activities internally or externally

of *future* political priorities and *past* performance data are often irrelevant in this context. Second, it might make a lot of sense to invest in underperforming units when undercapitalization is the cause of bad performance. When a police department is underperforming, more training and equipment might be needed, and thus more budget.

4   *To motivate.* How can organizations motivate line staff, middle managers, non-profit and for-profit contractors, stakeholders and citizens to do the things necessary to improve performance? Meaningful performance goals are a strong motivator. They give an indication of what is important for the organization or programme. The indicators may provide a sense of mission.

5   *To promote.* How can the manager convince political superiors, legislators, stakeholders, journalists and citizens that the organization is doing a good job? Performance information can be a strong instrument to demonstrate the relevance of the organization, to build goodwill and trust, and even to support budget increments.

6   *To celebrate.* What accomplishments are worthy of the important organizational ritual of celebrating success? Celebration rituals tie people together, give them a sense of their individual and collective relevance, and motivate future efforts. The result should be a strong organization with a sound organizational culture.

7   *To learn.* Why is something working or not working? While evaluation asks the question what works, learning asks the question *why* things (don't) work. Learning requires considerable interpretation of performance data. Data almost never speaks for itself.

8   *To improve.* What exactly should who do differently to improve performance? It is important to understand that improvement does not just happen. Somebody has to take purposeful action to transform the conclusions drawn from performance information into different practices. There are no recipes to get from performance information to performance improvement.

Behn argues that the first seven purposes are subordinate to the last purpose. He writes that 'for the measurement of performance, the public manager's real purpose – indeed, the only real purpose – is to improve performance. The other seven purposes are simply means for achieving this ultimate purpose' (Behn 2003: 588). Although many managers do indeed use performance information for improvement, research evidence suggests some other, somewhat less decorous purposes.

> *Enhancing power positions.* Francis Bacon wrote in 1597 that knowledge in itself is power ('ipsa scientia potestas est'). This also applies here. An organisation that has to provide performance information to outsiders is more vulnerable. The Labour government in England for instance used performance indicators in the early 2000s to strengthen control over the hospital sector.
>
> (Bevan and Hood 2006)

Symbolism. Measurement is modern and performance indicators thus can also be used for symbolic reasons – to be seen as modern. The purpose of measurement is not improvement, nor learning of any kind. Rather, measurement becomes a goal in itself.

(Vakkuri and Meklin 2006)

Behn suggested eight managerial uses and we have added two latent uses. In our text, we will further use a sparser, but not unrelated classification of purposes: *to learn*, *to steer & control* and *to give account* (see Table 6.2).

1 First, performance information may be collected in order to find out what works and why (not). The main function here is *learning*. The key question is how policy or management can be improved. Strategic planning and evaluation, business process re-engineering and benchmarking are examples of policy and management tools with primarily a learning orientation. Performance information can be used for process evaluation and outcome evaluation which envisages, respectively, service improvement and policy improvement.

2 Second, the *steering & control* function of performance information is about identifying and sanctioning institutions or public servants (to control and to motivate) and about allocating resources (to budget). Typical applications are management scorecards that monitor the performance of the organization. These systems mainly have a control orientation and are concerned with the present rather than future or past performance. The use of performance information for management tools such as performance based pay, performance budgeting and performance mandates falls into this category (Bovaird and Lœffler 2003; Henderson *et al.* 2005).

3 The third purpose is *to give account*. The key question is how to communicate with the outside world about performance. In recent decades, accountability mechanisms have shifted from a focus on legality (spend resources lawfully) to a focus on results (demonstrate what is coming out) (Kettl 2002). It was assumed that accountability for results would put external pressure on public organizations. In this sense, the orientation is not so much change or control, as survival. Performance measurement in this case is mainly about explaining past performance.

By requiring an organization or programme to give account, pressure is exerted. The underlying mechanisms are twofold. First, pressure can be created by showing results to the *general public*. In case of a public monopoly, the potential criticism of the public (and the media) is expected to wield enough pressure for change. Typical examples are citizen's charters and upgraded annual reporting (Bowerman 1995). In the case of (quasi-) markets, for instance in public (state) schools and hospitals, market pressures are provoked by publicizing rankings (Gormley and Weimer 1999). Second, pressure can be instituted by the political system. Performance contracts with agencies are a good

Table 6.2 *Three uses of performance information*

	To learn	To steer & control	To give account
Key question	How to improve policy or management?	How to be in control of activities?	How to communicate performance?
Focus	Internal	Internal	External
Orientation	Change/future	Control/present	Survival/past
Exemplary instruments	Strategic planning, benchmarking, risk analysis, business process re-engineering	Monitors and management scorecards, performance pay, performance budgeting	League tables, citizen's charters and annual reporting, performance contracts

example. These contracts give autonomy to agencies within a preset budgetary framework, provided that the agency commits itself to output or outcome targets (see for instance Greve *et al.* (1999) for a discussion on the Danish, UK and Dutch practice, Verhoest (2005) for a Belgian perspective, Laegreid *et al.* (2008) on Norway and Radin (2002) on the USA).

2 HARD AND SOFT USE

A crucial decision is whether performance information will be used in a hard or a soft way. The distinction refers to two dimensions. First, how tightly coupled are performance information and judgement (see Figure 6.1)? Hard use presupposes a tight coupling between performance information and judgement while soft use leaves more room. Dialogue and interpretation mediate final decision-making (Moynihan 2008). It is the difference between formula-based use and interpretative use. A performance contract that stipulates sanctions for an agency that does not reach its performance targets, regardless of context, is an example of hard use. A benchmarking exercise that requires some performance information to feed into discussions on how to do things differently is an example of soft use.

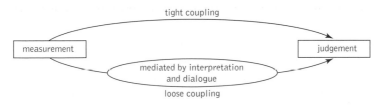

Figure 6.1 *Loose and tight coupling of performance information and judgement*

Other authors also have touched upon this distinction. Carter, Klein and Day (1992) used the metaphors of *dials* and *tin openers*. Performance indicators can be used in a 1:1 relation (like dials) between the results observed through measurement and the subsequent actions. Alternatively, performance indicators are used to open the tin, without revealing the contents of the tin. This is soft use, because the real interpretative work only starts and actions will only follow after interpretation.

The Public Administration Select Committee of the UK House of Commons made a similar distinction when they proposed to make a distinction between a measurement culture (hard use, formula based) and a performance culture (soft use, interpretation based). The conclusion of the report was that in the UK organizations were more concerned with measurement than with performance improvement. They recommended moving towards a performance culture. The proposal was not to abandon measurement, but to use performance indicators in a more sensible way (House of Commons Public Administration Select Committee 2003).

The second dimension of hard and soft refers to the consequences of the judgements that are based on the performance information. Some uses have a higher impact on organizations than others. Compare, for instance, major budget cuts with the publication of performance measures in an internal memo. Table 6.3 provides a non-exhaustive list of parameters that determine the impact of performance information on an organization.

Some uses have a soft inclination while others will tend to be hard, formula-based with high impact. Performance contracts have a propensity to be hard while benchmarking tends to be soft. Figure 6.2 plots the three categories of use on a grid. Yet, reality is contingent on the local context of the uses. It is definitely not the case that a specific use is *per definition* soft or hard. Formally, league tables of schools look quite similar across countries. Yet, it seems that their use is perceived much harder in some countries than in others. The reason is that in some countries parents use the league tables as one of the most important sources of information for school choice while in other countries other factors are taken into account.

Table 6.3 *Assessing the impact of performance judgements*

Low impact	High impact
Peripheral issues	Core business – distinctive competence
Not reputational	Reputation at stake
No budgetary consequences	Budgetary impact
No impact on autonomy	Infringes on autonomy
Congruent with organizational culture	Incongruent with organizational culture

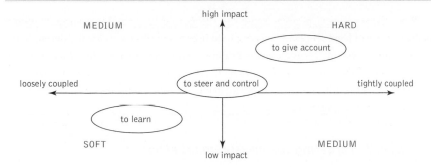

Figure 6.2 *Assessing the nature of use of performance information*

3 HARD VERSUS SOFT: IMPLICATIONS FOR THE DESIGN OF THE MEASUREMENT SYSTEM

Hard uses have a higher propensity to engender dysfunctional behavioural effects (see chapter 9). When there is a 1:1 relation between measurement and decision-making, the only way to influence the decision-making is to manipulate measurement. *Ceteris paribus*, soft uses only loosely couple measurement and decisions, and therefore are less threatening. If we assume that those who go through a measurement process prefer that favourable, or at least fair, decisions follow from measurement, then we must also take into account that they will try to influence decision-making. In case of hard use, there are three strategies in response to the indicators.

■ Strategy 1: *compliance*. In this case, the expression 'what gets measured, gets done' applies. Organizational and individual behaviour is aligned with the indicators. Management theory that stipulates the formulation of key performance indicators assumes that measurement will lead functional behaviour, i.e. a focus on what really matters. Yet, it is often forgotten that compliance is not the only behavioural option.
■ Strategy 2: *shirking*. A second strategy is to make it appear as if there is compliance by changing behaviours. Unlike the compliance strategy, behaviour is dysfunctional. Service or product quality for instance may suffer from an over-strong focus on production and service volumes.
■ Strategy 3: *misrepresentation*. Organizational and/or individual behaviour does not change, but is represented in a more flattering way. Because of the manipulation of the measurement system, the decisions are based on flawed information.

In the case of soft use, a fourth strategy can be added to this list: *explanation*. The organization trusts that after measurement, there will be sufficient opportunity to influence decision-making in order to get to a fair representation. As a result, there will be less pressure to shirk or misrepresent, but also less pressure to comply.

103

Since the propensity of organizations to resort to shirking and misrepresentation is higher in case of hard use, the choice for hard uses has implications for the design of the measurement system. Measurement systems need to be more robust. Measurement error, whatever the cause, cannot be corrected through interpretation and dialogue. We now return to the different steps in performance measurement discussed in chapter 4, and make a differentiation for use.

3.1 Step 1: Targeting the measurement effort

Since it is virtually impossible to measure everything, a reasoned decision on what to measure and what not to measure needs to be taken. The measurement effort should be targeted on the foreseen use. This decision can be based on several criteria such as intuitive indications of problems, added value of measurement, financial coverage, visibility of a service, etc. (see chapter 4). Table 6.4 differentiates the criteria for the uses of performance information.

To learn. Learning is about finding weaknesses and developing solutions. Intuitive indications of problems that need more evidence may therefore be the basis for measurement. A complaint on waiting lists may for instance trigger a systematic registration of waiting times for a service. Clearly, the added value vis-à-vis the information that is already available and the feasibility of measurement will be additional concerns when targeting the measurement effort.

To steer & control. A fair distribution of the indicators in the organization is a relevant criterion for this use. Management scorecards usually prescribe this approach (Kaplan and Norton 1996). Each division of the organization should provide some key performance indicators (KPIs) for management to monitor the operations. Managers are seen as pilots in a cockpit who take corrective action when an indicator signals a problem. Additional arguments could be to require more measurement from divisions with a higher financial importance (financial coverage) or divisions that employ a larger portion of the staff (staff coverage).

To give account. Accountability requirements are often imposed on organizations. In this case, the definition of the measurement object is predetermined: others have decided for the organization what it should measure. If, however, the organization is taking the initiative to give account, social visibility may be the criterion for selecting the measure-

Table 6.4 *Criteria for targeting measurement efforts on their foreseen uses*

To learn	To steer & control	To give account
Indications of problems	Distribution over divisions	Societal visibility
Added value	Financial coverage	Predetermined
Feasibility	Staff coverage	

ment object. An employment agency for instance may want to target measurement efforts on those target groups that are at the forefront of the policy debate. Usually, accountability initiatives are neither completely voluntary nor entirely predetermined. Accountability is negotiated and the measurement object is negotiated alongside. Negotiation is clearly part of performance contracts between agencies and departments, but the content of league tables or imposed reporting formats are also subject to negotiation and lobbying.

3.2 Step 2: Selection of the indicators

The second phase is the selection of the indicators. Indicators may be single indicators that refer to inputs, outputs, outcomes or the environment in which the organization operates. Indicators may also be ratio indicators that combine single indicators. Efficiency is input over output. Effectiveness is output over effect. Cost effectiveness is input over effect.

To learn. The indicator set has to cover the whole production chain of the organization. Underperformance could result from insufficient inputs, inadequate processes or unrealistic expectations of outputs and outcomes. Measurement will seldom univocally dictate answers. Interpretation through professional judgement and experience is needed to fill the gaps in the measurement system.

To steer & control. The indicators will principally have to be a combination of input and output indicators. Following the traditional politics/administration dichotomy, the main responsibility of public managers is to convert resources into products and services that politicians, policy-makers and ultimately citizens prescribe. Although scholars demonstrated that the line between politics and management is never that clear (see for instance Svara 1985 and Peters 2001), the distinction remains one of the leading principles in the design of administrative systems.

To give account. Outcomes are what matters for society, and therefore the optimal indicators for accountability should be outcome indicators (Hatry 1999). However, because of the potentially severe consequences of accountability for the organization, room for interpretation cannot be tolerated. In addition, outcomes have to be attributable to the organization's activities. These are qualities that outcome indicators seldom have. Therefore, output indicators are often used instead whereas the relation with outcomes is assumed (see Table 6.5).

Table 6.5 *Which indicators for which use?*

To learn	To steer & control	To give account
The whole 'production chain of the organization': from input to outcome	Mainly output and efficiency	Optimally outcome, with output as a second best

3.3 Step 3: Data collection

After the selection of the indicators, data needs to be collected. Organizations may use internal or external data sources. Internal data is produced by the organization itself while external data is purchased or obtained from other organizations. A broad array of data sources can be used (see Table 6.6).

To learn. Learning will require a wide range of data in order to cover the span, from input to outcome, of the performance measurement system. *Existing and additional administrative registrations* are useful to measure inputs, outputs and intermediate outcomes. *Self-assessments* can be used to measure internal processes. *Technical measurement* and *surveys* can provide insight into the outcome of the organization. Data from other organizations and *statistical institutions* will primarily be useful to establish causality and the influence of contextual factors on the outcome. *External observers* are the only data source that may be less useful. Learning postulates an intrinsic motivation and, therefore, the benefit of impartiality is less pressing than the need for ownership of the findings by those who will have to learn from it.

To steer & control. Measurement will mainly depend on *existing* and *additional registrations* and *record keeping* within the organization. This is consistent with the internal focus of management. If applicable, *technical measurement* is useful as a control device because of its unobtrusive character. When technical measurement is not feasible, *external observers* can take over the role of neutral bystander. Reliance on other organizations' data, *statistical data* and *survey data* is less useful for internal management since they rather comprehend outcome and contextual information. *Self-assessments* will also be less functional for steering & control because they are mostly project based and with a learning purpose.

Table 6.6 *Differentiation of the data sources according to the purpose of performance information*

	To learn	To steer & control	To give account
More useful	Existing registrations Additional registrations Surveys Self-assessments Technical measurement Other organizations Statistical, international and research institutions	Existing registrations Additional registrations Technical measurement External observers	Existing registrations Additional registrations Surveys Technical measurement External observers
Less useful	External observers	Surveys Self-assessments Other organizations Statistical, international and research institutions	Other organizations Statistical, international and research institutions Self-assessments

To give account. Administrative registrations are useful for accountability when organizations have to show which outputs they produced and which target groups and regions they have served. Additionally, *technical measurement*, *external observers* and *surveys* (for instance on client satisfaction) may be used. The subjective elements in surveys is however a problem for reliable accountability. Other organizations' data and data from *statistical institutions* will usually only play a peripheral role in contextualizing success and failure. Finally, *self-assessments* are not useful for the same reason as for the steering & control function.

3.4 Step 4: Analysis

The purpose of analysing data is to transform data into information on which decisions can be based. Regularly, interpretation and analytical processing are subliminal. Performance is for instance often compared with past performance in an inexplicit way. In order to fully explore the potential of the information, analysis should be an integral part of the measurement system. Chapter 4 referred to three approaches to analysis: norm setting, aggregation and statistical analysis. Table 6.7 differentiates the analytical approaches for different uses.

To learn. Learning will benefit from a broad range of assessments. Comparisons with *past performance* and confrontations with *scientific standards* can be a starting point for diagnosis of performance. Comparison with *other organizations* may set the organization on track of better practices elsewhere. In addition, *causal analysis* research can answer the question why a result is showing, and *disaggregation* can help to trace results back to divisions of the organization, target groups or geographical circumscriptions, which is key for remedying insufficient performance. Less useful for learning are symbolic norms and highly aggregated indices. The latter usually are not actionable.

To steer & control. Past performance is also of importance here. *Other organizations within the sector* can be a reference point for output levels while *organizations outside the sector* are mainly relevant for comparing the management functions of the organization. In particular cases, *scientific standards* are the point of reference. *International comparison* seems less useful. Foreign organizations mostly operate in an institutional and political context that is too different to be useful for daily steering & control. In order to fulfil the internal management function, *disaggregated* information will be needed. For instance, the allocation of resources based on performance data requires a detailed cost-accounting system that is capable of providing unit costs. *Causal analysis* of performance results is not the prime focus of this category of use. Usually, the causal assumptions will be working hypotheses.

To give account. Comparisons of current with *past performance* are also useful for account giving. Doing better is a not uncommon expectation for public organizations. Comparisons with *organizations within the sector* are a second important norm for accountability purposes. Organizational report cards (league tables) compare among others schools, hospitals, universities, police units and local communities. When the

Table 6.7 *Differentiation of the choice of analysis technique according to the purpose of performance information*

Use	Category	More useful	Less useful
To learn	Norm-setting	Time Other organizations within the sector Other organizations outside the sector Foreign organizations Scientific standards	Symbolic norms Aggregated
	Aggregation and breakouts	Disaggregated	
	Causal analysis	Causal analysis	
To steer & control	Norm-setting	Time Other organizations within the sector Other organizations outside the sector Scientific standards	Foreign organizations Symbolic norms
	Aggregation and breakouts	Disaggregated	Aggregated
	Causal analysis		Causal analysis
To give account	Norm-setting	Time Other organizations within the sector Foreign organizations Scientific standards Symbolic norms	Other organizations outside the sector
	Aggregation and breakouts	Aggregated	Disaggregated
	Causal analysis		Causal analysis

service provider is a monopolist in a country, *international comparisons* can be used. Furthermore, *scientific norms* can be used for accountability. For instance, a health agency may be expected to attain the vaccination grade that is required to avoid epidemics (which is not necessarily 100 per cent). Since symbolic norms may be used to keep an issue on the agenda, there is also an accountability aspect to it. Comparison with organizations from *different sectors* appears less appealing for accountability, given the fact that management should not be the core business of service delivery. Mol (2001), for instance, pointed to the negative effect of pinpointing accountability on some secondary processes in the Dutch military. Finally, the causes of performance usually are rather an implicit assumption than an explicit subject of *causal analysis*. In contrast to the learning and management function, accountability often requires *aggregated* information that allows for judgement at a glance by decision-makers.

3.5 Step 5: Reporting

The last step in the performance measurement process is the reporting of the information. With regard to reporting, a simple rule applies; the format should be suitable for the target group (Hendricks 1994; Rossi and Gilmartin 1980). Reporting of performance information to top management for instance will require other reporting formats compared to reporting to media or interest groups. Different reporting formats can make performance information suitable for different target groups. Two questions thus should be answered; who is using the information, and what is the right format for that target group? Differentiating for purposes implies answering the first question first; who should be the users of performance information if either learning, steering & control, or account-giving is the purpose. The next issue then is to find the right format.

To learn. Although learning can take place within several target groups, the main audience for learning purposes usually will be the *staff.* Contemporary implementation literature has confirmed the importance of professionals, street-level bureaucrats and front-line workers in the era of performance management; they still have to do the job (Hupe and Hill 2007; Noordegraaf and Abma 2003). The confrontation of performance information with professional judgement that is accumulated through daily practice is the core of the learning perspective. If we assume, together with implementation scholars, that most of this professional knowledge of how things work is owned at street level, it seems logical to target learning efforts primarily there. A good flow of information will assure that higher levels are kept informed and can act upon these learning efforts.

Outside of the organization, there may be interest in mainly *executive politicians* to learn from performance information for developing their policies. The evidence-based policy agenda (see chapter 3) supports this perspective. However, policy is not developed in a vacuum. Learning for policy from performance information is usually guided by advisory bodies and interest groups that will attempt to put their spin on the performance information. Finally, there may be some function for performance information in 'educating' *the public* about their behaviour. An environmental agency, for example, may heavily mediatize the number of interventions for illegal dumping in rivers and its detrimental effect on fauna in order to sensitize the public and render dumping socially unacceptable.

The reporting format is less important for learning compared to the other uses. As Moynihan (2008) argues in his dialogue theory, the process of measurement is as important as the outcomes. The main format will often be *oral witnesses.* In addition, in order to strengthen organizational memory, a case can be made to document learning outcomes in *specialized reports.* Such reports will also be needed when the findings need to be disseminated beyond the measurement group, i.e. the whole organization or policy sector.

To steer & control. Since steering & control is the main responsibility of management, higher *management* levels should be the prime target group. Management scorecards of the Balanced Scorecard game, with key performance indicators, are one of the most common reporting formats in this context. *Reports* can also be used, but in contrast to the specialized and irregular reporting of measurement for learning, steering & control will require recurrent reporting that follows a more standardized layout. *Oral witnesses* can supplement these sources and will particularly be required when management scorecards show unexpected results.

To give account. Since relations of accountability can be manifold, performance measurement may be relevant for a potentially broad set of actors. Accountability is a relationship in which an individual or agency is held to answer for performance that is expected by some significant 'other' (Romzek and Dubnick 1987). The ultimate significant other in a democracy is the general public, which can be reached through the *mass media*. Journalists are usually best reached through personal contact or press releases. Interest groups in essence have the same function of bridging the gap between the organization and the citizen, albeit usually for a particular concern. Since interest groups typically have fewer deadlines and are more specialized than journalists, *reports* and *interactive websites* can supplement oral witnesses.

Significant others in accountability relations however may also be located inside the political system, both in the executive and the legislative branch. *Annual reporting* and planning as well as budgets and accounts are typical accountability formats in this case (see Table 6.8). In addition, *supranational institutions* may hold governments accountable. The Maastricht criteria and the Lisbon indicators are examples of the European Union holding the member states accountable for their performance on a limited set of criteria. The aim is to align national policies to the European agenda without having to resort to regulation. The EU counts on the reputational damage of a bad score on the performance indicators for member states to react. In EU jargon, this approach to governance is known as OMC, the Open Method of Cooperation (Borras and Jacobsson 2004).

Table 6.8 *Differentiation of the reporting format according to the purpose of performance information*

	To learn	To steer & control	To give account
To whom	Staff Executive politicians Advisory boards Interest groups General public	The board of the organization The general public Top management	Mass media Interest groups Executive politicians Supra-national institutions Parliament
Format	Specialized reports Oral witnesses	Scorecards Recurrent reports Oral witnesses	Annual reports and planning Budget and accounts Specialized reports Interactive website Oral witnesses Press releases and publicity Scorecards

3.6 Quality assurance

Quality has three dimensions (Bouckaert 1993). First, quality implies the functionality of the measurement system; measurement should be fit for use. Second, quality implies indicators that are valid and reliable. A reliable indicator yields the same values for repeated measurements of the same object; and a valid indicator measures what is intended to be measured. The third quality dimension is legitimacy of a measurement system, which means that measurement should be supported by those who are supposed to use the information.

The criterion of functionality should be assessed first. Performance measurement systems that are dysfunctional should be abolished or redesigned. The other two criteria may be applied more variably accordingly to the purposes (see Table 6.9).

Before discussing the table, two remarks are needed. First, we use the categories 'moderately important', 'highly important' and 'critical', which does not look like a balanced scale. The reason is that a certain level of quality is required in all cases. It would be wrong to state that a particular quality characteristic is not at all important for a particular use. Yet, there is still variation in importance. Quality is relative and the marginal costs and benefits of more quality need to be taken into account. Hatry (2002) for instance argues that pressures from the professional community have overstressed the need for high levels of precision and response rates in customer surveys, which has driven costs up and discouraged practitioners. According to Hatry, the operational principle should be that it is better to be roughly right than to be precisely ignorant.

A second remark is that the quality dimensions may influence each other as independent and dependent variables. For instance, a high legitimacy within an organization may lead to high reliability because employees are mindful not to make mistakes in registration. Likewise, high validity may lead to high legitimacy because people feel the right things are measured. Untangling the dynamics between quality criteria is an empirical issue that would go beyond the scope of a textbook.

To learn. Learning poses the least strict conditions on validity and reliability. Performance information will be complemented by other information sources such as

Table 6.9 Differentiation of the quality dimensions according to the purpose

	To learn	To steer & control	To give account
Validity	Moderately important	Critical	Critical
Reliability	Moderately important	Important	Critical
Internal legitimacy	Critical	Important	Moderately important
External legitimacy	Critical	Moderately important	Critical

individual experiences of employees. This dialogue on the performance information can also seen as an *ex post* validity and reliability check. Crucial, however, is the legitimacy of the measurement effort. Without the conviction of staff that measurement may allow for evaluation and improvement, learning will not occur.

To steer & control. Validity and reliability are important for steering & control because sanctions and rewards as well as budget and staff are distributed based on measurement. We assessed validity to be critical and reliability only to be important. The reason is that steering & control usually requires the reiteration of measurement efforts in relatively short cycles (maximum one year, more often quarters). Reliability issues will thus emerge quite naturally and can be corrected in the short term. Validity problems on the other hand will be repeated with every measurement and can only be detected and corrected when the indicators are scrutinized. Legitimacy seems of lesser importance, since it is mainly the responsibility of the manager to control and to allocate resources, and not of the staff or external actors. It can be argued that given the internal focus of the measurement system, internal legitimacy is somewhat more important than external.

To give account. External accountability requires high validity and reliability, because of the high stakes of bad or good results for the organization. Given the behavioural effects that high-pressure systems may trigger (see chapter 9), bias and noise on measurement will distort the activities of the organization. While obviously external legitimacy is critical, internal legitimacy may be of second order importance. When the information will, for instance, be used for performance contracts with the organization, legitimacy for measurement in the whole organization may be less important. The main point is that the two sides of the contract, i.e. top management and the political level, support the indicators in the contract.

4 MULTIFUNCTIONAL MEASUREMENT SYSTEMS

The main argument until now has been that there is no 'one size fits all' measurement process. The design of the measurement system needs to be founded on the foreseen uses of measurement. When use is neglected while measuring, the performance information that comes out of the process has a high chance of being used or not used inappropriately. The differentiation of the design parameters however also introduces incongruence between the designs. The question then arises whether organizations can allocate different uses to one measurement process. Hence, a discussion on such multifunctional measurement systems is warranted.

At first, multifunction measurement systems appear not viable. The reason is that hard use drives out soft use; or once a measurement system is used for the harder purposes such as account giving, it can no longer be used for softer approaches such as learning. Learning requires room for dialogue in which those participating have to reveal their weaknesses. In account giving, room for interpretation should be as much as possible absent. Once performance information is used for accountability, participants in a measurement effort will anticipate the potential consequences by either trying to obtain favourable results (gaming) or by covering up unfavourable outcomes.

The solution may be to disconnect measurement processes, which results in a separate measurement process for different uses. In large organizations, these processes could be run by different organizational units. For instance, measurement for accountability could be the responsibility of the staff of the top managers, steering & control could be in the HRM or finance department while measurement for learning might be the responsibility of the quality manager. An additional advantage of parallel measurement processes is that performance information from one process can corroborate other results.

Although such a set-up may seem best, there are two risks attached to it. First, measurement may fall victim of what has been described in the literature as mushrooming (De Bruijn 2004). The number of indicators may become unmanageable. Second, the costs of measurement may accrue beyond reason. Measurement costs are overhead for most organizations (an exception being statistical offices), and as such it may divert resources from the front-line work.

A sensible solution seems to be an integration of the measurement processes in some steps and a separation in other steps. The main cost driver for measurement is data collection (step 3). In order to keep costs for measurement under control, without incurring the negative consequences of having a multifunctional measurement process, an integration of data collection could be considered. In fact, the building of electronic data warehouses with an integrated data management strategy is a step in this direction.

5 CONCLUSION

This chapter identified three uses of performance information – learning, steering & control and accountability. The uses put different levels of pressure on the organizations that are measuring performance. Learning generally implies soft use and accountability hard use. Steering & control lies somewhere in between. The performance measurement process will differ according to the envisaged use of performance information.

DISCUSSION QUESTIONS

1   Consider the use of indicators in a particular context: a police force, the university, hospitals, etc. How is the information used?
2   Which use (soft or hard) is more appropriate?
3   Evaluate the measurement system of an organization based on the use and the design parameters.

REFERENCES

Behn, R. D. (2003) Why measure performance? Different purposes require different measures. *Public Administration Review,* 63, 586–606.

Bevan, G. and Hood, C. (2006) What's measured is what matters: targets and gaming in the British health care sector. *Public Administration,* 84, 517–38.

Borras, S. and Jacobsson, K. (2004) The open method of co-ordination and new governance patterns in the EU. *Journal of European Public Policy,* 11, 185–208.

Bouckaert, G. (1993) Measurement and meaningful management. *Public Productivity & Management Review,* 17, 31–43.

Bovaird, T. and Lœffler, E. (2003) Evaluating the quality of public governance: indicators, models and methodologies. *International Review of Administrative Sciences,* 69, 313–28.

Bowerman, M. (1995) Auditing performance indicators: the role of the Audit Commission in the Citizen's Charter initiative. *Financial Accountability & Management,* 11, 171–83.

Carter, N., Klein, R. and Day, P. (1992) *How Organizations Measure Success: The Use of Performance Indicators in Government.* London, Routledge.

De Bruijn, H. (2004) *Managing Performance in the Public Sector.* London, Routledge.

Gormley, W. T. and Weimer, D. L. (1999) *Organizational Report Cards.* Cambridge, MA, Harvard University Press.

Greve, C., Flinders, M. and Van Thiel, S. (1999) Quangos – what's in a name? Defining Quangos from a comparative perspective. *Governance: An International Journal of Policy and Administration,* 12, 129–46.

Hatry, H. P. (1999) *Performance Measurement: Getting Results.* Washington, DC, Urban Institute Press.

Hatry, H. P. (2002) Performance measurement: fashions and fallacies. *Public Performance & Management Review,* 25, 352–58.

Hatry, H. P. (2008) The many faces of use. In Van Dooren, W. and Van de Walle, S. (eds.) *Performance Information in the Public Sector: How It Is Used.* Basingstoke, Palgrave Macmillan.

Henderson, L. J., Kamensky, J. and Morales, A. (2005) The Baltimore Citistat Program: performance and accountability. *Managing for Results 2005.* Lanham, MD, Rowman and Littlefield.

Hendricks, M. (1994) Making a splash: reporting evaluation results effectively. In Hatry, H. P., Wholey, J. S. and Newcomer, K. (eds.) *Handbook of Practical Program Evaluation.* San Fransisco, Jossey Bass.

House of Commons Public Administration Select Committee (2003) *On Target Government by Measurement.* London, House of Commons.

Hupe, P. and Hill, M. (2007) Street level bureaucracy and public accountability. *Public Administration,* 85, 279–99.

Kaplan, R. S. and Norton, D. P. (1996) *The Balanced Scorecard: Translating Strategy into Action Harvard Business School Press,* Boston, MA, Harvard Business School Press.

Kettl, F. D. (2002) *The Transformation of Governance.* Baltimore, Johns Hopkins University Press.

Lacgrcid, P., Roncss, P. G. and Rubccksen, K. (2008) Performance information and performance steering: integrated system or loose coupling? In Van Dooren, W. and Van de Walle, S. (eds.) *Performance Information in the Public Sector: How It Is Used.* Basingstoke, Palgrave Macmillan.

Mol, N. (2001) Performance indicators in the Dutch Department of Defence. *Financial Accountability and Management,* 12, 71–81.

Moynihan, D. P. (2008) *The Dynamics of Performance Management: Constructing Information and Reform.* Washington, DC, Georgetown University Press.

Noordegraaf, M. and Abma, T. (2003) Management by measurement? Public management practices amidst ambiguity. *Public Administration,* 81, 853–71.

Peters, B. G. (2001) *The Politics of Bureaucracy.* London, Routledge.

Radin, A. (2002) *The Accountable Juggler: The Art of Leadership in a Federal Agency.* Washington, DC, CQ Press.

Romzek, B. S. and Dubnick, M. J. (1987) Accountability in the public sector: lessons from the Challenger tragedy. *Public Administration Review,* 47, 227–38.

Rossi, R. J. and Gilmartin, K. J. (1980) *The Handbook of Social Indicators: Sources, Characteristics, and Analysis.* New York, Garland STPM Press.

Svara, J. H. (1985) Dichotomy and duality: reconceptualizing the relationship between policy and administration in council-manager cities. *Public Administration Review,* 45, 221–32.

Vakkuri, J. and Meklin, P. (2006) Ambiguity in performance measurement: a theoretical approach to organisational uses of performance measurement. *Financial Accountability & Management,* 22, 235–50.

Van Dooren, W. (2006) *Performance Measurement in the Flemish Public Sector: A Supply and Demand Approach.* Leuven, Belgium, Faculty of Social Sciences.

Verhoest, K. (2005) Effects of autonomy, performance contracting and competition on the performance of a public agency. *Policy Studies Journal,* 33, 235–58.

FURTHER READING

Hatry (1999), Behn (2003) and Hatry (2008) discuss the uses of performance information. Carter, Klein and Day (1992) made a distinction between the use of performance information as dials or tin openers. Moynihan (2008) suggests an alternative use of performance information, based on dialogue theory. De Bruijn (2004) speaks of more lively performance management systems.

Chapter 7

Users

Performance measurement efforts are not always specific to the target audiences they envisage. Yet, a clear understanding of the costs and benefits of performance information for the intended users is vital for performance management for two reasons. First, user profiles are connected to ways of use (learning, steering & control, accountability). Second, different users will require different choices in the design of the measurement process. The most visible manifestation is the reporting format of performance information, which needs to be carefully tailored to the needs of users.

In this chapter, we put ourselves in the position of the main users and ask whether much use is made of a type of performance information, why use is made of it and under what circumstances or conditions use is likely to occur. On the one hand there is an explosion in the availability of performance information, on the other the take up from different potential users is often weak. Therefore, it is useful to look at performance information from the users' end.

DIFFERENT USERS AND PERFORMANCE INFORMATION

Many uses of performance information have been identified earlier, but lists do not always specify users. For example, Hatry (1999) proposes ten uses only two of which – elected officials and citizens – are explicit users; see also Van Dooren's (2006) list of 44 uses in chapter 6. The stage of incorporation has earlier been distinguished, and is internal to public institutions. In the stage of the use of performance information, there is a broadening of the user audiences as it becomes more widely and publicly available and the interest is in the actual use of performance measures and indicators. In matters of use, it makes sense to talk about initial, intermediate and ultimate use. A basic distinction is between 'middlemen' (programme managers, senior officials in central agencies and ministries, and stakeholders who are the users and suppliers of specific services) and 'end users' (ministers, MPs and citizens) (Pollitt 2006).

In principle, performance information is indispensable to ministers for guidance, control and evaluation; to MPs to authorize expenses and follow-up by guaranteeing oversight on implementation and performance; to civil servants to take responsibility and be accountable; for citizens to the extent that they have an interest in economic, efficient and effective service delivery and policies. However, this obvious win/win/win/win for ministers, MPs, civil servants and citizens does not always materialize in practice (Pollitt 2006). A range of studies report communication disconnects and 'missing links' (Bouckaert and Halligan 2008). North American research on implementation and use indicates a gap between what is intended and what actually occurs (McDavid and Hawthorn 2006).

The main users of performance information divide into three basic groups: the civil servants who generate the material for use within their agency or reporting within the executive branch (e.g. to central agencies like a ministry of finance), the elected officials who are often depicted as the main audience, and various public actors – citizens, media and advocacy groups – that consume information (Van Dooren and Van de Walle 2008). The various users want different types of information for their respective tasks, and reflecting the several purposes of performance information: learning, steering & control, and reporting. A fuller list of potential users is given in Table 7.1, which also reflects the main use a particular user would emphasize (which does not imply that other uses are completely absent).

In the discussion of the users below, three questions are posed: do they use the performance information, why do they use it and under what conditions?

Table 7.1 *Users and their uses of performance information*

Users	Emphasis of uses	Type of performance information
Programme managers	Learning	Programme information, internal documents
Senior officials in central agencies and ministries	Steering & control	Programme information, internal documents
Service suppliers: delivery agencies	Steering & control	Programme information, performance assessments, scorecards
Ministers	Accountability	Programme performance, internal documents and reports on performance
Members of Parliament	Accountability	Reporting on performance, annual reports, forward estimates, reports on performance
Citizens	Accountability	Targeted publications
Other: • Media • International organizations • Advocacy groups	Accountability	Macro and sectoral analyses, annual reports with highlights, scorecards

PUBLIC MANAGERS

Performance information is used by decision-makers but the influence of outcomes and outputs information on decision-making is variable (see Box 7.1 for a tentative list). There are indications that the success of performance reporting is related to the information used for decision-making and improving programmes: departments with good performance reports scored high on the use of performance information for learning and for decision-making (Bouckaert and Halligan 2008). In the USA, a majority of surveyed officials reported that performance measures were used for guiding management decisions, but the proportion using this data ranged from 25 to 65 per cent (Newcomer 2007).

Public managers will want to use performance for learning purposes and for steering & control. Senior managers in large organizations will tend towards the latter use while middle managers and front-line supervisors may have more interest in learning purposes. Front-line supervisors are less dependent on performance information for steering & control. Both the physical and social distance between managers and workers is shorter

BOX 7.1 USE OF PERFORMANCE INFORMATION IN MANAGEMENT ACTIVITIES

■ Setting programme priorities
■ Allocating resources
■ Adopting new programme approaches or changing work processes
■ Coordinating programme efforts with other internal or external organizations
■ Setting individual job expectations
■ Refining programme performance measures
■ Setting new or revising existing performance goals
■ Rewarding staff
■ Developing and managing contracts

and therefore other management styles are feasible – think of the notorious management by walking around. For the same reason, front-line supervisors may be better at facilitating learning efforts. They have more situational knowledge that can be combined with measurement.

The use of performance information by managers is conditioned by several external factors. A study of middle managers of a regional administration tested a number of explanations of why middle managers incorporate and/or use performance information (Van Dooren 2005).

■ Measurability of the services of the organizations is a key factor for implementation. Organizations that have more routine-based services have a higher incorporation and use of performance measurement.

■ Political support for the measurement effort was unimportant for incorporation and for use. The absence of political interference was seized by middle managers as an opportunity to develop and use performance information. This finding may be context specific. In top-down measurement systems, support of political principals may be needed to set performance measurement in motion. Political authority is then the big stick.

■ Scale is important. Large organizations measure more. This observation leads to questions about whether a minimal capacity is needed for organizations to measure. Or, maybe, performance measurement is only functional in large organizations.

■ The lack of resources did not explain either incorporation or use. Those who measured, as well as those who did not measure, both perceived the lack of resources as a potential barrier to performance measurement. The provision of adequate resources always seems to be problem; some cope while others do not.

■ The linkage between goals and indicators seems to be of particular importance for use by middle managers. Decoupling did not however seem to impede incorporation. Once performance information is being used in practice, incoherence between indicators and objectives seems to become more problematic.

MINISTERS

Politicians use performance information for a range of reasons, often to do with advancing a cause or critiquing their opponents (Askim 2007). These uses should not be disposed of *because* they support a political agenda. On the contrary, political debate among opposition and majority on the (in)adequacy of public performance is a vital component of a functioning democracy. Provided that performance indicators are valid and the performance argumentation is not deceptive, the use of performance information by politicians in political controversy is definitely purposeful. Although the main users of performance information were expected to be elected officials, relatively little is known about the patterns of their use (McDavid and Hawthorn 2006).

For executive politicians, mainly accountability is important. Performance indicators are used to align the work of agencies with the policies of ministers. Executive politicians on the one hand and agencies on the other are in a principal–agent relationship. Performance indicators are often codified in performance contracts with the minister. In second order, ministers may also use performance indicators to evaluate and to develop new policy programmes. There is, however, a policy-making bottleneck in the electoral cycle in the months after the elections when new ministers have to write their policy documents. Time pressure often inhibits a careful use of performance information in outlining policy choices. The policy bottleneck is probably even more pressing for coalition governments that have to negotiate a policy agreement between parties within a time frame of some months.

Although performance contracts are found in many systems, the actual functioning of the indicators is conditioned by contextual factors. Goddard, Mannion and Smith (1999) for instance discuss how the use of soft information conditions the use of hard performance information. They distinguish between three models: (i) the use of 'soft' information as a complement to 'hard' information; (ii) the use of 'soft' information as a substitute for 'hard' information; and (iii) the use of 'hard' information as a safety net in the assessment of performance. They argue that one of the main functions of 'hard' information in performance assessment is to act as a safety net to identify the most prominent laggards by highlighting poor performance. They also argue that performance information is rarely used as a means to encourage good performance or to identify best practice.

MEMBERS OF PARLIAMENT

The OECD found from a survey of 27 out of 30 of its member countries that 24 countries provide outcome information to parliament, but in only five countries do MPs use it for decision-making and that in only two countries do budget committees use the information for allocation. Parliaments are clearly struggling with output and outcome information. Sterck (2007) found based on a comparative study of Australia, Sweden, the Netherlands and Canada that performance budgeting initiatives seldom lead to the promised improvements in accountability to the legislature. The focus of performance budgeting initiatives is mainly on changing the budget structure, but they do not seem successful in altering the budget functions. Often, the initiatives are too complicated.

An important issue with parliaments internationally is how increased information is used. Despite the growth of vigorous committee systems in Australia since 1970 – with over 3000 parliamentary reports presented – neither the institution nor the agencies in its environment have been able to make effective use of the vast amount of information now available. There is then a question of information overload confronting parliaments and how they can make effective use of their own reports as well as those of public organizations (Halligan, Miller and Power 2007).

The attention and interest of US congressional committees for performance information varies substantially from committee to committee. Some make considerable use of hearings and GAO studies to evaluate the effectiveness of programmes. Other committees are less likely to focus on the performance of programmes and are more likely to focus on oversight episodically or in an effort to promote a political agenda (Joyce 2005).

A problem with performance budgeting and management in the United States is that they do not engage the decision-making processes in national and state legislatures in large part because the executive branch undertakes reforms without the active involvement of the legislature. Performance information is typically introduced to legislative processes through reporting in the executive budget, and is unlikely to be influential because agencies of executive staff are not trusted as an information source. Legislators rely on 'heuristics and cues', trusting their own experience and that of their staff (Bourdeaux 2008). Similar evidence comes from the local level where Dutch aldermen place little value on and rarely use performance information in municipal reports. Instead they rely on informal and verbal communications and formal meetings with senior staff (Ter Bogt 2004)

It seems safe to conclude that overall the use of performance information by MPs did NOT fulfil the expectations of the performance measurement community. A better understanding of the factors that affect MPs' use of performance information may avoid further disillusionment (Bouckaert and Halligan 2008; Bourdeaux 2008; CCAF-FCVI 2006).

- Performance reports do not reflect their interests and world view: politicians often seek confirmation of their ideologically inspired beliefs rather than a rational cost benefit analysis. Even if they do engage in cost benefit assessments, the weighing of costs and benefits is ideologically inspired. Hence, if a performance report does not align with political interests, it will not be used. Hopefully, other politicians will pick up the numbers and introduce them in debates.

- Public performance reports lack credibility. Politicians may distrust performance information when it is produced by bureaucracies that they are supposed to scrutinize. Anecdotal evidence of gaming may seriously undermine credibility of government-wide performance reporting. The level of trust in the system varies across countries. If credibility of performance reports is affected, some mechanisms will be needed to reinstall trust. Investing in external audits to assure quality of information is a possibility.

- Few rewards or incentives to scrutinize government performance. Hard-working MPs that read performance reports, understand the technicalities, and challenge ministers and agencies usually do not get a lot of attention in the media. Reading performance reports usually does not win votes.

- Information overloads and time constraints. MPs usually get information from many sources and in many formats; hearings with trade unions, a note from the party, a complaint by a citizen, newspapers, lobbying by an advocacy group, some small talk in the local market . . . and finally a performance report.

- Public performance reports are not written from their perspective. Performance reports follow the agency or department logic and not the logic of an MP. Performance reports for instance tend to cover all the activities of the organization, while MPs may benefit more from a limited set of performance indicators that allow them to set the agenda or to assess the headlines of a policy.

- Reports focus on outcomes rather than inputs and outputs. Performance reports for parliaments often assume that MPs are mainly interested in outcomes. This assumption is based on the classic politics/administration dichotomy: politicians determine policies and mandate the administration to implement. It has been demonstrated however that the dichotomy is not followed in practice (see for instance Svara 1985). Politicians want to have at least something to say about inputs and outputs. MPs may interpret a performance report that only focuses on outcomes as undermining their capacity to control the executive (Sterck 2007).

Finally, policy sector dynamics are an insufficiently understood dimension which may explain variation of the use of performance information across parliamentary commissions. Evidence from Belgium demonstrates inter-sectoral variation (Van Dooren 2004). Performance information is more intensely used in the national housing committee and the welfare and public health committee and less used in the culture committee and the internal affairs committee. Figure 7.1 provides more detail and also shows the types of indicators that are being used.

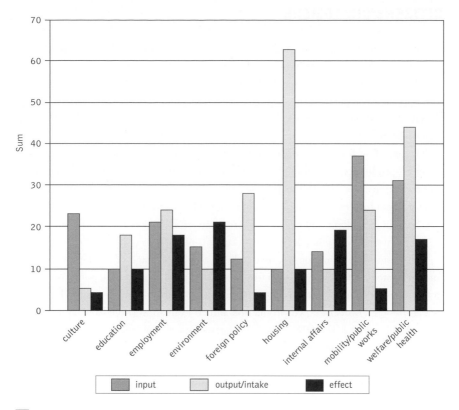

Figure 7.1 *An example of variation of MPs' use of performance information across sectors*

Source: Van Dooren 2004 (taken from an article in Public Management Review*)*

What might explain these differences? Van Dooren (2004) suggests four explanations for the Belgian context. A first explanation is the level of fragmentation in the policy sector. A sector with dominant organizations may be better able to develop a standardized measurement system whilst a sector with a high level of fragmentation may experience more consolidation problems. Second, different sectors may be confronted with different issues. Issues typologies can be useful here. Less performance information might, for instance, be expected in principle issues, e.g. moral, religious and constitutional matters. Third, the measurability of the dominant output in a policy sector may explain differences. Finally, some other factors related to the culture and established practices in a policy field may be of relevance. In this respect, it is important to identify the dominant profession in a field. Economists are probably more open to performance information than art historians.

CITIZENS/CUSTOMERS

Government performance information can be a very important tool for communication with citizens. Without any doubt, numbers of any kind are highly valued by citizens in our Western societies. Porter speaks of pursuit of objectivity (1995). Yet, when it comes to the actual use of performance reports, less enthusiasm is observed. A British attempt to make accessible (in supermarkets) a results-based annual report attracted scant interest (Pollitt 2006).

The use of performance information by citizens also fits in with renewed efforts to foster co-production (see Bovaird 2007 for an overview and a number of international co-production cases). Under this approach the public agency is decentred as the principal creator of public services, and clients contribute effort and time to producing services. The remixing of client and organizational motivations makes for a different type of engagement than when they are passive recipients of services (Alford 2002).

Until now co-production has mainly been about the stage of implementation. A further strategy is to take citizens actively on board at all stages of the policy cycle, and in the service delivery cycle, even giving them a say in the budget process. This results in a co-design, co-decision, co-production and co-evaluation (Bouckaert and Halligan 2008; Van Dooren *et al*. 2004). Box 7.2 suggests four models of citizen engagement in performance measurement.

Performance information also addresses the citizen in his or her capacity of customer of public services. This is for instance the case when governments create yardstick competition in public institutions such as schools, hospitals (Gormley and Weimer 1999). Competition will only occur when citizens behave as customers and shop around for the best school or hospital. Citizens are thus expected to find, read and use performance

---

BOX 7.2 MODELS OF PUBLIC ENGAGEMENT IN PERFORMANCE MEASUREMENT

■ *Performance management model*: public managers dominant, public role is minimal.

■ *Partnership model*: citizens and officials are in charge, public role is that of co-decision-maker.

■ *Community indicators model*: community leaders, multiple public roles in initiating, setting agenda and decision-making.

■ *Co-production model*: a more limited form of public engagement confined to contributions to service production, but with broader implications.

Ho 2007

information. For important decisions such as choosing a college, use by citizen/customers seems to be occurring. League tables are used, notwithstanding the often dubious quality of measurement (see Box 7.3).

The use made by citizens varies widely and various initiatives are highly rhetorical. Yet, if systems are to be based more on performance information, the question of how performance information connects to democracy and how it is relevant to consumer and other choices made by citizens becomes important. Much depends upon whether citizens notice and are prepared to think about using the information (rather than other more immediate media sources). Mechanisms for engagement therefore become significant for connecting citizens to processes that rely on performance information.

The ownership of performance management initiatives usually lies within the administration. However, administrators repeatedly complain about the lack of interest of the public in performance information – until things go wrong. This leads to frustration

BOX 7.3 POSING FOR THE SWIMSUIT ISSUE

Best demonstrates the use of performance information of schools by applicants for college admission. There are thousands of colleges in the USA and the application process costs money. The more elite schools will refuse access to most applicants, and therefore applications to several colleges are sent. But how do candidates make a choice among these colleges? Best argues that quality of education is not the prime criterion, since quality is hard to assess. Rather, students use a ranking published by the news magazine *US News & World Report*. Among college admission officers, the issue with the rankings is known as 'the swimsuit issue', since the indicators are highly cosmetic and do not seem to reflect quality. Different indicators are included in a complicated formula.

- Qualifications of the admitted students. Colleges that admit students with higher test scores are better.
- Indicators on the admission process: the number of admissions, the number admitted and the number who accept admission (students usually apply to different colleges). Low admission rates and a high acceptance rate lead to a higher score.
- Peer assessment. Two officials at each college have to assign scores to other institutions.
- Number of faculty members, spending per student, graduation rate.

Best 2004: 120

because there is a supply of performance information but no demand. An appealing approach to alleviate the problem is to make performance measurement more demand oriented. This implies the stronger involvement of citizens in the definition of performance (see Box 7.4).

There is also some evidence that citizens in their capacity as voters may take advantage of the availability of performance information to penalize incumbent councillors. The trend in some OECD countries to publish information on local services may be reflected in electoral support. In at least one, the United Kingdom, 'negativity bias' is apparent through a reduction in the aggregate vote for incumbents where there has been poor performance (James and John 2006).

BOX 7.4 CITIZEN-DRIVEN PERFORMANCE MEASUREMENT

One of the largest projects in this area is the Citizen-Driven Performance Measurement project at Rutgers University, NJ, financed by the Sloan Foundation. The programme's approach emphasizes citizen involvement to ensure that what is measured is what matters to citizens and that the data is not corrupted by the natural desire of officeholders to report favourable outcomes.

The project has been running for some years now and the first evaluations of its success have been made (Ho 2008). The main recommendations are:

- A certain level of trust and mutual respect between government officials and citizen representatives is necessary before any engagement can be launched. If government officials believe that citizens are only there to complain, or if citizens believe that government officials will not sincerely listen to their concerns and report performance honestly, the collaboration will be likely to fail.
- Citizens often have a different perspective on performance measurement than managers do. Generally, they are less interested in input and output measures, and are more interested in outcomes and in citizen perception of service quality, responsiveness, customer services, intra-jurisdictional equity, transparency and effectiveness in public communication.
- Despite the value of citizen participation, managers still need to manage and citizens cannot replace professional managers. Citizen input may contribute fresh ideas and new perspectives to management problems, but citizens ultimately will have to rely on or collaborate with government officials to implement the ideas.

- ■ Citizen participation in performance measurement does not necessarily guarantee better services and more satisfactory performance. Citizen-initiated performance measures may highlight the concerns and critical issues of a programme from the citizens' perspective, but the measures by themselves are insufficient to guarantee good management and greater public investment to improve services.
- ■ A citizen–official partnership in performance measurement can also be highly fragile. It not only requires government leaders to take risk and make government performance issues more transparent to the public, but also community leaders to commit time and resources to support the project, participate in meetings and work closely with government officials to learn about performance issues that can sometimes be highly technical and managerial in nature.

MEDIA

Finally, some other users are discussed. The media is a significant user of performance information in several forms including league tables and trends in service levels. While a number of observers have commented upon the disconnect between improved performance based on statistics and public perceptions of the quality of services – attributing the gap substantially to the media's role in shaping public perceptions – Flynn (2007) has examined the position of the media more systematically. He concluded that the UK government's biggest disappointment was the disconnection between improvements in performance and the level of public satisfaction. When polled, members of the public base their opinions on the standards of public service on factors other than the measurable performance targets carefully crafted by government.

Media do pick up bits of performance information, but it's very difficult to predict which pieces of performance information will be taken out of the performance report. There is a substantial literature however on news values of events (Galtung and Ruge 1965). Timely, unexpected, sudden, negative, unambiguous, personal, conflict-prone events are more likely to be picked up in the media, to name a few criteria. If performance information has to figure in the media, it needs to be adapted to increase the news value. Performance information can, for instance, be personalized by also showing a case or a witness. The release of performance information should fit the media cycle. There has to be a consistent storyline behind the numbers and focus should be on the unexpected results.

127

CONCLUSIONS

Like chapter 6, this chapter dealt with the use of performance information. The perspective shifted however from the organizational perspective to the perspective of the users. It is important to be very specific about the users that are envisaged by the measurement system. Use of performance information is conditioned by the specific context and incentive structures in which users operate. In order to avoid non-use, a good understanding of the conditional nature of use by users is vital. The next chapter focuses on non-use.

DISCUSSION QUESTIONS

1   Assume the role of a business consultant who has to promote the use of performance information among middle managers and front-line supervisors in a large agency; how would you go about it?

2   Should politicians be an important target group for performance information?

3   What performance information is picked up by the newspapers of the day? What are the qualities of the information that probably led to use by the media?

REFERENCES

Alford, J. (2002) Why do public-sector clients coproduce? Toward a contingency theory. *Administration & Society,* 34, 32–56.

Askim, J. (2007) How do politicians use performance information? An analysis of the Norwegian local government experience. *International Review of Administrative Sciences,* 73, 453–72.

Best, J. (2004) *More Damned Lies and Statistics,* Berkeley, University of California Press.

Bouckaert, G. and Halligan, J. (2008) *Managing Performance: International Comparisons.* London, Routledge.

Bourdeaux, J. (2008) Integrating performance information into legislative budget processes. *Public Performance & Management Review,* 31 (4), 547–69.

Bovaird, T. (2007) Beyond engagement and participation: user and community coproduction of public services. *Public Administration Review,* 67, 846–60.

CCAF-ECVI (2006) *Users and Uses: Towards Producing and Using Better Public Performance Reporting: Perspectives and Solutions.* Ottawa, CCAF-FCVI.

Flynn, N. (2007) *Public Sector Management.* Thousand Oaks, Sage.

Galtung, J. and Ruge, M. H. (1965) The structure of foreign news: the presentation of the Congo, Cuba and Cyprus crises in four Norwegian newspapers. *Journal of Peace Research*, 2, 64–90.

Goddard, M., Mannion, R. and Smith, P. C. (1999) Assessing the performance of NHS hospital trusts: the role of 'hard' and 'soft' information. *Health Policy*, 48, 119–34.

Gormley, W. T. and Weimer, D. L. (1999) *Organizational Report Cards.* Cambridge, MA, Harvard University Press.

Halligan, J., Miller, R. and Power, J. (2007) *Parliament in the 21st Century: Institutional Reform and Emerging Roles.* Melbourne, Melbourne University Press.

Hatry, H. P. (1999) *Performance Measurement: Getting Results.* Washington, DC, Urban Institute Press.

Ho, A. (2007) *Engaging Citizens in Measuring and Reporting Community Conditions: A Manager's Guide.* Washington, DC, IBM.

Ho, A. (2008) Citizen involvement in reporting PI. In Van Dooren, W. and Van de Walle, S. (eds.) *Performance Information in the Public Sector: How It Is Used.* Basingstoke, Palgrave Macmillan.

James, O. and John, P. (2006) Public management at the ballot box: performance information and electoral support for incumbent English local governments. *Journal of Public Administration Research and Theory*, 17, 567–80.

Johnson, C. and Talbot, C. (2008) UK parliamentary scrutiny of public services agreements: a challenge too far? In Van Dooren, W. and Van de Walle, S. (eds.) *Performance Information in the Public Sector: How It Is Used.* Basingstoke, Palgrave Macmillan.

Joyce, P. G. (2005) Linking performance and budgeting: opportunities in the federal budget process. In Kamensky, J. M. and Morales, A. (eds.) *Managing for Results.* Washington, DC, IBM.

McDavid, J. C. and Hawthorn, L. R. L. (2006) *Program Evaluation and Performance Measurement: An Introduction to Practice.* Thousand Oaks, Sage.

Newcomer, K. (2007) How does program performance assessment affect program management in the federal government? *Public Performance & Management Review*, 30, 332–50.

Pollitt, C. (2006) Performance information for democracy: the missing link? *Evaluation: The International Journal of Theory, Research and Practice*, 12, 39–56.

Porter, T. M. (1995) *Trust in Numbers: The Pursuit of Objectivity in Science and Public Life.* Princeton, NJ, Princeton University Press.

Sterck, M. (2007) The impact of performance budgeting on the role of the legislature: a four-country study. *International Review of Administrative Sciences*, 73, 189–203.

Svara, J. H. (1985) Dichotomy and duality: reconceptualizing the relationship between policy and administration in council-manager cities. *Public Administration Review*, 45, 221–32.

Ter Bogt, H. J. (2004) Politicians in search of performance information? Survey research on Dutch aldermen's use of performance information. *Financial Accountability & Management*, 20, 221–52.

Van Dooren, W. (2004) Supply and demand of policy indicators. *Public Management Review*, 6, 511–30.

Van Dooren, W. (2005) What makes organisations measure? Hypotheses on the causes and conditions for performance measurement. *Financial Accountability & Management*, 21, 363–83.

Van Dooren, W. (2006) *Performance Measurement in the Flemish Public Sector: A Supply and Demand Approach*. Leuven, Faculty of Social Sciences.

Van Dooren, W., Thijs, N. and Bouckaert, G. (2004) Quality management and the management of quality in European public administrations. In Loeffler, E. and Vintar, M. (eds.) *Improving the Quality of Eastern and Western European Public Services*. Aldershot, Ashgate.

Van Dooren, W. and Van de Walle, S. (2008) *Performance Information in the Public Sector: How It Is Used*. Basingstoke, Palgrave Macmillan.

FURTHER READING

An overview of several user perspectives is found in the edited volume *Performance Information in the Public Sector: How It Is Used* (Van Dooren and Van de Walle 2008). For a perspective on politicians, there are empirical studies by Ter Bogt (2004), Van Dooren (2004), Askim (2007), Sterck (2007), Johnson and Talbot (2008) and Bourdeaux (2008). Pollitt (2006) provides a more reflective perspective on the link between performance and democracy. Citizen involvement in performance management has been developed by the National Centre for Public Productivity at Rutgers University. A good study of report cards and league tables is published in Gormley and Weimer (1999).

Chapter 8

Non-use

LEARNING OBJECTIVES

■ To understand the phenomenon of non-use-despite-availability and to appreciate its consequences.

■ To be able to reflect on causes of non-use in practice, based on theoretical explanations.

KEY POINTS

■ Organizations are regularly not using performance information, although information is available.

■ Insufficient quality of performance information is only one among several explanations.

■ Psychological, cultural and institutional barriers may also have an impact.

■ Non-use has negative side-effects.

When decision-makers say they 'don't use' performance information, what does this actually mean? Does it mean they generally do not sit down with a 200-page performance report and a cup of coffee? This is quite likely. Henry Mintzberg, when studying managers, showed that managers did not generally get their information from reading reports, but by talking to other people (Mintzberg 1975). Likewise, the conclusion of the (all in all, scarce) research on how politicians use performance information, appears to be that performance reports are neither read nor valued (Pollitt 2006; Ter Bogt 2004).

Chapter 6 argued that organizations can use performance information for three reasons: learning, steering & control, and accountability. This chapter asks why organizations do *not* use performance information. It seems unlikely that they do not want to learn, steer & control or be accountable. Yet, performance information is often not picked up despite its potential benefits. The discussion of non-use touches upon some fundamental theoretical insights into how information is processed. Such insights may be particularly useful for providers of performance information, who have to develop performance information that is fit for use.

The chapter first portrays some empirical evidence on the issue of non-use, after which the causes of non-use are explored: insufficient quality of performance information and psychological, cultural or institutional barriers. Finally, some consequences of non-use of performance information are discussed.

1 NON-USE

Performance information may not be used simply because it is not available. The reasons why there is no performance measurement can be manifold. Previously, chapter 2 pointed to limited measurability as a potential explanation. Chapter 6 discussed the envisaged uses for measuring performance. If organizations do not see the benefits, they are very unlikely to engage in a measurement effort.

In this section, however, the focus is on those instances where performance information is available and is even incorporated, but is not or not significantly used. Moynihan argues that performance management is a 'good government reform' which is hard to oppose. Implementation, however, is much more difficult and support for performance is therefore often 'a mile wide but an inch deep' (Moynihan 2008: 192). Examples would be performance budgets that are not used in budget negotiations or performance-based annual reports that are not at all read or taken into account by funders of an agency.

Some US survey studies have documented the non-use of performance information. Research conducted by the GAB Governmental Accounting Standards Board (Government Accounting Standards Board n.d.) found that few government entities used performance measures for planning, resource allocation and programme management. Berman and Wang (2000) surveyed county managers in the US about the breadth and depth of their performance measurement practices. Only counties that at least performed some performance measurement were included in the analysis. Some items on what Berman and Wang call programme outcomes, but which in our terminology are indications of the use of performance information, are included in their survey. The percentages in Box 8.1 thus reflect the number of counties that agree with a number of statements. The last item for instance states that 15.5 per cent of the counties that are measuring performance see a value in improving timeliness.

It is remarkable that not even the highest score reaches 50 per cent, which implies that in more than half of the counties, performance measurement is not used for creating awareness for accountability. Only 35 per cent acknowledge that performance measurement leads to improved accountability and 26.6 per cent see a potential for

BOX 8.1 SOME SURVEY EVIDENCE ON USE AND NON-USE

	Agreement
Increased awareness about the need for accountability	48.0%
Increased ability to determine service efficiency	45.0
Increased ability to determine service effectiveness	43.0
Increased ability to determine service timeliness	40.0
Established performance target levels for programmes/services	40.0
Clarified agency or programme goals and objectives	37.2
Improved accountability of programme performance	35.6
Ability to achieve improvements despite resource constraints	32.5
Increased commitment to excellence	31.5
Improving group decision-making capabilities	26.6
Determined long-term budget needs	23.6
Eliminated services that are no longer needed	16.1
Improve timeliness of management decisions	15.5

findings from Berman and Wang 2000

improved decision-making. No more than 16 per cent use performance information to eliminate services and to improve timeliness of decisions.

In judging these numbers, the glass can be half full or half empty. It can be argued that the use of performance information is a gradual learning process. Melkers and Willoughby (2005) report somewhat higher use in a 2005 study, which may confirm the existence of some learning effects. Moreover, it can be debated whether it is realistic and even desirable to expect organizations to use performance information for all the items listed by Berman and Wang (2000). It may suffice that an organization strongly supports a small number of uses rather than doing something on everything. Under this assumption, low numbers are not as problematic as they may appear to be. On the other hand, it seems at least worrying that some of the more far-reaching uses of performance information such as improving group decision-making capacity, long-term budgeting and critically assessing the relevance of programmes are not accepted.

Additional evidence of non-use is provided by Ter Bogt, who studied the use of performance information by politicians. He concluded that:

> sources of performance information which the aldermen made by far the most use of were informal, verbal consultations and formal meetings with top managers, i.e. civil servants. They much less frequently used formal, written information in

budgets, annual reports, and interim reports, and other sources of formal and informal information.

(Ter Bogt 2004: 250)

This study reminds us of the fact that performance measurement is one source of information among many. The non-use of formal knowledge such as performance information does not imply that decisions are not informed. These findings should however prompt a reflection on the relation of formal, written information to other more informal sources (see Box 8.2).

BOX 8.2 NON-USE OR USE UNDER THE RADAR? DECOUPLING OF INDICATORS AND GOALS

In some cases, it is probably concluded too easily that performance information is not used. Researchers typically look for the ideal typical use in performance management systems. This ideal type propagates the formulation of strategic and operational goals that have to guide the formulation of indicators. Such a system, it is argued, has to be integrated. It typically consists of a hierarchical cascade of goals and indicators. Hence, when there are no indications of use in formulating and monitoring objectives, it is concluded that information is not used.

The theoretical perspective of loose coupling may however cast another light on the use of performance information. Orton and Weick (1990) conclude from a literature review on the subject that from a Weberian bureaucratic perspective, the recurring surprise is that organizations routinely exhibit looseness. From a decoupling perspective, the recurring surprise is that organizations routinely exhibit coupling (p.218). We therefore should not be surprised that performance information is not used in an integrated command and control structure. Nevertheless, it may well be that information is used in other locations in the organization.

Some empirical evidence with regard to performance measurement exists. Brignall and Modell (2000) suggest that decoupling of (as opposed to integration between) performance indicators and goals is a viable strategy for seeking simultaneous legitimacy of multiple constituencies. Johnsen (1999) concluded from a case study of four Norwegian municipalities that in complex settings a decoupled implementation mode may be more successful than a coupled one. Laegreld, Roness and Rubecksen (2008) document a case of decoupling in the Norwegian national performance management scheme (Management By Objectives and Results).

2 WHY IS PERFORMANCE INFORMATION NOT USED?

Why do Americans (until now) not buy small cars? Is it because the cars are not good enough, not safe enough? Is it a manifestation of bounded rationality, where the environmental costs are not taken into account? Or is it a matter of culture? Is a large car an expression of success in an individualistic society? Or, finally, is it a matter of formal and informal rules? Is the tax regulation more generous for large cars compared to for instance Europe? A simple question triggers different answers: about the quality of the product, the psychological limitations, cultural aspects and institutional variation.

Let us now turn to the question why information is not used. Since empirical evidence on the issue is rare, some middle range theories are used to suggest potential answers. Four potential explanations are explored, being aware of the fact that several other theories may yield additional insights. The first explanation of non-use is about the information itself, the second about the user of the information and the third and fourth about the cultural and institutional context of information and information use respectively.

2.1 Explanation: insufficient quality

More than three decades ago, Mintzberg (1975) observed that many managerial tasks involve judgement rather than formal analysis. Managers therefore prefer rapid, informal and speculative information to entirely accurate information. Current leadership studies do not seem to suggest a more analytical profile for the contemporary manager. According to Van Wart (2003), leadership literature from the 1990s onward formulates the need for vision, entrepreneurialism and charisma. Such labels usually do not embrace an understanding of the technical quality of performance data as a key competence for leaders. On the contrary, for substantial knowledge of their business, public managers are expected to rely on professional staff. For managers, it seems, quality of information is not a prime concern for use.

We should however not entirely dismiss the idea that non-use is somehow influenced by the quality of the performance information. A useful scheme to understand the role of technical quality in the decision of managers to use performance information is provided by Weiss and Bucuvalas (1980). They suggest that decision-makers when confronted with new information are performing two tests; a *truth test* and a *utility test*. For each test, there is the more conventional understanding as well as a more counterintuitive claim (see Table 8.1) (Van de Walle and Van Dooren 2010).

(1)   Decision-makers appraise the truth of information in terms of its technical merit as evidenced by the professional standards of the measurement process. This is the conventional wisdom held by the measurement profession. Many government or consulting reports treat the non-use of information as something that can easily be fixed though a number of practical and technical changes (Van de Walle and Bovaird

135

Table 8.1 Truth and utility tests of new information

	Truth test	Utility test
Conventional wisdom	I Does the *process* of measurement evidence high quality?	III Does the performance information help to *solve problems*?
Alternative explanation	II Are the *findings* of performance measurement in line with previous evidence?	IV Does it *enlighten* in the long term?

Source: based on Weiss and Bucuvalas 1980

2007). The spontaneous reaction to non-use is a plea for more technical training of those who have to use the data. Wholey (2002) however asserts that technical know-how is not enough. An extensive training in strategic planning, programme evaluation and the use of performance information is also required. As we discussed above, the impact of technical quality should thus not be overstated.

(2)   Decision-makers also test the truth of information by checking the conformity of the findings of performance measurement with their prior understanding and experience. Decision-makers are exposed to a variety of evidence such as direct observation, descriptive accounts, programme data, routine statistics, colleagues' reports, as well as a body of previous research, and they use their stock of knowledge to judge the truth of the findings (Weiss and Bucuvalas 1980: 308). Confronted with a performance statistic, say for instance high dissatisfaction of users of public transport, a manager of a transportation agency will typically react off the cuff saying things like 'I don't believe that', or else 'I am not surprised'. At that moment, he or she is performing a first truth test. Note that the quality of the measurement process is less relevant here.

Three alignment scenarios of measurement findings with prior knowledge can be distinguished. In case of *non-alignment*, performance information contradicts prior knowledge. In case of *semi alignment*, some performance results are counter-intuitive while others are not. The case of *full alignment* reflects performance information that endorses previously held beliefs about performance. Each scenario can lead to use or non-use, depending on the context (see Table 8.2).

(3)   The utility test also consists of two judgements. Information is assessed by the extent to which it provides explicit and practical direction on matters decision-makers can do something about. Information has to be actionable and has to increase the problem-solving capacity of decision-makers. It also is expected to reduce uncertainty. As a result, the utility test tends to disfavour statistical analysis. The application of statistical standards to performance information show precisely the limits of the

Table 8.2 *Alignment scenarios and the use of performance information*

Scenarios of alignment with prior knowledge	Performance information is used because . . .	Performance information is not used because . . .
In case of non-alignment	Performance information allows challenging the status quo. Unexpected findings at least attract attention and may be instrumental to 'rock the boat' and change power distribution between actors.	Performance information is deemed unrealistic.
In case of semi alignment	Performance information can support a compromise in policy-making or substantiate incremental steps in policy change.	Performance information is not providing direction.
In case of full alignment	Performance information reinforces standpoints and beliefs already held.	Performance information is not seen as having an added value.

information (expressed by probabilities and confidence intervals) and this is not what decision-makers in search of certainty and evidence may want to hear.

(4)   Utility can also be seen as the capacity of performance information to challenge current practices and suggest new perspectives and orientations. This is what Weiss (1979) calls the *enlightenment* function of information. The latter concept points to the fact that performance information may slowly and unnoticeably alter the definition of policy problems and solutions. Unlike the other three boxes of the quadrant, enlightenment cannot easily be traced back to an individual decision-maker. The metaphor of a 'test' performed by a user is less applicable here.

2.2 Explanation 2: psychological barriers

A second set of explanations can be found in the psychological barriers that limit human information-processing capabilities. The most important insights were probably provided by Herbert Simon, father of the now generally accepted concepts of *bounded rationality* and *satisficing*. His theory provides a perspective on why performance information may not be used. The general argument is that performance measurement systems assume an idealistic model of the rational decision-maker. Simon speaks of the model of the *Economic Man,* which he opposes to the more realistic model of the *Satisficing Man.* Performance measurement processes that take the satisficing model into account have more chances of their information being used.

The Economic Man model is represented in Table 8.3. Based on complete information of the environment, the courses of action and the consequences, a decision-maker will maximize value by processing all information in the light of a stable set of preferences. This view assumes almost superhuman capabilities of the human brain. In actual decision-making, the environment is ambiguous, courses of action are unstable and consequences and risks are unknown. Moreover, preferences are usually not even temporarily stable and can not be rank-ordered.

These observations led Simon to define the model of Satisficing Man (1997). The term 'satisficing' is a combination of 'satisfy' and 'suffice'. A decision-maker will search for alternatives that are good enough, instead of searching for maximal utility. The failure of omniscient rationality is largely a failure of knowing all the alternatives, uncertainty about relevant exogenous events, and inability to calculate consequences (Simon 1979). Hence, rationality is bounded by incomplete information, insufficient processing capacities and the pervasive impact of uncertainty.

Simon does not portray the model of Economic Man as undesirable. He in fact considers it an appropriate normative model of decision-making with a precise definition of rationality. However, since the economic model inadequately describes *actual* decision-making processes, it can not be taken for granted. The model of Economic Man is the ideal, while the model of Satsificing Man is a realistic residual.

What does this imply for the design of a performance measurement system? The main lesson from Simon's work is that bounded rationality rather than full rationality should be the point of departure. Measurement systems need to be designed based on the assumption that users have limited processing capacities and limited computational skills and objectives. This implies, for instance, that efforts to present performance information in a decision-relevant format should be firmly ingrained in the measurement system. The observation of unstable preferences leads to questions about the flexibility and adaptability of the measurement system. The combination of stringent coupling

Table 8.3 *Rational decision-making according to Simon*

The model of the Economic Man (Simon 1997)

The decision-maker knows all the relevant aspects of the decision environment.

The decision-maker knows all the courses of action.

The decision-maker knows all the consequences of those alternatives with certainty, or knows the probability distribution of risks.

The decision-maker has a known, and temporarily stable preference function for all sets of consequences.

The decision-maker has the computational skills.

The decision-maker maximizes the satisfaction of his values by choosing the alternative that is followed by the most preferred set of consequences.

between indicators and objectives on the one hand and a volatile environment on the other may yield performance information that is quickly superseded.

Although Simon's work can lead to a major critique of performance measurement, it also provides a rationale. Since pure rational decision-making is preferred over satisficing search-behaviour, performance measurement may be seen as a step towards more rationality. Although measurement always deals with past performance, it may to some degree reduce uncertainty over future performance. Performance measurement is able to provide decision-makers with more information on the decision environment, courses of action, consequences and risks. Moreover, the dialogue around the indicators may lead to a crystallization and stabilization of preferences (Moynihan 2008).

To conclude, Simon's psychological perspective suggests that performance measurement does have the potential to improve decision-making. However, this potential will only materialize when performance measurement professionals explicitly acknowledge the existence of bounded rationality, and do not take rationality for granted.

2.3 Explanation 3: cultural barriers

A third set of explanations for non-use is rooted in cultural theory (Schedler and Proeller 2007). The causes of non-use are sought in the mismatch between the use of performance information and the cultural traditions of a society, administration or organization. When performance measurement is a cultural *Fremdkörper*, the chances for use are minimal.

The general definition of culture includes three elements that are shared among people: cognitions, values and affects. *Cognitions* are the empirical perceptions of reality of how the world works. For instance, some cultures stress individual choice and responsibility as the cause of criminal behaviour, while other cultures put an emphasis on the social conditions surrounding the individual. *Values* are the convictions of how it *should* work. For instance, some cultures seem more tolerant towards repression in order to fight crime than others. *Affects* reflect the emotional involvement in cognitions and values. Cultural symbols such as the flag and the national hymn represent a set of cognitions of what a country is, and values about what it should be. Yet, they do not evoke the same affective reactions in all cultures.

Cultural theory yielded numerous analytical schemes that allow describing the potential mismatch between the use of performance information and cultural elements. The cultural theories of Bendix, Sartori, Hofstede and Douglas and their relevance for the use of performance information are selected from this theoretical affluence.

Bendix (1974) differentiated between *entrepreneurial cultures* that emphasize personal bargaining and negotiation (e.g. Great Britain) versus *bureaucratic cultures* that are based on the acceptance of impersonal rules (e.g. continental Europe). Performance-based accountability (see chapter 6) may better fit entrepreneurial cultures. Personal achievement of top managers is the basis of accountability and can, or rather should, be exposed. In bureaucratic cultures, on the contrary, accountability is mainly about following rules and authority. Performance-based accountability may be at cross purposes with this tradition of rule-based accountability. The case where good performance coincides with a mild infringement of rules and authority is often felt to be much more problematic in bureaucratic cultures.

Sartori (1969) describes the traditional distinction between *rationalist, deductive cultures* and *pragmatic, empirical cultures*. The former tend to approach problems with coherent argumentation derived from theory while the latter rely on evidence and testing. Precedent prevails over theory. Learning from performance information may be easier in pragmatic, empirical cultures than in rationalist, deductive ones. The openness to consider performance information with a wide outlook and to challenge dominant frameworks based on empirical observation is better embodied in empirical cultures.

Hofstede (2005) distinguishes five components of culture: (1) *power distance* reflects the extent to which the less powerful members of organizations accept and expect that power is distributed unequally; (2) *collectivism*, as opposed to *individualism*, is the degree to which individuals are integrated into groups; (3) *masculinity*, as opposed to *femininity*, is the level of competitiveness and assertiveness; (4) *uncertainty avoidance* reflects the tolerance towards uncertainty and ambiguity; and (5) *long-term orientation*, as opposed to *short-term orientation*, is the degree to which cultures value thrift and perseverance and denounce respect for tradition, fulfilling social obligations and protecting one's 'face'.

Some of Hofstede's dimensions are relevant for understanding the use of performance information. For instance, performance-based pay has a strong competitive element and therefore is more aligned with a masculine culture. On the contrary, performance dialogues for learning purposes require consensual and emphatic attitudes typical of feminine cultures. Another example is the impact that a long-term orientation may have on the target setting and performance evaluation. The occurrence of the dysfunction of myopia (see chapter 9) may be less likely in a long-term culture. Finally, the culture of risk avoidance may prohibit learning from performance information, which almost inevitably requires a degree of experimentation.

Douglas (1996) developed the widely applied group-grid theory of culture (see, for instance, Hood (2000) for an application in public administration). The first dimension, *group*, is similar to the distinction between individualism and collectivism that Hofstede proposes. It is intended to show the role of group pressure upon individuals stemming mainly from moral compulsion and the degree of group integration. Compare for instance group pressure in a small rural town with the anonymity of a metropolis. The German saying, *Stadtluft macht frei*, perfectly expresses the sense of freedom some experience in anonymous city life opposed to the oppressive informal rules of country life. *Grid*, the second axis, refers to the constraints created by the formal and informal rules that are imposed upon the group members. Compare, for instance, dense rules of dining in a three-star Michelin restaurant with a picnic in a public park.

The combination of the two dimensions yields four ideal-typical cultures (Hood 2000) (see Figure 8.1).

140

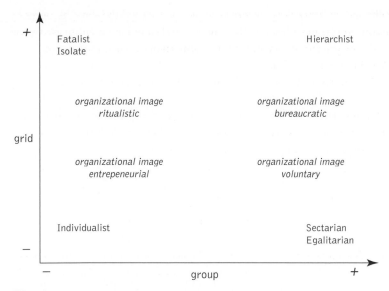

Figure 8.1 *The group-grid scheme of culture*

(1) An *individualist culture* scores low on both group and grid. The financial sector in Wall Street may serve at an example. Burroughs and Helyar's (2003) book, *Barbarians at the Gate*, vividly describes the cold-blooded 1988 leverage buyout of RJR Nabisco and the extreme individualism that characterizes a sector where everybody is working for himself. The stress is on individuals as self-interested rational choosers. Organizational problems are defined in terms of faulty incentive structures and lack of price signals and remedies are sought in market-like mechanisms, competitions and league tables. It is assumed that individuals need more information to support choice. The organizational image therefore is entrepreneurial.

(2) A *fatalist culture* scores high on grid but low on group and reflects a situation where people follow rules in a group or society, but without a sense of belonging. The North Korean mass manifestations to honour the leaders of the country may serve as an example of ritualistic adherence to rules without group loyalty. Fatalists define organizational problems in terms of unpredictability and unin-tended effects. The strong emphasis on fate leads to a minimal anticipation to problems. At most, there is an *ad hoc* response after the event. The organizational image is ritualistic.

(3) *Egalitarian cultures* have a high sense of belonging to a group, but do not have a low grid of rules. There is a relatively clear idea on who is in or out, but within the group, members are equal and free. A classic example is the hippie movement of the 1960s but many voluntary organizations also fall into this category. Problems are defined in terms of inadequate group and power structures.

141

Egalitarians will more than others blame the system and the abuse of power by top-level government leaders. Participation and communitarianism are typical safeguards against system failure. The organizational image is voluntary.

(4) Finally, *hierarchists* have both high group and grid. A common example is a combat unit in an army that combines camaraderie with strict formal and informal rules. The traditional Weberian bureaucracies would also largely fit this description. Hierarchists put the accent on expertise, planning and forecasting, and management. Failure should be addressed by building more expertise, tighter procedures and greater managerial grip.

Performance measurement systems will operate in a fundamentally different way according to the culture.

(1) *Individualist cultures* may adopt performance incentives and performance pay. Many NPM reforms assumed an individualist culture and proposed better (read: performance-based) incentive structures. Osborne and Gaebler's *Reinventing Government* (1993), for instance, has a subtitle about the entrepreneurial spirit that is transforming the public sector.

(2) *Fatalist cultures* will in all probability adopt ritualistic performance measurement exercises. Window-dressing tactics are likely.

(3) *Egalitarian cultures* may more easily adopt performance dialogue, but have more problems with performance information that is highly broken out. Such detailed performance information would reveal differences within the group, which egalitarian cultures have difficulties with. Obviously, performance pay and individualized incentives are out of the question.

(4) *Hierarchists'* stress on professionalism would require that performance information is integrated in the professional corpus of the organization. Performance information that runs counter to the accepted professional definitions and norms will meet resistance from the professions. In addition, the stress on regulation might lead to performance information that gets a regulatory character.

2.4 Explanation 4: institutions

Finally, performance measurement systems also operate in different institutional contexts that may explain non-use (Van Dooren 2008). March and Olsen (1989) distinguish between two logics of action that are shaped by two kinds of institutions: normative and regulatory. Dimaggio and Powell (1983) describe the pressure that arises from three types of institutions: power structures, norms and shared cognitions. Here, the focus is on regulatory and normative institutions.

(1) *Regulatory institutions* reflect the power distribution in a politico-administrative arena. Institutions constrain and regulate behaviour through rule-setting, monitoring and sanctioning (Scott 2001). Rules can be informal (with reputational

sanctions) or formal (police and courts). Compliance follows from the calculation of costs and benefits of each alternative. March and Olsen (1989) speak of the logic of the consequences, which is in essence preference based.

One of the main ideas of the New Public Management doctrine was the combination of managerial freedom with performance agreements. This notion was reflected in the catchphrases 'let managers manage' and 'make managers manage' (Kettl 2002). New Public Management somewhat courageously assumed a balance between intrinsic motivation and managerial craftsmanship on the one hand and extrinsic incentives and accountability on the other. It remains unclear however how this balance between managers and political principals comes about.

The concept of power, an often forgotten dimension in the NPM literature, may be useful in this regard. Roughly speaking, managers want enough freedom 'to do the job'. This quest for autonomy does not only concern management issues, as NPM literature suggests. Often, managers also seek strategic autonomy on policy matters (Verhoest *et al.* 2004). In some contexts, managers may use performance indicators to chalk out their territory, to set the boundaries of political interference. Politicians, who disagree with the limitation of their scope of action, will not use the performance information; not because the information is not good or useful, but because it infringes on political interests.

Politicians, on the other hand, want as much supervision over the bureaucracy as possible. They are afraid that the discretion of managers might enable them to obstruct policies. Political principals therefore search for means to control the bureaucracy and to make them manage. Performance indicators sometimes are mainly a tool for political control over the bureaucracy. Managers who are subjected to this pressure may attempt not to use the performance information, not because the information is not good or useful, but because it infringes on managerial interests.

The bipolar representation of the power struggle between managers and politicians is deceptively simple. In reality, performance indicator regimes play a role in at least five power games. Performance indicator regimes potentially shift the balance of power between:

1 the executive and legislative
2 executive politicians and administration
3 staff and line agencies
4 tiers of government
5 leadership and front-line workers.

(2) *Normative institutions* are the values, norms and roles that guide behaviour (Scott 2001). *Values* are the conceptions of the desirable and standards to which existing structures and behaviour can be assessed. *Norms* specify how things should be done and reflect opinions about proper means and ends. *Roles* are the values and norms for specific persons or classes. March and Olsen (1989) talk about the logic of appropriateness. Unlike for coercive institutions, there is no rational

calculation. The normative institutions constrain and enable rational calculations because they set the rules of the game and they structure choice. Normative institutions are identity based instead of interest based.

Professional identity is mainly shaped through education. Doctors, lawyers, anthropologists and engineers, to name a few, acquire the values, norms and roles typical of the profession. The non-use of performance information can be explained by the normative pressure from the professional norms. The question, therefore, is whether performance indicator regimes align with the norms and values of the profession or infringe on them. It can be hypothesized that:

1 Highly technocratic professions will be able to use their technical competence as a line of defence against in their view too simplistic performance indicators.
2 Professions that are measurement-minded may have fewer problems with performance indicator regimes.
3 Professions that are well-organized in professional associations will have better opportunities to voice their disagreement with the managerial doctrine (see Box 8.3).

BOX 8.3 PERFORMANCE INFORMATION AND INSTITUTIONAL READINESS

Institutions can strongly affect the proper use of performance information and hence the success of performance management. Schick (1998) argues that most developing countries are not ready to implement performance management. The World Bank *Public Expenditure Handbook* (1998) echoed this argument stating that performance management will only succeed if it is built on, or builds in, the basics (p.82). In an article titled 'Why most developing countries should not try New Zealand's reforms', Schick outlines his argument. Developing countries have to follow a 'logic of development' and performance-oriented reforms are only the last step.

First, progress in the public sector requires parallel advances in the market sector. As long as the economy operates according to informal norms and property rights are defined more by practice than by contract, the government is not likely to make much headway in installing rule-based public management. Formalizing the market sector does not ensure reciprocal changes in public institutions, however.

Second, modernizing the public sector means establishing reliable external controls. As old-fashioned as external controls may seem to be, they are building blocks for a formal, rule-based, honest public sector. Operating in an externally controlled environment is an essential phase in the development process. It gives managers the skills to manage on their own, builds trust between central controllers and line managers and confidence between citizens and government, and encourages managers to internalize a public ethic of proper behaviour. As these basic conditions of formal management take root, it should be possible for central controllers to ease the regulations by giving line managers broader discretion in operating their programmes.

Third, politicians and officials must concentrate on the basic process of public management. They must be able to control inputs before they are called upon to control outputs; they must be able to account for cash before they are asked to account for cost; they must abide by uniform rules before they are authorized to make their own rules; they must operate in integrated, centralized departments before being authorized to go it alone in autonomous agencies.

3 CONSEQUENCES OF NON-USE

The explanations for the non-use of performance information can be manifold. To conclude this chapter, we discuss some of the effects of the non-use of performance information. This is somewhat of a lacuna in the performance literature. Many studies are concerned with the dysfunctional, perverse effects of the *use* of performance information, often (implicitly) assuming that non-use is preferable. The dysfunctional effects of the *non-use*, however, are not studied. Two consequences are discussed: over-claiming on 'best practice' in reforms and 'short institutional memories'.

3.1 Over-claiming on 'best practice'

One of the most notable lacunas of performance information in the public sector concerns public management and governance. In policy sectors such as environmental policy, employment and education, much more information is available. This leads the OECD to conclude that there is a paradox at the heart of the international movement in favour of performance-oriented management reform (OECD 2006).

> The reformers insist that public sector organisations must reorient and reorganise themselves in order to focus more vigorously on their results. They must count costs, measure outputs, assess outcomes, and use all this information in a systematic process of feedback and continuous improvement. Yet this philosophy has clearly not been applied to many of the reforms themselves, which have thus far been evaluated relatively seldom and usually in ways that have some serious methodological limitations.
>
> (Pollitt and Bouckaert 2004: 140)

145

In the absence of performance data on what works, reformers develop an almost religious belief in 'best practice', with a substantial risk of context reduction as a consequence.

Concerns about inappropriately enthusiastic and uncritical acceptance of managerial and policy reforms are echoed within policy sectors such as health, where Marmor *et al.* (2005) find that:

> There is . . . a considerable gap between promise and performance in the field of comparative policy studies. Misdescription and superficiality are all too common. Unwarranted inferences, rhetorical distortion, and caricatures – all show up too regularly in comparative health policy scholarship and debates.

They warn of costly policy errors based on misconceptions of experience abroad (Marmor *et al.* 2005: 343).

3.2 Weak institutional memories

A review of US government reforms suggests that:

> the deluge of recent reform may have done little to actually improve performance. On the contrary, it may have created confusion within government about what Congress and the president really want, distraction from needed debates about organisational missions and resources, and the illusion that more reform will somehow lead to better government.
>
> (Light 1997)

Others might strongly challenge these propositions. However, with limited time series data, it is all but impossible to determine the degree to which such alleged reversals or reform overloads have occurred. Mobility of staff and structural reforms lead to institutional memory loss.

Pollitt (2000) sees a role for record-keeping in avoiding such memory loss. Record-keeping can reinforce organizational memories under the condition that, first, significant data or decisions are documented; second, records do not get lost; third, they can be quickly accessed; and fourth, someone thinks of using them. If records are not limited to inputs (e.g. budgets and staff) or decisions, and include performance, institutional memory is without a doubt reinforced.

4 CONCLUSION

The question why performance information is not used, notwithstanding its availability, provides some interesting insights into how performance information is processed by users. This chapter suggested various theoretical approaches to grasp these dynamics; truth and utility testing, bounded rationality, cultural theory and institutionalism. A good understanding of the theory behind the use of performance information is not only of academic interest, but is vital for designing successful measurement systems in practice.

DISCUSSION QUESTIONS

1 Is non-use problematic and why (not)?
2 Consider a well-known performance indicator (viewing figures for a public broadcasting company, traffic casualties, educational performance (e.g. in the OECD's *Education at a Glance*). Why are these indicators used in some circumstances and not in others? Use theoretical explanations.

REFERENCES

Bendix, R. (1974) *Work and Authority in Industry*. Berkeley, University of California Press.

Berman, E. and Wang, X. (2000) Performance measurement in US counties: capacity for reform. *Public Administration Review,* 60, 409–20.

Brignall, S. and Modell, S. (2000) An institutional perspective on performance measurement and management in the 'new public sector'. *Management Accounting Research*, 11, 281–306.

Burroughs, B. and Helyar, J. (2003) *Barbarians at the Gate*. New York, Harper Business.

Dimaggio, P. J. and Powell, W. W. (1983) The iron cage revisited: institutional isomorphism and collective rationality in organizational fields. *American Sociological Review,* 48, 147–60.

Douglas, M. (1996) *Natural Symbols: Explorations in Cosmology*. London, Routledge.

Government Accounting Standards Board (n.d.) *Performance Measurement at the State and Local Levels: A Summary of Survey Results*. Washington, DC, GASB.

Hofstede, G. J. (2005) *Cultures and Organizations: Software for the Mind*. New York, McGraw-Hill.

Hood, C. (2000) *The Art of the State: Culture, Rhetoric, and Public Management*. Oxford, Oxford University Press.

Johnsen, A. (1999) Implementation mode and local government performance measurement: a Norwegian experience. *Financial Accountability & Management,* 15, 41–66.

Kettl, F. D. (2002) *The Transformation of Governance*. Baltimore, Johns Hopkins University Press.

Laegreid, P., Roness, P. G. and Rubecksen, K. (2008) Performance information and performance steering: integrated system or loose coupling? In Van Dooren, W. and Van de Walle, S. (eds.) *Performance Information in the Public Sector: How It Is Used*. Basingstoke, Palgrave Macmillan.

Light, P. C. (1997) *The Tides of Reform*. New Haven, Yale University Press.

March, J. G. and Olsen, J. P. (1989) *Rediscovering Institutions: The Organizational Basis of Politics*. New York, Free Press.

Marmor, T., Freeman, R. and Okma, K. (2005) Comparative perspectives and policy learning in the world of health care. *Journal of Comparative Policy Analysis: Research and Practice,* 7, 331–48.

Melkers, J. and Willoughby, K. (2005) Models of performance-measurement use in local governments: understanding budgeting, communication, and lasting effects. *Public Administration Review,* 65, 180–90.

Mintzberg, H. (1975) *The Nature of Managerial Work*. New York, HarperCollins.

Moynihan, D. P. (2008) *The Dynamics of Performance Management: Constructing Information and Reform*. Washington, DC, Georgetown University Press.

OECD (2006) *Issues in Output Measurement for Government at a Glance*. Paris, OECD.

Orton, J. D. and Weick, K. E. (1990) Loosely coupled systems: a reconceptualization. *The Academy of Management Review,* 15, 203–23.

Osborne, D. and Gaebler, T. (1993) *Reinventing Government: How the Entrepreneurial Spirit is Transforming the Public Sector*. Boston, Addison Wesley.

Pollitt, C. (2000) Institutional amnesia: a paradox of the 'information age'? *Prometheus,* 18, 5–16.

Pollitt, C. (2006) Performance information for democracy: the missing link? *Evaluation: The International Journal of Theory, Research and Practice,* 12, 39–56.

Pollitt, C. and Bouckaert, G. (2004) *Public Management Reform: A Comparative Analysis*. Oxford, Oxford University Press.

Sartori, G. (1969) Politics, ideology, and belief systems. *American Political Science Review,* 63, 398–411.

Schedler, K. and Proeller, I. (2007) *Cultural Aspects of Public Management Reform*. Amsterdam, Elsevier.

Schick, A. (1998) Why most developing countries should not try New Zealand's reforms. *World Bank Research Observer,* 13, 123.

Scott, W. R. (2001) *Institutions and Organizations*. Thousand Oaks, Sage Publications.

Simon, H. A. (1976) *Administrative Behavior: A Study of Decision-Making Processes in Administrative Organizations*. New York, Free Press.

Simon, H. A. (1979) Rational decision making in business organizations. *American Economic Review,* 69, 493–513.

Simon, H. A. (1997) *Administrative Behavior: A Study of Decision-Making Processes in Administrative Organizations*. New York, Free Press.

148

Ter Bogt, H. J. (2004) Politicians in search of performance information? Survey research on Dutch aldermen's use of performance information. *Financial Accountability & Management,* 20, 221–52.

Van de Walle, S. and Bovaird, T. (2007) *Making Better Use of Information to Drive Improvement in Local Public Services: A Report for the Audit Commission.* Birmingham, School of Public Policy.

Van de Walle, S. and Van Dooren, W. (2010) How is information used to improve performance in the public sector? Exploring the dynamics of performance information. In Walshe, K., Harvey, G. and Jas, P. (eds.) *Connecting Knowledge and Performance in Public Services: From Knowing To Doing.* Cambridge, Cambridge University Press.

Van Dooren, W. (2008) Performance indicators: a wolf in sheep's clothing? Paper presented at the symposium 'Changing Educational Accountability in Europe' (24/25 June 2008) WZB – Berlin. Berlin, Wissenschaftszentrum Berlin für Sozialforschung.

Van Wart, M. (2003) Public-sector leadership theory: an assessment. *Public Administration Review,* 63, 214–28.

Verhoest, K., Peters, B. G., Bouckaert, G. and Verschuere, B. (2004) The study of organisational autonomy: a conceptual review. *Public Administration and Development,* 24, 101–18.

Weiss, C. H. (1979) The many meanings of research utilization. *Public Administration Review,* 39, 426–31.

Weiss, C. H. and Bucuvalas, M. J. (1980) Truth tests and utility tests: decision-makers' frames of reference for social science research. *American Sociological Review,* 45, 302–13.

Wholey, J. S. (2002) Making results count in public and nonprofit organizations. In Newcomer, K., Jennings, E. T., Broom, C. and Lomax, A. (eds.) *Meeting the Challenges of Performance Oriented Government.* Washington, DC, ASPA.

World Bank (1998) *Public Expenditure Handbook.* Washington, DC, World Bank.

FURTHER READING

Non-use has not been studied extensively. Some surveys on use may give indications on non-use (Berman and Wang 2000; Government Accounting Standards Board n.d.; Melkers and Willoughby 2005). A start for further reading on the suggested theoretical explanations would be Weiss and Bucuvalas (1980) on truth and utility tests, Simon (1976) on the psychological barriers, Hood (2000) for an application of group-grid theory to public administration and March and Olsen (1989) on different institutional logics. Pollitt (2000) is a good reference on institutional memory and amnesia.

Chapter 9

The effects of using performance information

LEARNING OBJECTIVES

- To have an insight into the dynamics that bring about effects of using performance information.
- To develop a theoretically grounded and nuanced opinion on the effects of measurement.

KEY POINTS

- The use of performance information can have functional and/or dysfunctional effects.
- The manifestation of effects depends on the way performance information is used: learning, steering & control, or accountability.
- Strategies to tackle dysfunctional effects should focus on the motive and/or the opportunity of dysfunctional behaviour.

NPM doctrine led managers to believe that 'what gets measured, gets done'. It seems that many made the logical error of inferring that 'what does not get measured, does not get done'. In conjunction with the NPM reform agenda, performance management acquired some faddish traits. Public managers jumped the bandwagon while management consultants further paved the way. The global management consulting market was worth $51 billion in 1996. In 2002, this figure had risen to $119 billion (Saint Martin 2005).

The study of the effects of performance measurement has polarized around the proponents and critics of the broader New Public Management agenda. In this chapter, we will not take sides. It starts with the observation that measurement is seldom unobtrusive and thus changes behaviour. The question that follows is whether these behavioural effects are functional or dysfunctional for performance. Next, the conditions under which functional and/or dysfunctional effects are likely to occur are summarized. We end with some thoughts on how to remedy dysfunctional effects.

1 MEASUREMENT CHANGES BEHAVIOUR

Performance measurement in organizations affects behaviour of its members in a fundamental way. A study of the effects of performance measurement thus has to reconsider its impact on the behaviour of managers, professionals, operators, clients and stakeholders. Performance measurement is seldom unobtrusive. This should not come as a surprise, however. Social sciences have long established the behavioural effects of measurement.

In the 1930s, Elton Mayo (1933) showed that the mere fact of being observed influences behaviour. This effect, later coined as the Hawthorne effect, was discovered in a research project that was initially staged to study the impact of illumination on workers' productivity in an industrial plant. It showed that productivity rose in either the higher-light or lower-light conditions, but in both conditions it dropped again after some time. The Hawthorne research team tested the effect of other variables such as maintaining clean work stations and clearing floors of obstacles. The same pattern, however, was found. It was concluded that the mere fact of being observed, at least in the short term, changes behaviour and performance.

In 1941, Rugg demonstrated the impact of the wording of a question on responses. Using a split-ballot method, he asked one sample of the US population whether respondents felt that the USA should forbid speeches against democracy while asking the second sample whether the USA should allow public speeches against democracy. Table 9.1 shows the remarkably different numbers for logically identical answers. Apparently, people would rather not allow something than forbid. As this study demonstrates, obtrusiveness of measures is an established research agenda in social research methodology. The awareness of being part of a research design alters behaviour. The issue of social desirability in survey research probably is one of the most well-known manifestations of obtrusiveness.

In 1956, Berliner studied uneven production cycles in the planned economy of the Soviet era, which appeared to be a behavioural effect of measurement and targets. Typically, Soviet plants produced more than 50 per cent of their production in the last

Table 9.1 One of Rugg's (1941) experiments on wording survey questions

Survey item	Response	%
Should allow speeches against democracy	yes	21
Should not forbid speeches against democracy	no	39
Should not allow speeches against democracy	no	62
Should forbid speeches against democracy	yes	46

ten days of the month. Such 'production spurts' caused inefficiencies and coordination problems. Yet, the central administration could not control the problem. Berliner demonstrated that monthly production targets combined with strong performance incentives for managers caused the spurts. Managers of local plants received considerable bonuses of up to 100 per cent of the base wage for meeting targets. Additional bonuses were provided when targets were surpassed. However, in the latter case, the next production target would be set at a higher level ('the ratchet effect'). As a result of this system, managers were inclined to do everything they could to meet targets without surpassing them too much. Therefore, they put pressure on all production factors (personnel, machines, etc.) at the end of the month to reach the targets. The first weeks of the next month were used to maintain machines, allow for vacation of staff, etc. Measurement and the seemingly arbitrary choice of the accounting period (i.e. monthly targets) fundamentally altered the business cycle.

The behavioural effects of performance measurement are essential for perform-ance-based NPM applications. For NPM, the informational value of performance measurement is often overshadowed by the value for steering behaviour of organizations and individuals (see chapter 6). As a result, functionality of performance measurement is increasingly more assessed in terms of the behavioural effects that follow from its use than based on the information it yields.

2 FUNCTIONAL BEHAVIOURAL EFFECTS

In general terms, we define a phenomenon as being functional if its consequences contribute positively to a larger structure (Merton 1949). Performance measurement thus would be functional when it contributes to the goals of a larger structure such as the organization, the policy sector, the whole of government or even society at large. Functionality of performance measurement is an empirical question that can be answered differently at different levels. The functional behavioural effects we discuss below mirror the three uses of performance measurement we identified in chapter 5. The effects could be seen as criteria for success of the use of performance information. We therefore ask three questions for which a positive reply would point to a functional behavioural effect.

2.1 Does the use of performance measurement trigger learning and innovation?

In the absence of a market test, public organizations have the tendency to grow continuously. Parkinson firmly formulated this trend in an essay in the *Economist* in 1955. Based on staff statistics of the British Navy and the Colonial Office, he concluded that the yearly growth in administrative staff invariably was between 5.17 per cent and 6.56 per cent, irrespective of any variation in the amount of work to be done. Work accumulates to the extent that there is time available. Although this so-called Parkinson's

Law seems a bit presuming, it is clear that the public sector more than the private sector tends to accumulate slack resources. Performance measurement may create transparency and in this way trigger change and innovation (De Bruijn 2004).

Much of the evidence of functional behavioural effects is case based. Moynihan (2008) finds some evidence in the US states of Vermont and Virginia of benefits of performance management in the respective Departments of Corrections. Basic goals and philosophies of programmes were questioned, an employee-centred culture was reinforced, communication between community and institutional staff was improved, and new leaders were socialized. Moynihan notes that these effects were not prescribed by the performance management handbooks, but were nonetheless of prime importance.

Moynihan also assesses the Programme Assessment and Rating Tool (PART). The US Office of Management and the Budget (OMB) is the nucleus in this performance management initiative. The aim of PART is to assess the performance of federal programmes on a regular basis. Preliminary evidence suggests, according to Moynihan, that PART is having an influence on decision-making within the OMB, albeit minor. The main weaknesses of PART, i.e. its ambiguity and partisan nature, are at the same time its main strengths. PART allows that different parties, with different ideologies, come to different but logical conclusions. These rationales are the core of the policy dialogue that is triggered by the process. Richard Nathan of the Rockefeller Institute is quoted as saying that PART should not be seen as a tool to simplify the policy world. Instead, it should be seen as a way of complexifying decisions and prompting a serious dialogue about performance.

Benchmarking groups are another seemingly successful and upcoming practice. The idea is relatively simple. A number of organizations decide to get together in order to compare their performance. The first sessions are used to define the subject and to define indicators. Next, every organization gathers the information. A third party, usually a consultant or an academic, analyses the information and draws some tentative conclusions. In the final sessions, the results are discussed and matched to good practices within the organizations. At the end of the process, the benchmarking group decides which results can be released.

Some examples. The *Kommunale Gemeinschaftsstelle für Verwaltungsmanagement* (KGSt), the largest German local government association, has a project to foster benchmarking groups among its members. Participation is voluntary and participants pay a fee for the KGSt guidance that covers the costs. Since its inauguration in 1996, more than 200 benchmarking groups have been formed and almost 1000 different municipalities have participated. In 2002, 28 of the largest Dutch executive agencies – they handle 50 per cent of the public budget – formed a formal benchmarking organization, the *Rijksbrede Benchmarking Group*. They developed benchmarks in a variety of sectors: public safety, administrative affairs, housing, waste management, etc. In recent years, the number of benchmarks and benchmark providers (read consultants) has boomed. The proliferation has led the Dutch local government association to award a hallmark to those providers that meet certain standards (see Box 9.1).

153

> ## BOX 9.1 QUALITY CRITERIA FOR PROVIDERS OF BENCHMARKS ACCORDING TO THE DUTCH LOCAL GOVERNMENT ASSOCIATION (VNG)
>
> Requirements for a benchmark provider
>
> 1   The provider establishes (with the participants) the objective of the benchmark and integrates it in the design of the benchmark.
> 2   The data remains the property of the particpants.
> 3   The indicators are selected in cooperation with the participants.
> 4   The imputed data is checked for validity.
> 5   The benchmarks process schedules meetings with the participants.
> 6   The provider offers the opportunity to participate for several years.
> 7   The benchmarking exercise is evaluated.
> 8   The provider pays ample attention to improvement and performance of the participants.
> 9   The provider allows for interpretation of the data by participants.
> 10   The participants evaluate the process and the benchmark in a positive way.
> 11   The provider takes into consideration that participants have to ask for high-level commitment.
> 12   There is a willingness to disclose the methodologies and definition of the indicators.
> 13   Different points of view on the organizational processes are considered.
> 14   There is attention to the coordination of different benchmarks.
> 15   The provider is willing to align his/her approach with the methodology and definitions of the innovation monitor (a VNG project to coordinate benchmarks).

2.2 Does the use of performance measurement improve steering & control in the organization?

As we argued above, management in a public sector organization is fundamentally different from management in a private company. While private managers are mainly concerned about the bottom line of making sustainable profits, public managers are confronted with a top line of regulation, political interference and budget constraints (Wilson 1989). As a result, public managers can only to a limited degree let performance indicators drive the decisions on how to steer & control their operations.

Hence, there are many cases where steering & control has improved thanks to performance management initiatives. Let us first review some cases beyond the Anglo-Saxon world using the *PA@Babel database* (which holds English abstracts of non-English journals). Performance budgeting is implemented and used in the Belgian social security administration. Some significant improvements in service delivery have been reported that can be largely attributed to performance management. Waiting times between the first day of unemployment and the disbursement of the first unemployment benefit were reduced from several months to a few weeks, which makes a big difference for claimants who have just lost their job (Baeck and Van Neyen 2003). Bräunig (2007) demonstrates the benefits of benchmarking for controlling purposes in German social security. In France, the performance budgeting initiative (LOLF) has led to centralization in the justice sector, but also to budget cuts (Marshall 2008).

Lumijärvi (2001) points to the utility of the Balanced Scorecard in managing police units, provided that the scorecard is tailor-made to the context and needs of the organization. Vitezic (2007) as well as Verheijen and Dobrolyubova (2007) point to the benefits of performance management in Slovenia and the Baltic states.

One of the best documented performance management success stories is the New York Police Department's CompState programme. In Box 9.2, Mayor Giuliani of New York explains how the system helped reduce crime through better allocation of resources. The system was perceived to be so successful that other New York city departments implemented similar systems for public parks and recreation (parkStat), for health (healthStat) and for the corrections department (O'Connell 2001). Philadelphia has a schoolStat system and the city of Baltimore implemented a citywide system (CitiStat).

BOX 9.2 MAYOR RUDOLPH GIULIANI ON COMPSTAT

The CompStat programme is . . . [a] programme that has had a big impact on the level of crime. I used to be the associate attorney general. I was in charge of dissemination of national crime statistics. So, I've been involved in crime numbers for 20 years. And it seemed to me that we were doing something wrong in the way in which we measured police success. We were equating success with how many arrests were made. A police officer was regarded as a productive police officer if he made a lot of arrests. He would get promoted. A police commander in a precinct would be regarded as a really good police commander if his arrests were up this year. This wasn't the only measure of success, but it was the predominant one.

Arrests, however, are not the ultimate goal of police departments or what the public really wants from a police department. What the public wants from a police department is less crime. So it seemed to me that if we put our focus on crime reduction and measured it as clearly as we possibly could, everybody would start thinking about how we could reduce crime. And as a result, we started getting better solutions from precinct commanders. We have 77 police precincts. Every single night they record all of the index crimes that have occurred in that precinct and a lot of other data. We record the number of civilian complaints. We record the number of arrests that are made for serious crimes and less serious crimes. It's all a part of CompStat, a computer-driven program that helps ensure executive accountability. And the purpose of it is to see if crime is up or down, not just citywide, but neighborhood by neighborhood. And if crime is going up, it lets you do something about it now – not a year and a half from now when the FBI puts out crime statistics. After all, when you find out that burglary went up last year, there's nothing a mayor can do about it because time has passed and the ripple of criminal activity has already become a crime wave.

Now we know about it today. And we can make strategic decisions accordingly. If auto theft is up in some parts of the city and down in others, then we can ask why. And that will drive decisions about the allocation of police officers, about the kinds of police officers. This is one of the reasons why New York City has now become city #160 on the FBI's list for crime. Which is kind of astounding for the city that is the largest city in America. Think about the other 159 cities: Many of them have populations that are 300,000, 400,000, 500,000. And on a per capita basis, some of them have considerably more crime.

quoted in O'Connell 2001: 9

2.3 Does the use of performance measurement shape accountability based on performance?

The success of performance measurement for accountability rests on the pressure that measurement puts on organizations to critically assess their operations, to question established routines and to search for innovative solutions. The reasoning is that accountability should be based on performance rather than on inputs or mere compliance with rules and regulation.

This pressure can emanate from the general public and the media, from the political principals or from both. Without any doubt, the publication of performance information increases pressure on organizations. The next section will discuss several instances where this pressure has proved to be dysfunctional. Empirical evidence of whether accountability schemes really lead to better accountability is scarce. Yet, some cases are documented.

- A survey of performance practices in US counties by Berman and Wang (2000) found that an increased awareness about the need for accountability was one of the major outcomes of performance measurement schemes. Perhaps building *awareness* for accountability is what performance measurement efforts should hope for. Is it realistic to expect full performance accountability? In other words, is the glass half full or half empty?

■ Brezzi, Raimondo and Utili (2008) report on a financial performance incentive in a programme to develop the depressed regions of southern Italy. Regions that score well on 12 performance indicators could get financial rewards. A sum of €2.6 billion, accounting for 6 per cent of the programme's resources, was allocated in this way. It is assessed that significant results and modernizations can be attributed to the incentive system.

■ Also in Italy, local governments can voluntarily engage in social reporting, which is seen as a means of democratic accountability. According to Marcuccio and Steccolini (2005), these efforts do lead to more transparency, although authorities tend to overstress their strengths and are inclined to play weakness down by referring to the unique context they operate in.

■ Leighton (2008) argues that the call for performance-based accountability is inescapable. The spill-over of private sector scandals such as Enron and WorldCom has affected public trust. Hence, credible performance reporting is key. He argues that quality of reporting in Canada has improved over the last years in response to these challenges. The guidelines and audits of the Treasury Board and the Office of the General Auditor have reinforced this development.

Overall, it seems that better accountability as a functional behavioural effect is the least promising prospect for performance measurement. Full accountability, according to Thomas (2008), requires not only transparency, but also positive or negative consequences. The OECD provides an overview of the potential positive or negative consequences of accountability for results (see Table 9.2). Many of the proposed incentives, however, are either unrealistic or may inhibit improvement rather than bring

Table 9.2 *Incentives based on accountability for results*

Mechanisms	Positive incentives	Negative incentives
Funding	Increase funding Maintain status quo Provide bonuses Increase staff budget	Reduce funding Eliminate funding Cut salaries Cut staff budgets
Flexibility	Allow retaining and carrying over of efficiency gains Allow flexibility to transfer funds between line items in the budget Exempt agency from reporting requirements	Return funding to the centre Restrict the ability to transfer funds Increase reporting requirements Order audits
Reputational	Public recognition of performance	Public criticism

Source: based on OECD 2008: 174

it about. Is it reasonable to stop funding a regional hospital when no other hospitals are nearby? What will be the consequences of cutting staff budgets of a school that failed to improve teaching methods? Probably, it means a higher pupil/teacher ratio which further diminishes the capacity for change. What happens if management of a badly performing immigration service is confronted with additional reporting? Probably, managers will have to lock themselves in their office to fulfil reporting obligations and as a consequence, they are further alienated from what happens on the floor.

It is thus not surprising that there is a lot of hesitation to use incentives for performance. OECD surveys (2008: 162) found that finance ministries hardly ever eliminate programmes when performance targets are not met. Moreover, between 2005 and 2007, the numbers of countries that claimed to do this further declined. Accountability failures are dependent on many factors that are often not included in the measurement system and that go beyond the reach of the organization that is held accountable. The main limitation of performance measurement is its inability to provide a conclusive answer to the performance question. As a consequence, performance measurement and performance accountability may prove to be incompatible in many cases.

3 DYSFUNCTIONAL BEHAVIOURAL EFFECTS

In the previous section, we discussed some of the functions of performance measurement. The dysfunctions refer to those effects that undermine the goals of the larger structure. The literature on the dysfunctions of performance measurement seems to be much richer than that on the functions. A multitude of effects of performance measurement has been described. Before we discuss a number of them in more detail, a categorization of dysfunctional behavioural effects is proposed.

Dysfunctional effects are caused by either manipulation of the measurement process or a manipulation of the organizational output (see Figure 9.1). The first set of effects mainly leads to measurement that is not a good representation of reality. Yet, the real quantity, quality and nature of the output of the organization are not affected. When measurement is pure window dressing, skewed measurement will not impact the day-to-day operations of the organizations. This category is represented by (1) on Figure 9.1.

Some dysfunctions alter the daily operations of the organization through the behaviour of organizational members. In this case, outputs of a different quantity, quality or nature

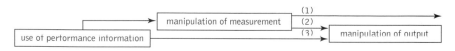

Figure 9.1 *Effects of the use of performance information*

Source: Van Dooren 2006

are pursued. These dysfunctions may materialize even with a perfect measurement system – category (3) on Figure 9.1. However, with an imperfect measurement system, the chances of such operational dysfunctions are higher – category (2) on Figure 9.1. Flawed measures may indeed be a catalyst for distorted operational practices.

We now have a classification of measurement dysfunctions as well as a first scheme of how dysfunctions might interact. Before we discuss the effects, a final word on the intentionality of the occurrence of the effects is needed. Are these effects just 'happening', or are they the result of deliberate tactics of those who are confronted with performance information? The term 'manipulation' of measurement suggests the latter and all the effects described below can be planned for. However, this does not exclude the possibility that some effects are unplanned side effects rather than the result of a grand manipulative design.

3.1 Distortion of performance information

Manipulation of measurement comes in many guises. There are at least seven ways of manipulating the measurement process (Bouckaert and Balk 1991; Smith, 1995b).

(1) *Over- and underrepresentation*. The measured value may not correspond with the real value and may provide a perception of more or less performance. Examples of both can be found in bibliometric analysis, which attempts to measure scientific impact through citation analysis (Garfield and Welljams-Dorof 1992). On the one hand, the phenomenon of citation circles – academics who strategically decide to cite each other's work – may lead to overrepresentation. It brings about an overestimation of the impact of those authors. On the other hand, the obliteration phenomenon leads to underrepresentation. This phenomenon refers to a process in which breakthrough advances – for example Einstein's theory of relativity – are cited less frequently over time. These landmark discoveries are incorporated into the generally accepted body of scientific knowledge. They are assumed, and therefore no longer cited. The measured value underestimates the real impact.

(2) Bouckaert and Balk (1991) refer to the *Mandelbrot disease* as a second instance of failing measurement (see chapter 2). By looking at increasingly fine resolutions, more and more lengths are approximated, and the total estimate of length appears to increase to infinity. This process also takes place in performance measurement. More measurement may lead to higher values because phenomena are observed that were not seen before. The number of violations of human rights reported by Amnesty International may rise because of a real deterioration of the situation in the field. Yet, a higher number may also be caused by the establishment of new observatories. Similarly, homicide statistics – although hopefully not approaching infinity – may be higher in countries that routinely perform more post-mortem investigations. Whenever the magnitude of the underlying phenomenon is unknown, Mandelbrot is watching.

159

(3)   Third, the number of indicators in a set often risks inflating. This process is often termed the '*mushrooming*' of indicator sets. Too many indicators may indeed be problematic since the users of the information can no longer see the wood for the trees. In principal–agent relations, the creation of such an information overload may be a tactic of an agent to obfuscate real performance to the principal. Agents then exploit the information asymmetry that is typically to their advantage in principal–agent relations. For principals, this tactic is very difficult to counter. After all, the agent *is* providing huge amounts of information. The indicators are, however, only one, and not even the most important, component of the information asymmetry. The capacity to make sense of the performance indicators is a more significant dimension of information asymmetry than the indicators themselves. Hence, the agent erodes the principal's sense-making capacity by providing more indicators than a principal can handle, while maintaining the image of cooperation and transparency.

Moreover, a large indicator set conveniently raises the chances of excelling at least on some dimensions. This is particularly problematic for accountability purposes. Box 9.3 describes the case of the Lisbon process of the European Union. In a very explicit way, it is shown that too many indicators erode their regulatory capacity.

Notwithstanding the potential problems, the addition of increasingly more indicators is often a remedy for at least two other dysfunctional effects which we will discuss below: cream skimming (selecting the intake) and myopia or tunnel vision (focusing on the measured activities only). As a result, the definition of an optimal number of indicators is ineffectual. Organizations need to find this out through experience. The Audit Commission in the United Kingdom, for instance, gradually reduced the number of indicators for local government from 242 in 2000 to 166 in 2002 (Bouckaert *et al.* 2003).

(4)   Performance information that is intensively used may get *polluted* (Bouckaert and Balk 1991). This mainly refers to the terminology of the indicators. Different people interpret the concepts and definitions (slightly or substantially) differently. For some, performance refers to output; for others, performance is outcome; and for still others, it means both. The notoriously nebulous measure of public trust for instance has been interpreted as a measure of openness (OECD 2005), of performance (Afonso *et al.* 2006) and of integrity (Pope 2000), while in essence it only measures the disposition of people towards government (Van de Walle and Bouckaert 2003). As a consequence, people talk at cross-purposes and the effectiveness of performance measurement erodes significantly. Although this dysfunction may well be the result of a spontaneous social mechanism, it is not unthinkable that actors deliberately create terminological confusion.

(5)   Performance information may be manipulated by *unjustifiable aggregation or disaggregation* data (see chapter 6) (Perrin 1998). Composite indicators have the benefit of simplicity. Decision-makers with limited time or the general public with limited insight into complex policy matters are helped with a universal assessment of performance. Yet, by choosing and weighting the measures, organizations may hide

BOX 9.3 TOO MANY INDICATORS? THE CASE OF THE LISBON PROCESS IN THE EUROPEAN UNION

At the Lisbon European Council in spring 2000, the European Union set the 'strategic goal for the next decade: to become the most competitive and dynamic knowledge-based economy in the world capable of sustainable economic growth with more and better jobs and greater social cohesion' (paragraph 5 of the Council conclusions) (European Commission 2000). This agenda has been monitored following the Open Method of Coordination (OMC). Each year, member states are held accountable for the progress as measured by means of a set of indicators. It is expected that these progress reports will push countries in the right direction. The indicator set started off with 35 indicators covering employment, innovation, economic reform and social cohesion. Soon, the set expanded to 42 indicators that now also cover environment as well as some general economic indicators. Besides the selection of structural indicators, hundreds of other indicators are collected in complementary processes.

After three years, the EU commissioned a mid-term review of the process, led by former Dutch minister-president Wim Kok. The proposal was to reduce the number of indicators to 14 in order to increase their ability to put pressure on nations. The mid-term review report states that 'more than a hundred indicators have been associated with the Lisbon process, which makes it likely that every country will be ranked as best at one indicator or another. This makes the instrument ineffective . . . The European Commission should present the Heads of State or Government and the wider public annual updates on these key 14 Lisbon indicators in the format of league tables with rankings (1–25), praising good performance and castigating bad performance – naming, shaming and faming' (European Commission 2004: 43). For accountability, too many indicators are clearly a problem.

problematic aspects of their performance. The reverse scenario is to look for more detail when aggregate measures are not satisfactory. For example, attention to an overall increase in crime rates in a city can be diverted by pointing to an improvement in a previously troubled quarter.

(6)   *Misrepresentation* is the deliberate manipulation of data – ranging from creative accounting to fraud (Smith 1995a). There is a thin line between under- and over-representation on the one hand (point 1 above) and misrepresentation on the other. The distinction lies in the illegal character of misrepresentation as opposed to under- and overrepresentation. A public theatre that deliberately counts more visitors than actually attended a performance may be an example. Financial information systems combat

misrepresentation by installing extensive internal control systems, supplemented by internal and external audit systems (Raaum and Morgan 2001). For non-financial information, there is usually not such an extensive control structure. Misrepresentation thus has to be prevented in a different way. Some authors propose to relying more on trust-based systems (Grizzle and Pettijohn 2002; Power 1999).

(7)   *Misinterpretation* is the incorrect inference about performance brought about by the difficulty of accounting for the full range of potential influences on performance (Smith 1995a). This dysfunction is particularly applicable to outcome measures. The ultimate impact of government output in society is often only visible in the long term. Moreover, societal change is seldom ascribable to one single agency or department. Low unemployment figures for instance may be the result of a good training programme. Yet, the economic climate is without doubt also an important determinant. Moreover, tough inspection on moonlighting may add to the overall result of declining unemployment. Although this complexity is generally accepted, it is often forgotten when indicators need to be interpreted.

3.2 Distortion of output

Manipulation of output is a second category of behavioural responses to the use of performance information. Unlike the manipulation of measurement, the manipulation of output alters the daily operations of the organization. Measurement is not (necessarily) skewed, but the underlying reality changes. This set of dysfunctions has an effect on what citizens directly or indirectly experience from public services. Therefore, the impact of manipulation on the nature, quality or quantity of outputs is more far-reaching than manipulating the statistics.

(1)   *Measure fixation* is the pursuit of success as measured rather than as intended. Smith (1995a) gives the example of the 'hello' nurse in English hospitals. A nurse at the counter had to make a first contact with patients in order to meet a five-minute waiting time requirement, after which the patient was guided to another waiting room. Although the target is being met, this is clearly not an improvement of service delivery. University rankings are another example (Best 2001; Gormley and Weimer 1999). To obtain good rankings, universities may primarily try to improve prestige and not programme quality. Frederickson (2001) mentions several strategies such as attracting academics who publish in respected journals, nurturing a doctoral programme with a good outplacement in recognized education programmes, participating visibly in associations, attracting an important journal editorship, developing a well-oiled alumni organization, developing visibly one or two specializations, having at least one faculty member publishing in the popular press, and having at least one 'grantsman-rainmaker' in the faculty. Measure fixation may be avoided by including more indicators. However, by adding indicators the risk of mushrooming crops up.

Measure fixation may have two consequences: oversupply and/or a decline in quality.

(a) Oversupply is the provision of more products and services than needed. Oversupply of measured activities is reinforced by the incentive structure of measurement. This is especially the case when unit costs are calculated in order to reimburse producers – as is the case in several European health systems. The medical accounting system stimulates medical overproduction. When fixed costs are considerable, as is the case for medical equipment, it usually is easier to reduce cost per unit by increasing output rather than decreasing input. As a result, the total output inflates (Dawson and Street 2000).

Oversupply of certain outputs often goes hand in hand with the neglect of other, unmeasured outputs and activities. In particular intangibles such as training and advice may be ignored. Blau (1963) gives an example of an employment agency where interviewers were motivated to complete as many interviews as possible. While doing so, they paid insufficient attention to other activities such as locating new jobs.

(b) A second consequence of measure fixation is the loss of quality. Qualitative aspects of public services are usually more difficult to measure and therefore risk receiving less attention. Heinrich (1999) for instance observed that robust attention for cost-per-placement considerations in a job-training programme had a negative impact on service quality. Another example is situated in a British hospital, where waiting-time targets led to cancellations, long waiting times before appointments could be made, and a lack of follow-up visits (House of Commons Public Administration Select Committee 2003).

(2) A second dysfunction is *myopia* (Bouckaert and Balk 1991). The long-term view is excluded by a fixation on short-term goals. A myopic strategy usually favours curative services above preventive services – for example crime solving rather than crime prevention. Prevention is an example of an activity with results that are by definition intangible. In fact, the results are what did *not* happen. Another example is Blau's (1963) study of a court where the target of eight cases a month per person leads to the adjournment of difficult cases in favour of easy cases. The initial prioritization criterion, relative urgency, was replaced by another criterion, relative ease of processing. In the long term, obviously, the difficult cases accumulate. This effect is also found in the private sector, where companies (and their top managers) are driven to constantly improve quarterly results under pressure of stock markets and short-term incentive schemes. The 2008 financial crisis uncovered in a dramatic way the neglect of long-term risks.

(3) Third, *sub-optimization* refers to a situation where an optimal situation at unit level leads to a sub-optimal situation at higher levels. The pursuit of local organizational

objectives goes at the expense of more general objectives (Bouckaert and Balk 1991; Hood 1974). This dysfunction often appears when the attainment of an outcome is the responsibility of a sequence of actors. Public security is an example of such a chained outcome. The first step is prevention; public places need to be well lit at night, people in shopping areas need to be alerted for pickpockets, and social workers have to locate and remedy social hardship. Next, the police need to patrol and make arrests. The public prosecutor has to institute legal action and the courts have to pass judgements. Finally, the prisons have to detain convicts and the social services have to run programmes to reintegrate detainees into society. A high number of arrests, including less important offences, may be optimal for a police force, but sub-optimal for the overall outcome of public safety. Since the public prosecution service and the courts have to process all the arrests, the often limited capacity of the judicial system may become inadequate, and the more serious crimes may remain unsolved.

(4)   A fourth dysfunction is *cream skimming* (also called *cherry picking*) (Behn and Kant 1999; Grizzle and Pettijohn 2002). When confronted with output measures, organizations may be tempted to select the intake. Job training programmes for instance have been demonstrated to select those unemployed who are most likely to find a job (Anderson *et al.* 1993; Heckman *et al.* 1997). Although this strategy may be economically efficient, it usually contrasts with the public goals of the programmes that propagate equity of access to services.

An extreme manifestation of selection of intake is a full disinvestment in the services for which the target will never be reached. Rather than attempting to make these worst cases as good as they can get, they are written off. We might call this dysfunction *adverse skimming*, since the worst are left out instead of the best being taken in. The performance of railroad companies, for instance, is typically assessed by measuring the percentage of trains arriving on time. A railroad company might rather have one train being much too late or even cancelled than many trains being a little late. In terms of service delivery, the latter option may be more acceptable.

(5)   A fifth dysfunction of performance measurement is *complacency*. Organizations will often strive towards adequate performance rather than excellence since excellence also implies risks. The French phrase *pour vivre heureux, vivons cachés* (in order to live happily, we need to live concealed) is emblematic of this position. Typically, organizations fear two consequences of excellent performance. On the one hand, there is the threat of budget cuts. It is often difficult to demonstrate that good performance is the result of good management and policy, and not of excessive resources. On the other hand, excellence may trigger ratchet effects (Bevan and Hood 2006). Exceptional performance levels of year t may be considered normal in year $t+1$. Because standards of assessment shift upwards, it will become more difficult to excel in the future. Fear of the ratchet effect may cancel out the incentives that a measurement system is believed to introduce (Courty 2004).

164

(6)   An excessively rigid measurement system may finally lead to *organizational paralysis* (Bouckaert and Balk 1991; Smith 1995a). Performance measures potentially guide behaviour and, as such, they have regulatory power. In the same way that too detailed regulation may squeeze out all freedom of action and innovation, overly rigid performance measurement systems may ostracize the necessary discretion in organizations. Too detailed time registration systems and performance contracts, for instance, may inhibit experimentation. Time registration systems that make every failure visible and its costs computable will run counter to demands for innovation, which inherently require some tolerance towards failure.

3.3 Performance target paradox

The result of the behavioural effects – functional and dysfunctional – is that performance will cluster around the target. Throughout time, an indicator loses its capacity to discriminate between good and bad performers because organizations adapt their performance. Meyer and Gupta (1994) call this the performance paradox (see also Van Thiel and Leeuw 2002). We will use the term performance *target* paradox, because the effect that Meyer and Gupta describe should be attributed to the measurement of performance and not to the pursuit of performance as such. More precisely, it should be attributed to the practice of target-setting based on performance indicators. As we discussed above, this is only one dimension of the use of performance information.

Figure 9.2 graphically represents the performance target paradox. We assume that performance is normally distributed and that a target is introduced on the average. The performance target paradox predicts that underperformers will change their behaviour in a functional or dysfunctional way to meet the target, while those that are performing better than the target will lower performance levels in order to avoid the ratchet effect. Some worst cases even may be abandoned (adverse skimming). The distribution clusters around the mean, with a slight increase in worst cases to account for adverse skimming.

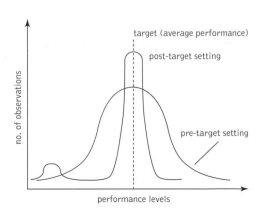

Figure 9.2

Performance target paradox – the tendency towards target

4 CONDITIONALITY OF FUNCTIONS AND DYSFUNCTIONS

The sections above have put the functions and dysfunctions of measurement in a behavioural perspective. Individual behaviour, however, is encapsulated in a complex configuration of institutions that determine the conditionality of functions and dysfunctions. We limit the discussion here to the incentive structure that is embedded in the use of performance. However, it goes without saying that other structural and cultural characteristics will also play a role. Since targets are often imposed in a hier-archical context, the acceptance of hierarchy (Bendix 1974) might foster a culture where target-based performance measurement thrives well. It seems plausible that cultures with a higher acceptance of hierarchy (such as England) will more quickly engage in target-setting. Bureaucratic cultures such as France and Germany, on the contrary, may be less receptive for target-based governance arrangements (see Box 9.4).

BOX 9.4 ENGLISH EXCEPTIONALISM ACCORDING TO *CANDIDE*

Hood argues that the use of performance targets in England is rather exceptional (Hood 2007). No other country in the world uses them with the same vigour. He refers to Voltaire's 1759 work *Candide ou l'optimisme* to illustrate the cultural background to this extraordinary position (Voltaire 2006). Here, we include the translated excerpt of Voltaire's work.

> Talking thus they arrived at Portsmouth. The coast was lined with crowds of people, whose eyes were fixed on a fine man kneeling, with his eyes bandaged, on board one of the men of war in the harbour. Four soldiers stood opposite to this man; each of them fired three balls at his head, with all the calmness in the world; and the whole assembly went away very well satisfied.

> 'What is all this?' said Candide, 'and what demon is it that exercises his empire in this country?' He then asked who was that fine man who had been killed with so much ceremony. They answered, he was an Admiral. 'And why kill this Admiral?' 'It is because he did not kill a sufficient number of men himself. He gave battle to a French Admiral; and it has been proved that he was not near enough to him.'
> 'But,' replied Candide, 'the French Admiral was as far from the English Admiral.' 'There is no doubt of it; but in this country it is found good, from time to time, to kill one Admiral to encourage the others.'

Voltaire 2006

In chapter 6, we identified three uses of performance information – to learn, to steer & control and to give account – which have different assumptions. *Use for learning* assumes that people are intrinsically motivated to perform well and to seek responsibility. The use of performance information for research and learning has the lowest impact on the degrees of freedom of the organization. *Use for steering & control* is mainly about allocating resources and taking corrective actions when performance is lagging behind. The use for steering & control may have a significant impact on the degrees of freedom within an organization. However, the managers of organization still control the performance information as well as the message that performance information gives to the outside world. The third purpose is *accountability*. The main proposition is that the public sector should be accountable to the citizens/taxpayers and politicians and therefore performance of public bureaucracies should be disclosed to politics and public.

It can be assumed that both functional and dysfunctional effects will be conditioned by the use of performance information. Figure 9.3 represents some rudimentary working hypotheses.

(a) There is a linear relationship between the intensity of use and intensity of effects.
(b) The gradient is steeper for higher pressure uses; accountability > learning; and accountability > steering & control.
(c) No use implies no effects (the curve starts in the origin).
(d) The function is similar for different kinds of behavioural effects.

Empirical evidence for these relations is limited. Research comparing different uses of performance information is virtually absent. Nonetheless, some counterhypotheses can be formulated vis-à-vis the working hypotheses.

(a) The relation may not be linear. In case of very intense uses of performance information, measures may fall more quickly (see the performance target paradox),

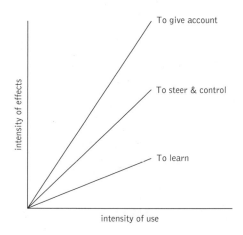

Figure 9.3
Central thesis of conditionality:
use determines effects

167

and therefore the intensity of the effects may decline since measurement no longer shows variation. If this should be the case, the relation would be parabolic rather than linear.

(b) The gradient may not necessarily be steeper for accountability use than for steering & control, since both uses potentially have high stakes. Use for learning may be fundamentally different in this respect.

(c) Measurement without use may nonetheless trigger effects when people believe that the information *can* be used. This will again mainly be the case for accountability and steering & control and less so for learning. If this is the case, the curve does not start in the origin.

(d) The relation between effect and use may be different depending on the particular use and effect under study. It may well be that intensive use for learning triggers very intense functional effects without having dysfunctional effects.

5 HOW TO REMEDY DYSFUNCTIONAL EFFECTS?

The description of the dysfunctions of measurement raises the issue of how to remedy these effects. Up to this point, the line of reasoning has been that use for accountability and/or steering & control has a more pressing and direct impact on the organization than use for learning. The direct stakes in terms of budget allocations, bonuses or sanctions are higher. Therefore, the former uses provide a *motive* for altering behaviour as purposed by the indicators. A motive for dysfunctional behaviour however needs to be combined with an *opportunity* for altering output – as anyone who every now and then watches a detective is perfectly aware. It is not always possible to manipulate performance indicators.

Table 9.3 provides constraints that may limit the propensity of dysfunctional behaviour, as well as some counteracting strategies. The analysis is based on interviews with middle managers in regional government administration (Van Dooren 2006). The constraints that limit opportunity and motives are to a large extent given that cannot be influenced in the short term. The counteracting strategies are deliberate actions that aim at taking away opportunity and/or motive for dysfunctional behaviour.

Table 9.3 *Constraints and counteracting strategies for dysfunctional behaviour*

A. Opportunity – constraints	B. Motive – constraints
No control over intake	Habit formation and predictability
Characteristics of the service	Consequential loop (boomerang effect)
Administrative and sectoral networks	Intrinsic motivation
C. Opportunity – counteracting strategies	D. Motive – counteracting strategies
ICT's	Abandon targets
Control	Set absolute targets
Qualitative assessments	Set general targets

5.1 Constraints on the opportunity for dysfunctional behaviour

First, organizations need to have an impact on the intake. Only then will effects such as cherry picking be possible. Schools, for instance, that are obliged to enrol students on a first-come-first-served basis will not be able to seek pupils with strong socio-economic profiles. An emergency unit of a hospital is not supposed to control its intake when ambulances pull up with badly injured patients. Similarly, courts cannot refuse persons seeking justice. This is a fundamental constituent of the rule of law.

Second, the characteristics of the service may limit the opportunity for gaming. This is, for instance, the case for adverse skimming. A complete disinvestment in a service will only be possible when the importance for individual beneficiaries of that service is limited. Therefore, it may be easier 'to park' a case if several people are minimally affected than when few people are heavily affected. Delaying an already delayed train a bit more may meet less resistance than setting aside a dossier for subsidizing a school or paying a wage. In the latter cases, the disadvantaged will almost always appeal to the courts. Similarly, a decline in quality of services as a result of number fixation will be noticed more quickly in personal services than road construction, for example.

A third limitation is caused by exposure of the production process to peers in administrative and sectoral networks. Dysfunctional behaviour may be quickly identified by other organizations within administrative and social networks. In general, public organizations are embedded in a web of relations within the administration as well as within politics and society. In some policy sectors, the social distance between societal actors, politicians and the administration is closer than in others. This is particularly the case when a policy sector is highly institutionalized with strong umbrella organizations. In this case, the opportunity to alter output to obtain favourable scores is reduced because of peer insight into the production function of the organization.

5.2 Constraints on the motive for dysfunctional behaviour

First, increasing experience in working with performance information leads to habit formation. The use of performance information becomes more predictable over time and as a result it may also become less threatening. Obviously, predictability may also increase the opportunity for dysfunctional behaviour, since actors learn how to play the game. Opportunity and motive work against each other in this case.

Second, the motive may be affected because of the consequential loop of dysfunctional behaviour. A public organization, or even an individual employee, may be directly affected at a later stage by gaming at an earlier stage. For instance, pursuing quantity at the expense of quality may result in a higher workload because more appeals are lodged with administrative courts. Inferior quality may return like a boomerang. Obviously, this is not always the case. A noteworthy counter-example is low quality in paying allowances or tax inspections. When low quality means that decisions are made in favour of the beneficiary, cases will not return.

169

Third, there is substantial evidence that intrinsic motivation in public bureaucracies is still substantial (Perry and Hondeghem 2008). In particular in highly professionalized services, professional standards outweigh the pressure to obtain high performance scores. Dimaggio and Powell (1983) would call this normative isomorphism.

5.3 Strategies to reduce the opportunity for dysfunctional behaviour

First, information and communication technology (ICT) may strongly reduce the opportunity for skewing performance measures. ICT is increasingly used for process management. Since all dossiers need to be stored in computers, data can be broken down to the individual employee and the individual dossier. Control and audit opportunities are much stronger. In addition, standardization of online forms reduces the opportunity for misclassification – deliberate or not.

Second, traditional control techniques may be employed. A common technique is to double-check a sample of registrations in the measurement system. In addition, analysis of outliers or unlikely results may be a useful approach. The perceived probability of being controlled may strongly affect the opportunity for dysfunctional behaviour. In this respect, a certain reverberation of the controls being executed in the organization makes sense.

Third, in addition to measurement, public organizations may resort to qualitative assessments. This can be done through focus groups and conversations with staff and stakeholders. Corroboration of measurement results with other sources of knowledge can be a very effective way to uncover gaming. Note that such corroboration is already built into the use for learning.

5.4 Strategies to take away the motive for dysfunctional behaviour

Strategies for taking away the motive are all directed towards target-setting. The most obvious strategy is to abandon targets, and to primarily aim at triggering dialogue and learning effects. This is a good strategy if learning is the purpose of measurement and the measurement system is designed along these lines. If not, without a target people will often rely on other ways of sense-making when confronted with the data. The most likely point of reference will then be last year's performance or performance of comparable units. If this is the case, the motive gets back in by the back door, but remains implicit.

Another strategy is to formulate an absolute standard (e.g. 100 per cent precision, zero-tolerance for corruption, etc.). There is usually a strong symbolic dimension to an absolute target. The message is that the organization, for instance, does not tolerate corruption, even when corruption levels are low. In this sense, the target is mainly used to set the agenda. However, as a yardstick, an absolute target is not useful and again, the implicit standard is not clear.

Yet another strategy is to phrase the targets in general terms. Rather than a precise number, the targets are formulated in terms of an increase or decrease of the results. There is a target, but not as strict as a numerical standard. Here, too, it is better to be roughly accurate than precisely wrong. In addition, the standard is made explicit, which should largely take away the conspiratorial character of introducing measurement and build trust in the system.

6 CONCLUSION

The use of performance information influences behaviour in functional and/or dysfunctional ways. The dysfunctional effects usually get more airplay in the academic field than the functional ones. A balanced view however takes both into account. The occurrence of effects depends on the way performance information is used, besides some general cultural and institutional variables. Finally, it is argued that dysfunctional effects can be tackled by taking away the motive or the opportunity to behave dysfunctionally.

DISCUSSION QUESTIONS

1   Assume the role of a counsellor in an employment agency. You are evaluated based on the number of unemployed you counselled for. What would you do to get a favourable evaluation?
2   Assume the role of an advisor in an oversight agency that has to define some indicators for a broadcasting company. Which indicators would you define? Can they be manipulated?
3   Is it realistic to develop a functional performance accountability regime?

REFERENCES

Afonso, A., Schuknecht, L. and Tanzi, V. (2006) *Public Sector Efficiency: Evidence for New EU Member States and Emerging Markets.* Lisbon, Technical University of Lisbon.

Anderson, K. H., Burkhauser, R. V. and Raymond, J. E. (1993) The effect of creaming on placement rates under the Job Training Partnership Act. *Industrial and Labor Relations Review,* 46, 613–24.

Baeck, K. and Van Neyen, S. (2003) Risicobeheer bij de Rijksdienst voor Arbeidsvoorziening: een nieuw element binnen het geïntegreerd beheersmodel. *VTOM,* 8: 3, 26–35.

Behn, R. D. and Kant, P. A. (1999) Strategies for avoiding the pitfalls of performance contracting. *Public Productivity and Management Review,* 22, 470–89.

Bendix, R. (1974) *Work and Authority in Industry.* Berkeley, University of California Press.

Berliner, J. S. (1956) A problem in Soviet business administration. *Administrative Science Quarterly,* 1, 86–101.

Berman, E. and Wang, X. (2000) Performance measurement in US counties: capacity for reform. *Public Administration Review,* 60, 409–20.

Best, J. (2001) *Damned Lies and Statistics: Untangling Numbers from the Media, Politicians, and Activists.* Berkeley, CA, University of California Press.

Bevan, G. and Hood, C. (2006) What's measured is what matters: targets and gaming in the British health care sector. *Public Administration,* 84, 517–38.

Blau, P. (1963) *The Dynamics of Bureaucracy: A Study of Interpersonal Relationships in Two Government Agencies.* Chicago, University of Chicago Press.

Bouckaert, G. and Balk, W. (1991) Public productivity measurement: diseases and cures. *Public Productivity & Management Review,* 15, 229–35.

Bouckaert, G., De Peuter, B. and Van Dooren, W. (2003) *Meten en vergelijken van bestuurlijke ontwikkeling: Een monitoringsysteem voor het lokaal bestuur in Vlaanderen,* Brugge, Die Keure.

Bräunig, D. (2007) Benchmarking als sachzielorientiertes Controllinginstrument am Beispiel von Sozialversicherungsträgern. *Zeitschrift für öffentliche und gemeinwirtschaftliche Unternehmen,* 30: 4, 373–89.

Brezzi, M., Raimondo, L. and Utili, F. (2008) Using performance measurement and competition to make administrations accountable. In Delancer Julnes, P., Berry, F. S., Aristigueta, M. and Yang, K. (eds.) *International Handbook of Practice-based Performance Management.* Thousand Oaks, Sage.

Courty, P. (2004) An empirical investigation of gaming responses to explicit performance incentives. *Journal of Labor Economics,* 22, 23.

Dawson, D. and Street, A. (2000) Comparing NHS hospital unit costs. *Public Money and Management,* 20: 4, 58–62.

De Bruijn, H. (2004) *Managing Performance in the Public Sector.* London, Routledge.

Dimaggio, P. J. and Powell, W. W. (1983) The iron cage revisited: institutional isomorphism and collective rationality in organizational fields. *American Sociological Review,* 48, 147–60.

European Commission (2000) *The Lisbon European Council – An Agenda of Economic and Social Renewal for Europe.* Contribution of the European Commission to the special European Council in Lisbon, 23–24 March 2000. Brussels, European Commission.

European Commission (2004) *Public Finances in EMU.* Brussels, Office for Official Publications of the European Communities.

Frederickson, H. G. (2001) Getting ranked. *Change,* 33, 48–55.

Garfield, E. and Welljams-Dorof, A. (1992) Citation data: their use as quantitative indicators for science and technology evaluation and policy-making. *Science and Public Policy,* 19, 321.

Gormley, W. T. and Weimer, D. L. (1999) *Organizational Report Cards.* Cambridge, MA, Harvard University Press.

Grizzle, G. A. and Pettijohn, C. D. (2002) Implementing performance based budgeting: a system dynamics perspective. *Public Adminsitration Review,* 62, 51–62.

Heckman, J., Heinrich, C. and Smith, J. (1997) Assessing the performance of performance standards in public bureaucracies. *American Economic Review,* 87: 2, 389–96.

Heinrich, C. J. (1999) Do government bureaucrats make effective use of performance management information? *Journal of Public Administration Research and Theory,* 9, 363–93.

Hood, C. (1974) Administrative diseases: some types of dysfunctionality in administration. *Public Administration,* 52, 439–54.

Hood, C. (2007) Public service management by numbers: Why does it vary? Where has it come from? What are the gaps and the puzzles? *Public Money and Management,* 27, 95–102.

House Of Commons Public Administration Select Committee (2003) *On Target Government by Measurement.* London, House of Commons.

Leighton, B. (2008) Recognizing credible performance reports: the role of the Government Auditor of Canada. In Delancer Julnes, P., Berry, F. S., Aristigueta, M. and Yang, K. (eds.) *International Handbook of Practice-based Performance Management.* Thousand Oaks, Sage.

Lumijärvi, I. (2001) Tasapainoitettu mittaristo (BSC) poliisitoiminnan arvioinnin ja kehittämisen työkaluna. *Hallinnon Tutkimus* 20, 72–80.

Marcuccio, M. and Steccolini, I. (2005) Nuovi modelli di accountability nelle amministrazioni pubbliche: un'analisi empirica del contenuto del bilancio sociale degli enti locali. *Azienda Publica,* 18, 665–88.

Marshall, D. (2008) L'impact de la loi organique relative aux lois de finances (Lolf) sur les juridictions. *Revue Française de l'Administration Publique,* 125, 121–32.

Mayo, E. (1933) *The Human Problems of an Industrial Civilization.* New York, MacMillan.

Merton, R. K. (1949) *Social Theory and Social Structure: Toward the Codification of Theory and Research.* New York, Free Press.

Meyer, M. W. and Gupta, V. (1994) The performance paradox. *Research in Organizational Behavior,* 16, 309–69.

Moynihan, D. P. (2008) *The Dynamics of Performance Management: Constructing Information and Reform.* Washington, DC, Georgetown University Press.

O'Connell, P. E. (2001) Using performance data for accountability: the New York City Police Department's CompStat model of police management. *The PricewaterhouseCoopers Endowment for the Business of Government.* Washington, DC, PricewaterhouseCoopers.

OECD (2005) *Strengthening Trust in Government.* Paris, OECD.

OECD (2008) *OECD Public Management Reviews: Ireland.* Paris, OECD.

Perrin, B. (1998) Effective use and misuse of performance measurement. *American Journal of Evaluation,* 19, 367.

Perry, J. L. and Hondeghem, A. (2008) *Motivation in Public Management: The call of Public Service.* Oxford, Oxford University Press.

Pope, J. (2000) *Confronting Corruption: The Elements of a National Integrity System.* Berlin, Transparency International.

Power, M. (1999) *The Audit Society: Rituals of Verification.* Oxford, Oxford University Press.

Raaum, R. B. and Morgan, S. L. (2001) *Performance Auditing: A Measurement Approach.* Altamonte Springs, FL, Institute of Internal Auditors.

Rugg, D. (1941) Experiments in wording questions: II. *Public Opinion Quarterly,* 5, 91–2.

Saint Martin, D. (2005) Management consultancy. In Ferlie, E., Lynn, L. E. and Pollitt, C. (eds.) *The Oxford Handbook of Public Management.* Oxford, Oxford University Press.

Smith, P. (1988) Assessing competition among local authorities in England and Wales. *Financial Accountability and Management,* 4, 235–51.

Smith, P. (1995a) On the unintended consequences of publishing performance data in the public sector. *International Journal of Public Administration,* 18, 277–310.

Smith, P. (1995b) Performance indicators and outcome in the public sector. *Public Money and Management,* 13–16.

Thomas, P. G. (2008) Why is perfomance based accountability so popular in theory and so difficult in practice? In KPMG (Ed.) *Holy Grail or Achievable Quest: International Perspectives on Public Sector Performance Management.* Toronto KPMG.

Van de Walle, S. and Bouckaert, G. (2003) Public service performance and trust in government: the problem of causality. *International Journal of Public Administration,* 26, 891–914.

Van Dooren, W. (2006) *Performance Measurement in the Flemish Public Sector: A Supply and Demand Approach.* Leuven, Faculty of Social Sciences.

Van Thiel, S. and Leeuw, F. L. (2002) The performance paradox in the public sector. *Public Performance & Management Review,* 25, 267–81.

Verheijen, T. and Dobrolyubova, Y. (2007) Performance management in the Baltic States and Russia: success against the odds? *International Review of Administrative Sciences,* 73, 205–15.

Vitezic, N. (2007) Beneficial effects of public sector performance management. *UPRAVA: mednarodna znanstvena revija za teorijo in prakso,* 5, 7–27.

Voltaire (2006) Candide. *Project Gutenberg.*

Wilson, J. Q. (1989) *Bureaucracy: What Government Agencies Do and Why They Do It.* New York, Basic Books.

FURTHER READING

In the 1990s, Bouckaert and Balk (1991) and Smith (1995a) pointed to the dysfunctional effects of performance measurement. One of the most cited recent studies of the dysfunctional effects of performance management is Bevan and Hood's analysis of the British health care sector (Bevan and Hood 2006). See Van Thiel and Leeuw (2002) on the performance paradox. A recent study that documented some functional effects of performance management is Moynihan (2008). Cases of functional effects can also be found under the best practice banner on for instance the website of the IBM Center for the Business of Government. From the canon, the case studies by Blau (1963) should have priority on the reading lists.

Chapter 10

The future of performance management

LEARNING OBJECTIVES

- To understand some of the paradoxes and challenges of performance management.
- To be able to form a well-founded opinion on where to go next with performance management.
- To put the concepts and discussions of the book into practice while reflecting on the future.

KEY POINTS

- Performance management is widespread, but some challenges remain.
- Better implementation may solve some of the issues while another option is to fundamentally rethink the blueprint of performance management in order to better fit with complex environments.
- Three recommendations are suggested: performance management needs to be agile, close to the action and political.

It is always somewhat venturesome to title a chapter 'The future of . . .'. What we offer here is a somewhat tendentious extrapolation of current trends. More so than in other chapters, we take positions which are often hypothetical. The function in the context of a textbook is to trigger debate while making use of the frameworks and concepts of the previous chapters. Crystal ball gazing is a good way to challenge our thinking, but it comes with a disclaimer: it isn't necessarily so.

We first outline some paradoxes in performance measurement and management, which at the same time echo some of the challenges that performance management faces.

The second part asks the question how we can do better in the future. We discuss some of the implementation challenges for performance management. The third and last part suggests three ways to rethink performance management. Rather than focusing on the nuts and bolts of implementation, this section suggest a more fundamental redesign of performance management in a complex environment that is in permanent flux.

1 PARADOXES IN PERFORMANCE MEASUREMENT AND MANAGEMENT

1.1 Counting the uncountable

Allegedly, in Albert Einstein's office at Princeton University there hung a sign stating that 'Not everything that counts can be counted, and not everything that can be counted counts'. Performance measurement adepts sometimes forget about this insight. Managers and politicians inferred from the conviction *what gets measured, gets done* that *what does not get measured, does not get done*. This incorrect logical inference was reinforced by management consultants advocating the quest for the ultimate set of Key Performance Indicators (KPIs): see for instance Kaplan and Norton (1996) on the Balanced Scorecard. Many employees inferred that services not subjected to a KPI are not that important. It is not uncommon for divisions in large organizations to lobby to get their activities into the KPI set. They know, what is counted, counts.

The last decade, several performance management experts have argued for a focus on measuring outcomes instead of outputs or processes (Hatry 2002; Perrin 2003). The argument is that only outcomes are 'real' key results, i.e. results that matter for society. It does not matter how many police patrols are negotiating the streets (which is an output); citizens want safety (which is an outcome). Therefore, performance measurement should primarily focus on outcomes. Yet, and therein lies the paradox, outcomes are in many instances very hard to count. We know that what is measured gets attention, but we also know that many important dimensions are immeasurable.

1.2 Distrusting professionals, but relying on them

Performance management doctrine has an ambiguous attitude towards expertise and professionals. On the one hand, professionals are the key to better performance. In fact, the NPM phrase 'let managers manage' reflects a confidence in the professionalism of managers. Similarly, it is expected that managers are entrepreneurs and leaders that bring out the best in the staff under their supervision, not in a command and control style, but by empowerment. On the other hand, the performance movement expresses a certain distrust in professionals. Davies and Lampel (1998), assessing performance management in the British National Health Service, argue that managers needed performance information in order to intervene successfully in the doctor–patient relationship. Hence, a plethora of indicators has been developed in order to

176

counterbalance doctors' professional knowledge. Radin (2006) provides the example of the British Research Assessment Exercise (RAE) which audited the research quality of universities based on a number of performance indicators such as the number and type of publications. Rather than trusting the professional researcher, quality is counted. Similarly, Radin points to the No Child Left Behind initiative in the public schools in the USA. She asserts that the most vigorous critique was of the standardized tests that allegedly did not leave enough room for teachers' discretion.

There is a clear paradox. On the one hand, trust in professionalism is vital in an increasingly complex society. On the other, we are reluctant to grant this trust and hence we fall back on control and audit. In circles of auditors, the adage '*in god we trust, the rest we audit*' is well appreciated. According to Power (1999) these audits are to a large extent ceremonial – he speaks of rituals of verification. Many audits are mainly about creating an illusion of control. Similar arguments can be made for other performance measurement initiatives in both public and private sectors.

1.3 Paralysis by analysis

Decision-makers have to process a lot of information: budgets, audits, impact analyses, evaluation studies, memoranda from interest groups, laws and jurisdiction, personal communication, etc. . . . An almost superhuman analytical capacity is required to process all these sources. Performance information comes on top of this pile, and so the risk of information overload increases even more. Although performance management is devised to improve decisions, it may well lead to paralysis. It should thus not come as a surprise that practitioners consider selectivity in measurement to be one of the key challenges for implementing performance management (Mayne 2007).

1.4 The best non-workable system?

Stating that, up to now, everything has failed but that performance management will succeed may sound like a position close to hubris. The failure of PPBS, ZBB (zero-based budgeting), MBO (management by objectives) and other such initiatives to become institutionalized can be attributed to the inability of those processes to integrate themselves into the decision-making processes that really matter to managers and stakeholders, most particularly the budget process. Accordingly, under the GPRA, the goal was to ultimately place performance metrics at the centre of resource allocation, personnel evaluations and other processes that matter (Posner and Fantone 2007). This almost results in the TINA-paradox: There Is No Alternative. Managing performance is necessary, useful, indispensable but impossible to attain. Ingraham talks about performance as a siren for modern government (2005). Probably, the expectations of what performance management can do should be better attuned to reality.

177

1.5 *If everyone is accountable, no one is*

Given the continuing overriding commitment to performance and to striving to improve performance frameworks, several agendas are advanced for governments internationally that together move the performance approach beyond current limitations. The relevance of trends depends on developmental paths, but the general imperative is for greater collaboration and sharing across boundaries while seeking to maintain system integration. Actors from all spheres – the executive, legislature, the citizen and the administration – are expected to share responsibilities.

There is increasing awareness that public organizations cannot be effective on their own. A considerable literature on collaboration, partnerships and networks has developed – see for instance Milward and Provan (2000), Vangen and Huxham (2001), Koppenjan and Klijn (2004), Agranoff (2005) and a recent special issue of *Public Management Review* on network effectiveness (Mandell and Keast 2008). As a result of collaboration, the responsibilities for performance are shared as well. Hence, when many organizations participate, it becomes more difficult to hold a single organization accountable for results. And if many are accountable, the risk occurs that no one takes responsibility for failure and everybody for success.

Should we then stick to traditional accountability schemes with one principal and one agent? Probably not. Willingness to collaborate can erode when single accountability schemes are maintained. Denhardt and Aristigueta (2008) demonstrated that typical approaches to performance management are impacting partnerships and collaborations. Performance-based accountability systems will tend to undermine collaborative efforts unless they are accompanied by other strategies for providing an impetus for alignment and collaboration across agencies.

1.6 *Performance management does not equal performance*

Apart from some documented best practice, there is little evidence on whether performance management actually contributes to performance. Indubitably, however, other organizational factors besides performance management do have an impact on performance. An OECD literature study assesses the drivers of performance (Van Dooren *et al.* 2007). Decentralization for instance appears to be a structural feature of public administration that positively influences performance. Attention for the soft dimensions of HRM is an example of a management practice that influences performance. Performance pay systems on the contrary mostly seem to have a negative effect. Other variables such as budgeting flexibility, coordination efforts, unionization, openness of the recruitment system can be expected to have an influence on performance as well. Finally, and maybe blindingly obvious, a lack of resources may affect the performance of public organizations.

We do not argue that performance management does not lead to performance. Evidence is mostly lacking to substantiate either a positive or a negative relation. Research in this area faces the challenging task of not only collecting empirical evidence on the relation between performance management and performance, but also of contextualizing empirical evidence.

2 TOWARDS BETTER IMPLEMENTATION

Few argue against the aims of performance management. Hatry (2008), for instance, finds it hard to believe that performance management will not continue far into the future. Nonetheless, as we argued in other chapters in this book, performance management is not without its problems. Practitioners, management consultants as well as academics have sought solutions in response to the paradoxical and often problematic nature of performance management. Yet, the solutions that are proposed have a different bearing on performance measurement and management.

A first cluster aims to mitigate the implementation problems. The main argument is that better results in performance management can be attained by taking care of some unfavourable organizational conditions and making some adjustments to the measurement and management system. The message is 'to have a second go' with an essentially good system. The blueprint of performance management is good; it only has to be done better. A second cluster of responses, discussed in the next section, is to fundamentally rethink performance management. The assumptions as well as some of the core design issues of performance management are put into question. Here, the message is not just to try it again, but to do it differently.

2.1 Improve the quality of performance information

We argued in this book that quality of performance information alone does not guarantee the use of performance information. Yet, it definitely *can* be an important factor. Attention paid by organizations to quality matters is not always evident. Some research suggests that often only modest attention is paid to quality assurance practices in the area of performance measurement (Mayne 2007). Hatry (2008) argues that an investment in the many dimensions of quality can ratchet up the use of performance information.

- ■ Validity of the performance indicators. Do the indicators measure what is relevant and important about the particular issue or service?
- ■ Quality of the data. Is the quality of the data collected for each of the performance indicators of sufficient accuracy?
- ■ Timeliness of the data. Is the performance data collected and reported in a sufficiently timely fashion so the information is available when needed?
- ■ Analysis of the data. Has at least some basic analysis been undertaken of that data to put it into meaningful form, such as by providing breakouts of the aggregate data

and by providing legitimate comparisons so that users can interpret the extent to which the measured levels of performance represent good or poor outcomes?

■ Presentation of the performance information. Is the information presented in a form that the user groups can understand and interpret and in an easy to read format?

Besides these punctual criteria, quality may also refer to the ethical attitude of measuring bodies (Bouckaert and Halligan 2008). Integrity, independence and transparency relate to the quality and integrity of performance information and the institutions responsible for them. Credibility of performance information is in the eye of the user related to the credibility of the provider. There are two major institutions responsible for safeguarding integrity: audit offices and statistical offices. The cascade of a solid internal control system, which is assessed by an internal audit office under the guidance of an internal audit committee, which itself is assessed by an external audit office, sometimes even a Supreme Audit Institution, is designed to provide assurance about the quality of performance information. In some instances the cascade is successful, while in other cases quality assurance is mainly a bureaucratic snowball.

The role of statistical bureaus will become more important. Statistical agencies are recognized as having the capacity to look beyond single organizations. With an increasing span and depth of performance information, there is a need to look beyond outputs to societal outcomes. A key issue for the future is to combine audit standards with statistical standards and make these useful for managing performance.

2.2 Leadership

An OECD 2005 survey (Curristine 2005b) found that strong (political) leadership is key to explaining success in performance management. Someone has to put his or her shoulder behind a performance management effort and develop a measurement strategy. Preferably, this person carries some weight. However, leadership as a concept is ill-specified, and hence the interpretation of the OECD survey results is more complicated. The issue of leadership raises a host of questions: who should the leader be? What traits are important for performance leadership? Where does leadership in performance come from and how to sustain it?

Behn (2004) regards performance leadership as a capacity of public managers. He opposes the performance leadership model to a focus on performance systems and structures. He writes that 'rather than to develop public managers with the leadership capacity to improve the performance of their agencies, we have sought to create performance systems that will *impose* such improvements' (p.3). This approach echoes the need to trust public managers as management professionals. Performance leadership, in this view, aligns best with the managerial and learning perspectives on the use of performance.

2.3 Ownership

Another somewhat magical word in the management discourse is ownership. Implementation failures are regularly said to be caused by a lack of it. Mayne (2007), for instance, notes that a system built on filling in performance information forms for others, with no apparent use for those down the line, is unlikely to be robust and survive over time. Better implementation of performance measurement and management requires that those who are affected by the system have to accept and internalize the system.

Different uses suggest different challenges in creating ownership. High stakes use, such as performance contracts and league tables, necessitate a thorough *ex-ante* dialogue with the *owners-to-be* in order to define indisputable and robust indicators. Inevitably, such hard uses will feature relatively more top-down implementation characteristics. Softer uses such as benchmarking circles and other learning efforts require an effort to avoid a noncommittal attitude. Bottom-up processes will be relatively more important in these instances.

2.4 Setting realistic expectations

The perception of success depends on expectations. Belgian football teams are usually quite happy when Milan or Madrid only set them back a goal or two. Similarly, politicians celebrate a loss in parliamentary seats as if it was a victory if they did better than the projected by opinion polls. The often perceived failure of performance management is no exception to this rule.

Performance management reforms are often victims of over-commitment. Many people need to be convinced in order to introduce a performance management system: politicians, top and middle managers, professionals and front-line workers, to name a few. Hence, an understandable strategy is to create high expectations and to play down the costs. Yet, although this strategy may prove successful in the short term, it almost definitely will boomerang in the medium term. Typically, costs of a performance management system are tangible and become apparent relatively shortly after the introduction of the system. Benefits on the other hand are intangible and may only appear in the longer term. Disillusionment with performance systems that do not (yet) deliver may undermine confidence and hence the failure of the performance management effort may become a self-fulfilling prophecy.

2.5 Adequate training and skills development

A further strategy to improve implementation is to provide training and to develop skills of both producers and consumers of performance information (Wholey 1999). The most widespread training efforts are in the technicalities of performance measurement and are oriented towards producers of performance information. Statistical and design skills are the main objective of these initiatives. Arguably, we can also envisage skill development at the receiving end. Users of performance information such as politicians, top managers and even citizens could be target groups. Obviously, the nature of such training courses needs to be different. It should primarily focus on the capability to recognize credible performance information and to understand the ways in which it can be sensibly put into use. It should also focus on the limitations of performance information.

2.6 Integration

Integration, coordination, formalization, consistency, coherence, routine-building and alignment are some of the most common keywords for those who want to fix performance management without questioning its blueprint. Box 10.1 provides an example of a machine-based view of performance management, with a strong focus on an intensification of integration efforts. Although the importance of integration and coordination is undeniable, we should also acknowledge the limitations. Complexity and change regularly tear carefully coordinated systems apart. The desire to coordinate all efforts in advance may lead to delay and even deadlock. In some instances, it may make more sense to remedy the consequences of ill-coordinated performance efforts than to embark on excessively ambitious coordination efforts (see also Laegreid *et al*. 2008).

BOX 10.1 A MACHINE-BASED VIEW OF PERFORMANCE MANAGEMENT

Accenture, a leading management consultant, published its view on performance management (Accenture 2006). The recommendations and challenges reflect the machine-based rhetoric.

Performance management processes should relate to each other, but often do not. Instead of being managed and viewed as end-to-end mission enablers, most of these management processes operate separately, driven by their own unique set of players and dynamics.

Drivers for all performance management processes lack consistency. All management processes should be driven by the ultimate outcomes they are meant to achieve. While strategic plans will articulate what the programme or organization is supposed to achieve, the rest of the management processes tend to focus more on dollars spent than on what is accomplished with them. For example:

Programmes lack integration through all levels of the organization. Strategic-level goals and associated metrics, now required by many large government organizations (United States, Canada, Australia, France), are set by top executives. A different, lower level of the organization carries out the detailed management processes, but the strategic goals are rarely driven down into the organization.

3 RETHINKING PERFORMANCE MANAGEMENT

Several studies have proposed new ways of doing performance management. Radin (2006) and Moynihan (2008) studied the American performance management movement, with a particular focus on the Government Performance and Results Act (GPRA) and the Program Assessment and Rating Tool (PART). De Bruijn (2004) mainly analysed experiences in the Dutch public sector. The UK House of Commons (2003) investigated English practices.

The House of Commons' request to move from a measurement culture towards a performance culture captures the road ahead for next generation of performance management. Too often, performance management is devised following *a machine-based engineering logic*. Performance management is locked into formal and over-bureaucratic systems. At the same time, performance management has slipped through the fingers of those managers, officials and professionals who are supposed to benefit from it. Future performance measurement and management will need to move away from systems thinking and engineering logics. How then could next generation be conceived? We first argue that a reconsideration of the assumptions of performance management is needed. Next we discuss the implications for performance management founded on this alternative set of assumptions.

3.1 Rethinking the assumptions of the performance movement

The context of public administration is complex and ambiguous. Kravchuk and Schack (1996) explain what complexity means: indeterminate objective functions, multiple administrative layers, collective action problems, system overloads and information overloads, and an increasing scope and scale of operations. Noordegraaf and Abma (2003) add that current performance management, which they label management by measurement, only fits the rare unambiguous contexts of public administration. There are many sources of ambiguity: history (what has happened?), intentions (what must be done?), technology (what can be done?), and participation (who is present?) (March and Olsen 1976). Defined as such, not many unambiguous contexts will be found. Since ambiguity is everywhere, the prospects for performance management in this view are rather limited.

An alternative approach is to rethink performance management to make it '*ambiguity proof*'. This can only be done by taking complexity and ambiguity as a given, and to rebuild performance management on this foundation. Complexity should be the assumption of performance management and dealing with complexity should be its ambition. Radin (2006), analysing performance management in the USA in recent decades, concludes her insightful study with a plea to rethink the assumptions of the performance movement. Many problems with performance measurement and management can in her view be attributed to these faulty points of departure. Seven issues need reconsideration to better fit with real world experience (see Table 10.1).

183

Table 10.1 *Rethinking the assumptions of the performance movement*

Issue	Classic assumptions	Alternative assumptions
Intelligence	Clarity, universal principles, literal meanings	Multiple sources, situational knowledge, literal *and* symbolic meanings
How the world works	Linear cause–effect relations Clear (or at least clarifiable) goals Planned	Complexity, interdependence and unplanned change
Organizational theory	Generic principles, internal focus	Focus on the environment of the organization
Professionalism	Distrust Control is needed	Essential to programme operation Discretion is needed
Values, politics and power	Value-neutral, apolitical, widely shared	Value-laden, highly political and controversial
Information	Information is available, neutral and conclusive	Information is partially available and often costly, value-laden and mostly inconclusive
Mode of organization	Performance-based control	Alternative modes of control
Markets and prices	Performance indicators as currency in quasi markets, competition based on performance specifications	Competitive tendering, competition based on process or input specifications
Hierarchy and authority	Performance indicators as coercive rules	Traditional regulation
Networks and trust in professionalism	Incompatible	Custom, tradition, reciprocity, professionalism, trust

Source: based on Radin 2006: 241–2

3.2 Rethinking performance management

A review of assumptions requires a rethinking of the blueprint of performance management. Three important implications are discussed below: performance management needs to be agile, close to the action, and political.

3.2.1 Performance management needs to be agile in order to deal with complexity

Kravchuck and Schack (1996) refer to Ashby, a cybernetics scholar, who posited that only complexity can absorb complexity. Rigid information systems will not be able to apprehend and understand rising complexity in the environment. In the most extreme cases, chaos will appear to reign due to the ever-increasing gap between experience and the knowledge base as provided by the information system. Information (what we believe to know) and practice (what we experience) risk becoming separated worlds; one orderly, where objectives are set and performance targets are reached, and one chaotic, where people are mainly concerned with muddling through the day. The 2008 crisis in the financial sector demonstrated the consequences of rigid performance management in increasingly complex settings. There was total panic when the financial sector started to realize that the information system of the rating agencies did not at all reflect real risks.

The main implication is that performance information should be used for learning, and less so for accountability. Performance-based accountability requires stability for the period for which targets are set. Not many fields remain stable for three to six years. Research in New Zealand and Australia has proven that it is very difficult for governments to live up to the stability requirement and that accountability erodes accordingly (Carlin 2006; Gregory and Lonti 2008). In addition to stability, accountability requires relatively univocal performance measures that do not allow for much interpretation. The performance indicators have to be accurate reflections of performance. Learning does not require the same stability and robustness. On the contrary, performance measurement is part of a permanent dialogue in order to make sense of complexity. Hence, indicators can and should be adjusted in response to contextual changes and new insights.

If performance management moves away from accountability, other forms of organizational control need to be reconsidered. A well-established distinction is between market-, hierarchy- and network-based systems (Bradach and Eccles 1989). Performance-based accountability aligns itself with either hierarchical or market-based control. League tables that attempt to provide quasi markets are an example of the latter. Performance targets are an example of hierarchical rule.

There are three alternatives to performance-based accountability (see Table 10.2). The most obvious is to revert to the administrative default mode which is traditional regulation. Market-based control can be instituted by competitive tendering or competition based on process or input specifications. Trust-based control systems can be a good alternative to performance-based accountability. Trust-based systems rely on traditions, on professions, on standard operating procedures which seem to be functional. They are very cost-effective and there is a considerable ownership within the vertical responsibilities.

3.2.2 Performance management needs to be 'close to the action'

Organizations typically have an undercurrent of repeated decisions they have to make. To these recurrent cycles, a constant stream of unique one-off decision processes is added. In recent decades, the weight of the stable, recurrent processes has decreased.

Table 10.2 *Alternatives for performance-based accountability*

Mode of organization	Performance-based control	Alternative modes of control
Markets and prices	Performance indicators as currency in quasi markets, competition based on performance specifications	Competitive tendering, competition based on process or input specifications
Hierarchy and authority	Performance indicators as coercive rules	Traditional regulation
Networks and trust in professionalism	Incompatible	Custom, tradition, reciprocity, professionalism, trust

Kettl (2002) argues that the traditional US public administration boundaries of mission, resources, capacity, responsibility and accountability must be managed in an increasingly complex and political context, necessitating additional negotiation and collaboration between systems and agencies. These complex parallel processes are in a unique way shaped by situational requirements of time and place.

Recurrent financial, HRM and contract cycles have been the main vehicle for incorporating performance information in decision cycles (see chapter 5). Without doubt, these cycles will remain the foundation of performance management in the future as well. Yet, top-down performance management on a yearly (as in the budget cycle) or monthly basis (as in many Balanced Scorecard systems) will need to be supplemented by flexible efforts to provide performance information on demand. Since complex, unique processes will gain importance, the timing and targeting of performance measurement will be challenged.

> Timing – 'guerrilla tactics': in complex policy and management processes, the demand for performance information can arise relatively unexpectedly. At the same time, it can fade away as quickly as it came about. In such a context, expert staff are needed to quickly infuse complex processes with performance information. It is vital that they are able to both capture the need and understand the availability of performance information.

> Targeting – 'decentralization of performance management': rather than devising top-down systems, performance management needs to be in the hands of middle managers and front-line supervisors who understand the situational requirements best.

For budgeting, this approach would suggest infusing performance information into budget negotiations on an *ad hoc* basis rather than systematically reporting performance in the budget document voted in parliament. Since the budget document is mainly an after-the-fact codification of political processes of negotiation that have taken place, performance budgets risk becoming a purely bureaucratic exercise. Some confirmation is found in an OECD survey of performance budgeting showing that countries use performance information to inform, but not determine, budget allocations (Curristine 2005b). Furthermore, it is argued that much 'linking' of this performance and financial information has been simply to provide them in the same report.

3.2.3 Performance management needs to be political

Some time ago, Innes (1990) observed that the only way to keep data-gathering out of politics is to collect irrelevant data. Performance management, including the use of performance information for policy-making, *has* to be political. Good performance information should strengthen the evidence base for solving political problems of who gets what, when and how – which is the classic definition of politics by Lasswell (1936). Issues of who gets what, when and how are at play at all levels: in government-wide policy-making, in policy sectors and networks, in organizational management and in micro-management. We thus do not imply that the political institutions (ministers, parliament, parties) have to interfere with all performance issues at all levels. We stress the importance of a recognition of the political nature of performance management.

- A first implication is that performance management should involve more, rather than fewer, actors. Performance learning, the preferred use in flexible performance management systems, will probably have the highest impact when different perspectives are drawn into the analysis.
- A second implication is that performance management should deal with controversy rather than suppress it. Performance information should not be an authoritarian argument to end conflicting views on where to allocate resources. Rather, it should underpin a careful argumentation of causes, consequences and priorities.

The previous paragraphs dealt with the political nature of performance management, and not so much with the political system. There are some efforts however to strengthen the role of performance information in the political system as well. Yet, such initiatives will only be successful when they acknowledge the different values and positions that political players assume. Performance information that promises to end political debates, to get political argumentation out of the political system, is irrelevant at best, and potentially harmful. Conflict is essential for the functioning of democracy and therefore performance information should primarily refocus political debate rather than curb it.

DISCUSSION QUESTIONS

1   What is in your view the future of performance management? Do we need better implementation or a fundamental rethink? Or is there no future at all?
2   Should performance management be more political? More decentralized?
3   Is engineering logic too dominant in performance management?

REFERENCES

Accenture (2006) *Accenture Point of View: Performance Management*. Washington, DC, Accenture.

Agranoff, R. (2005) Managing collaborative performance. *Public Productivity & Management Review,* 29, 18.

Behn, R. D. (2004) *Performance Leadership: 11 Better Practices That Can Ratchet Up Performance*. Washington, DC, IBM Center for the Business of Government.

Bouckaert, G. and Halligan, J. (2008) *Managing Performance: International Comparisons*. London, Routledge.

Bradach, J. L. and Eccles, R. G. (1989) Price, authority, and trust: from ideal types to plural forms. *Annual Review of Sociology,* 15, 97–118.

Carlin, T. M. (2006) Victoria's accrual output based budgeting system – delivering as promised? Some empirical evidence. *Financial Accountability & Management,* 22, 1–19.

Curristine, T. (2005a) Government performance: lessons and challenges. *OECD Journal on Budgeting,* 5, 127–51.

Curristine, T. (2005b) Performance information in the budget process: results of OECD 2005 questionnaire. *OECD Journal on Budgeting,* 5 (2), 87–131.

Davies, H. T. and Lampel, J. (1998) Trust in performance indicators? *Quality in Health Care,* 7, 159–62.

De Bruijn, H. (2004) *Managing Performance in the Public Sector*. London, Routledge.

Denhardt, K. and Aristigueta, M. (2008) Performance management systems: providing accountability and challenging collaboration. In Van Dooren, W. and Van de Walle, S. (Eds.) *Performance Information in the Public Sector: How It Is Used*. Basingstoke, Palgrave Macmillan.

Gregory, R. and Lonti, Z. (2008) Chasing shadows? Performance measurement of policy advice in the New Zealand government departments. *Public Administration,* 86, 837–56.

Hatry, H. P. (2002) Performance measurement: fashions and fallacies. *Public Performance & Management Review,* 25, 352–58.

Hatry, H. P. (2008) The many faces of use. In Van Dooren, W. and Van de Walle, S. (eds.) *Performance Information in the Public Sector: How It Is Used.* Basingstoke, Palgrave Macmillan.

House of Commons Public Administration Select Committee (2003) *On Target Government by Measurement.* London, House of Commons.

Ingraham, P. W. (2005) Performance: promises to keep and miles to go. *Public Administration Review,* 65, 390–95.

Innes, J. E. (1990) *Knowledge and Public Policy: The Search for Meaningful Indicators.* New Brunswick, Transaction Publishers.

Kaplan, R. S. and Norton, D. P. (1996) *The Balanced Scorecard: Translating Strategy into Action.* Boston, MA, Harvard Business School Press.

Kettl, F. D. (2002) *The Transformation of Governance.* Baltimore, Johns Hopkins University Press.

Koppenjan, J. F. M. and Klijn, E. H. (2004) *Managing Uncertainties in Networks: A Network Approach to Problem Solving and Decision Making.* London, Routledge.

Kravchuk, R. S. and Schack, R. W. (1996) Designing effective performance measurement systems under the Government Performance and Results Act of 1993. *Public Administration Review,* 56, 348–58.

Laegreid, P., Roness, P. G. and Rubecksen, K. (2008) Performance information and performance steering: integrated system or loose coupling? In Van Dooren, W. and Van de Walle, S. (eds.) *Performance Information in the Public Sector: How It Is Used.* Basingstoke, Palgrave Macmillan.

Lasswell, H. (1936) *Politics: Who Gets What, When and How?,* New York, Whittlesey House.

Mandell, M. and Keast, R. (2008) Introduction. *Public Management Review,* 10, 687.

March, J. G. and Olsen, J. P. (1976) *Ambiguity and Choice in Organizations.* Bergen, Universitetsforlaget.

Mayne, J. (2007) Challenges and lessons in implementing results-based management. *Evaluation,* 13, 87–109.

Milward, H. B. and Provan, K. G. (2000) Governing the hollow state. *Journal of Public Administration Research and Theory,* 10, 359–80.

Moynihan, D. P. (2008) *The Dynamics of Performance Management: Constructing Information and Reform.* Washington, DC, Georgetown University Press.

Noordegraaf, M. and Abma, T. (2003) Management by measurement? Public management practices amidst ambiguity. *Public Administration,* 81, 853–71.

Perrin, B. (2003) *Implementing the Vision: Addressing Challenges to Results-Focused Management and Budgeting.* Paris, Organisation for Economic Co-operation and Development.

Posner, P. L. and Fantone, D. M. (2007) Assessing federal program performance: observations on the US Office of Management and Budget's Program Assessment

Rating Tool and its use in the budget process. *Public Performance & Management Review,* 30, 351–68.

Power, M. (1999) *The Audit Society: Rituals of Verification.* Oxford, Oxford University Press.

Radin, B. A. (2006) *Challenging the Performance Movement: Accountability, Complexity, and Democratic Values.* Washington, DC, Georgetown University Press.

Van Dooren, W., Lonti, Z., Sterck, M. and Bouckaert, G. (2007) *The Institutional Drivers of Efficiency.* OECD/GOV technical papers. Paris, OECD.

Vangen, S. and Huxham, C. (2001) Enacting leadership for collaborative advantage: uncovering activities and dilemmas of partnership managers. *British Journal of Management,* 14, 61–76.

Wholey, J. S. (1999) Performance-based management: responding to the challenges. *Public Productivity & Management Review,* 22, 288–307.

FURTHER READING

Three texts that suggest more fundamental ways to rethink performance management are Kravchuck and Schack (1996), Moynihan (2008) and Radin (2006). The report of the UK House of Commons Public Administration Select Committee is also worth reading (House of Commons Public Administration Select Committee 2003). *Public Performance & Management Review* devoted a special issue to the future of performance management with relatively short and provocative contributions by key authors (vol. 25, issue 4). Hatry (2002) for instance discusses the fashions and fallacies in the field. A special issue of *Public Management Review* (Mandell and Keast 2008) discusses performance of networks. Exemplary studies that focus on implementation are by Mayne (2007) and Curristine (for performance budgeting) (Curristine 2005a).

Index